there's STILL no
such thing as

'NAUGHTY'

PARENTING THE PRIMARY YEARS

Simple Steps to Support Your
Child's Mental Health from 5—12

'We are exquisitely attuned to other humans, especially when we are growing up. Our relationships become physically and psychologically embedded in each of us – shaping how we feel and think about ourselves and the world. These relationships can anchor us, helping foster resilience against adversity. And they give us a secure base that allow us to take risks and explore the world. The human brain is fundamentally a social organ. It is what ensures our survival not only as individuals but as a species. This is why relationships really matter.'

Professor Eamon McCrory, Professor of Developmental Neuroscience and Psychopathology, UCL

KATE SILVERTON

there's STILL no such thing as

'NAUGHTY'

PARENTING THE PRIMARY YEARS

Simple Steps to Support Your
Child's Mental Health from 5–12

Lagom

First published in the UK by Lagom
An imprint of The Zaffre Publishing Group
A Bonnier Books UK company
4th Floor, Victoria House
Bloomsbury Square,
London, WC1B 4DA
England

Owned by Bonnier Books
Sveavägen 56, Stockholm, Sweden

Trade Paperback – 978-1-788706-75-9
Ebook – 978-1-788706-76-6
Audio – 978-1-788706-77-3

A CIP catalogue of this book is available from the British Library.

Designed and typeset by EnvyDesign Ltd

Printed and bound in Great Britain by Clays Ltd, Elcograf S.p.A.

1 3 5 7 9 10 8 6 4 2

FSC
www.fsc.org
MIX
Paper | Supporting
responsible forestry
FSC® C018072

Every reasonable effort has been made to trace copyright holders of material reproduced in this book, but if any have been inadvertently overlooked the publishers would be glad to hear from them.

Lagom is an imprint of Bonnier Books UK
www.bonnierbooks.co.uk

*To Liza, without whom I would
never have known.*

KATE SILVERTON is one of the UK's most familiar faces. A much-loved broadcaster and journalist, she's covered conflicts in Iraq and Afghanistan, rubbed shoulders with Hollywood's finest on the red carpet at the Oscars, and shone bright as one of the stars on *Strictly Come Dancing*.

A mother to two young children, in 2020, Kate made what many considered a brave mid-life decision to switch lanes and change careers. She explained that she had followed her heart and found joy, returning to her academic roots in child psychology.

Now a qualified child therapist, Kate combines her time supporting her family, volunteering in clinical practice to support children in need and working privately to help parents find their joy and harmony at home. Her first parenting book, *There's No Such Thing As 'Naughty'*, was an instant *Sunday Times* number-one bestseller.

Author's Note
Confidentiality is the bedrock of the therapeutic relationship. In addition to obtaining written permission to use other people's real-life parenting stories in this book, I have disguised identities, and, in some instances, material and scenarios from various parents and children have been attributed to one.

A Note on Terminology
The people who take on the tremendous responsibility of caring for children come in many forms and with different titles. I pay tribute to and recognise the selfless commitment of all those who play a role in raising or caring for children: parents and other primary carers, foster carers, adoptive parents, grandparents, kinship carers, step-parents, teachers, social workers and health workers. In this book, I refer to *parents* in the first instance to cover all those who take on this vital role purely for simplicity and clarity.

DEBORAH FOWLER'S first short story was published when she was seventeen. Since then, she has published over six hundred short stories, novels, a crime series and several works of non-fiction. Deborah lives in a small hamlet just outside St Ives and *A St Ives Christmas Mystery* was the first in a new series set against the beautiful backdrop of the West Cornish coastline.

Contents

Introduction

As a child therapist and as a parent with two primary-aged children, I know how difficult, demanding and exhausting the job can be.

'There is no joy left in my parenting,' Nikki, a new client, tells me in our first session. She says her son, who's six, is 'impossible to control'. He tells her he hates her and that she's boring, and Nikki confesses the hours she spends with him are the most difficult of her day.

She shakes her head in sadness and disbelief; this isn't how she imagined parenthood would be.

She asks me the three questions, we may often ask ourselves when we are finding the going tough.

'Did I do something wrong?'

'Is there something wrong with my child?'

And . . . 'Is it too late for things to change?'

I have written this book to bring hope (as well as answers), to strengthen the bond we have with our children and to restore harmony in our homes. If parents are in need of support, it's not because we're not capable; it's because the job is bloody hard work. The commitment and responsibilities are endless, yet we often parent in isolation, receiving conflicting advice and juggling the constant demands on our energy and time.

It's important to remember that it hasn't always been this way. Our ancestors raised their children in small communities, with every adult and adolescent invested in their care. The multigenerational parenting model made for a strong socialising force and supported parents to nurture their children intuitively, guided by ancient wisdom passed down through generations. In the absence of more community-led parenting, we've seen a rise in opinion-based policies and parenting practices that, however well-intentioned, often pitch us against our children and, sadly, our children against us.

None of us wants to be locked in battle with our children. Certainly it won't bode well for when they're much bigger-bodied teens. If we want to ensure our children's good mental health and enjoy a happy, healthy relationship with them for life, we must learn from recent discoveries about child development and, specifically, neurobiology. They shine an extraordinary light on why our children behave the way they do. What the research in these fields has revealed is both exciting and profound – and can literally change our lives.

This is why it's vital that science forms the bedrock of this book. As well as allowing us to trust our instincts and parent more confidently, it confirms what our ancestors intuitively knew: that our children are deeply *feeling* rather than thinking creatures. If we are to better understand them, we must become more deeply feeling creatures ourselves.

Understanding that our children's nervous system, not 'naughty', drives their behaviour allows us to reframe how we view child development and be more compassionate with our care.

Often, we continue to do things because 'that's how it's always been done'. More recently, the word 'discipline' has been associated with punishment or harsh measures to keep children 'under control'. Yet discipline derives from the Latin *discipulus*, which means 'to learn'. I'll demonstrate that we can *teach* our children how to behave <u>without the need for punishment at all</u>.

We can do it most effectively by using boundaries and modelling the behaviour we *want* to see, not demonstrating the behaviour that we don't.

What I share with you here is informed by everything I have learned from decades of my own personal psychotherapy, studying, parenting and from my clinical work with children. The information I share is evidence-based and the exercises are rooted in what is called trauma-informed practice. This is how I work with my own children and the young clients in my care.

As I did in my first book, *There's No Such Thing as 'naughty'*, I'll start by explaining the neuroscientific basis of behaviour using my simple analogy of the lizard, baboon and wise owl. I include new research and additional concepts for this book relevant to our children now they are older, including what I consider the ten crucial pillars of parenting – these are the central columns that support a child's strong mental and physical foundations.

My own brain likes order, and all the pillars neatly begin with C!

Construction

Calm

Containment

Connection

Creativity

Curiosity

Communication

Compassion

Contracts and Crisis Management

Community

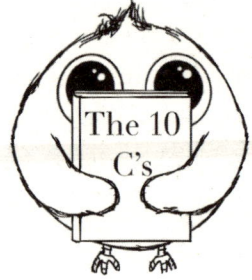

Each chapter covers a different pillar and I'll explain why they're so important for parents to put in place. In these pages, you'll find easy, quick practical exercises to do with your children, along with advice and scripts to try out. I'll share examples from my own parenting (especially the times when things have gone awry), as well as that of my husband and other families.

In Part Three, I'll show you how you can apply these 'Cs' to the situations that will test us both at home and beyond the front door. In the final chapter, we look at the importance of Community, with a rallying cry for parents to come together and share more openly if we are struggling, to seek support where we need it and offer our support to others who might need it too.

In coming together to advocate for our children, we can effect change and hold people and policies to account if they don't serve us, our children and their future health and wellbeing. We will see a different child when we change how we see our children. We will see changes in us as parents, too.

When I first met Nikki, she had lost all hope and confidence in her parenting. It took just four sessions for things to change. Learning about the neuroscience and, after modelling some practical exercises together, Nikki told me the small 'tweaks' I'd suggested had brought about a profound change at home. She said she felt less controlling and critical and her son was much calmer and loving towards her in turn. She declared, 'You are a magician! It's happened so quickly, it's as though I have a different child. Certainly, my son has a different me.'

I'm *not* a magician, but I do know how to bring magic back to our parenting. Science shows us how. In learning how to be playful rather than punitive, we trigger feel-good neurochemicals inside our children's brains. This allows them to experience joy in our presence and a deep sense of love and delight.

These feel-good neurochemicals lie, as the eminent neuro-scientist Jaak Panksepp described 'like Sleeping Beauty, waiting for someone to wake them up'.

I've written this book because my passion is for every parent to have the relationship with their children they always hoped to have and for their children to have the parenting experience they deserve. Our children do not have to be in crisis for us to reflect on how we might improve our efforts. It's what inspired me to do the research for my own family's benefit in the first place. Don't get me wrong, there are still days where I find myself gripping the sink, muttering 'FFS' under my breath while the children bicker behind me. But, as the poet and activist Maya Angelou so beautifully observed, 'When we know better, we do better.'

Science has opened the door for us to understand what we can teach our children and what they can teach us in turn.

I can't promise that the journey will always be smooth, but it doesn't need to be. In fact, it is often in our relational ruptures that we experience the greatest opportunity for repair. I *can* promise you that you'll find support and the answers to reassure you that we are never too late, we can always do things differently, and, just as there is no such thing as the perfect parent, there is (still) no such thing as the 'naughty' child!

We *can* be all the parents our children need and we are far more powerful than we know.

With this book, I hope you can also find comfort in knowing that, although we each sail our different boats, we no longer have to journey alone.

Kate Silverton, March 2024

PART ONE

Understanding Behaviour and Managing Emotions

Part One covers CONSTRUCTION, with a simple explanation of the science that reveals what's really behind your child's 'naughty' behaviour. We'll also look at how to find our own CALM amid the parenting chaos. Because if we're going to teach our children the art of emotional regulation, we need to model it too.

Chapter One

CONSTRUCTION – Why We're All in the Brain Development Business

Understand the brain and you will understand behaviour.

'I HATE him!'
'I hate YOU!'
'I'm HUNGRY!'
'She's MEAN!'
'I'm so BAD at this!'
'My tummy HURTS.'
'I WON'T wear those socks!'
'I don't WANT to go to school'
'And I'm NOT DOING THAT!'

Having 'survived' the first five years of parenthood, you probably assumed, as most of us do, that life would get easier once the pram was passed on and the kids were at school.

This morning, as he refereed a fight over who got the final Weetabix, my husband said that the people who told him the years from five to 12 were 'the best', either 'only had one child' or, he added dryly, 'they can't have been around much'.

There is hope, I promise. Even if the siblings you imagined would be best friends for life are currently only communicating via karate chop and you've found yourself googling 'anger management' after one too many meltdowns (yours, never mind the kids).

Our saviour comes in the perhaps unlikely form of neuroscience, specifically the scientific field of neurobiology. Revolutionary advances made in the research of our brain and nervous system development now give us concrete explanations for children's behaviour. And yes, that includes the hitting, biting, scratching, screaming, sobbing, sulking and sibling-baiting; incredibly, science reveals the mystery of it all. It completely dispels the notion of 'naughty' and in this first chapter I'll explain why.

As a child therapist and a parent to two primary-school-aged children, I do understand how infuriating, frustrating and even frightening our children's behaviour can be sometimes. I'll show you how you can contain their big behaviour safely and restore joy and harmony to your home. I'll show you why you don't need to battle your children to gain control and why you can command using the strength of your connection instead.

I share the practical and therapeutic tips, scripts and tools that I use in the therapy room and at home. It will have you translating your child's behaviour in seconds, as well as keeping your cool. Yes, even when your six-year-old is running around with his big boy pants on his head, refusing to go to bed, or your 11-year-old growls 'go away' when you attempt a gentle chat about her day.

In this chapter we look at 'construction': how our children's brains are built and how that impacts their behaviour. We explore the science that explains why, however mature they appear, standing proudly on the doorstep ahead of each new school year, your child will still sometimes struggle to handle their stress and successfully regulate their intense feelings and emotions. You will see that the reason your child behaves differently from you is that their brain is different from yours. Even at 11 years old your child will still navigate the world with a brain much less sophisticated than your own. Understanding 'construction' helps us to appreciate why.

BRAIN BOX

'Our brains develop in stages, with the more primitive parts developing first, the more sophisticated parts of our brain last. The part of the brain that allows us to mentalise, to fully consider how others see the world and their perspective of what is around them, isn't completely developed until we are in our twenties. It's why we must not view children of primary school age as the "finished article", they are far from it. Full understanding of what makes people tick only comes with a mature brain.'

— Professor Peter Fonagy, Professor of Contemporary Psychoanalysis and Developmental Science

Your child's brain is still developing, which is why their behaviour is still developing too. It means they WILL make mistakes and they'll need your help when they do. Just as we don't punish our children if they mess up their maths or get a spelling wrong (I hope!) we must offer guidance when they make mistakes with their behaviour, and model the conduct we want to see, not display the behaviour that we don't.

Understanding the neuroscience behind how our children's brains develop goes a long way towards helping us to show compassion when they display less developed behaviour. Anyone who cares for children should consider themselves in the brain development business and we want to do our job well because healthy brain development is fundamental for our children's good future mental health. If we are to understand our children (and ourselves too, by the way) we need to know the science.

The difficulty is that the science of the human brain can be as complex as the organ itself. Even the names given to essential structures seem better suited to *Star Wars* characters than the working parts inside my child's head. Think diencephalon, cerebral peduncle, pons, the arachnoid, not to mention the corpus callosum and cingulate gyrus. Little wonder it has been passing busy parents by! The human brain is considered one of the most complex biological organs in the known universe but our understanding of it doesn't have to be.

As a time-pressured parent myself I wanted a quick reference to remind *myself* 'there's no such thing as "naughty"' when my own children were 'acting out'! I conceived the simple analogy of a tree to represent the brain and three animals to represent its most influential regions. Clearly it uses a great deal of artistic licence to explain some incredibly fascinating science, but I have found it useful to have an accessible and visual reference to help me quickly remember how the different parts of the brain influence my children's (as well as my own) behaviour – particularly during moments of parental overwhelm!

The analogy is inspired by the psychiatrist Dr Bruce Perry's neurosequential model of brain development. I'd encourage you to take a look at his work, and indeed the work of all the scientists and clinicians referenced in the Brain Boxes on these pages. Their invaluable research forms the academic backbone of this book and has helped me to serve my own children as well as the young people in my clinical care.

In my analogy, the brain as a whole is represented by a large baobab tree, known across Africa as the 'Tree of Life'. The baobab is home to the three animals: a lizard, a baboon and a wise old owl. Each animal represents a different area of the brain and each influences different aspects of our behaviour. In reality, these regions of the brain are all interconnected and work together in most respects. While all these parts are present when your child is born, different parts and areas of the brain will develop at different rates.

In a new addition to the analogy for this book, our nervous system is represented by the roots of the baobab tree. Information is passed back and forth between our bodies and brains all the time via our nervous system. Understanding our nervous system and how our brains develop will explain everything about your children's behaviour. Let's start at the beginning to see why.

The Lizard, The Baboon and The Wise Owl ™

THE LIZARD

The first part of your child's brain to form began developing just a few weeks post conception. Known as

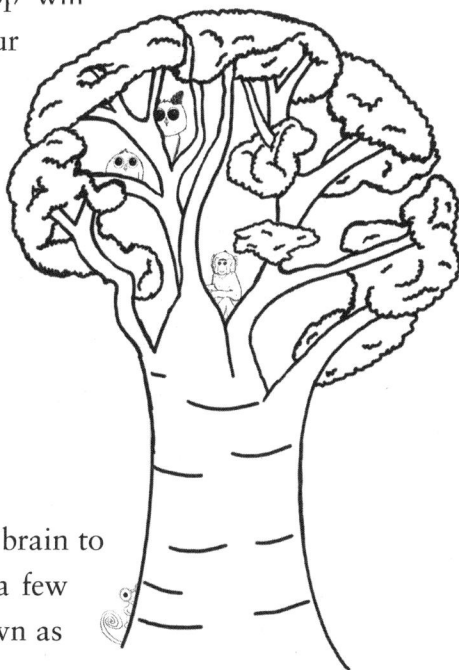

the brain stem, it kept your baby alive in the womb: regulating their breathing, heart rate, blood pressure, swallowing and sleeping patterns.

The brain stem is also involved in feeding, balance and coordination, and it plays an important role in your child's consciousness, awareness and movement. The brain stem and, later, the cerebellum and diencephalon, comprise what we might consider our 'survival brain'. Their function is purely to keep us alive. It's why they are involved in our children's stress response: how your child behaves when they feel threatened, challenged or afraid. Anxiety also has its origins here.

I visualise these parts of our brain as a lizard because they represent the most primitive parts of our brain and are remarkably like the brain that reptiles have – and which they have had for hundreds of millions of years.

Understanding their function helps us translate, and more easily support and soothe, our children's more anxious, defensive and erratic behaviour.

The brain stem connects your child's brain to the rest of their body via the spinal cord, so it also forms part of their nervous system. Just as it kept your child alive in the womb, so the brain stem, or 'lizard', keeps them alive today. It oversees all the behaviour we're less conscious of, including for example, how many breaths you take as you read this page.

Working with other parts of the brain, what I think of as the lizard is constantly scanning your child's (and again, your own) internal environment, checking to ensure their system is in balance; whether they need food or drink, whether they have an infection to fight, or if they've had enough sleep. The lizard – imagine it sat alone and exposed at the bottom of the tree – is alert to the environment around it too, sensing what your child can hear, see, taste, feel and smell. Just like a lizard in the wild, it reacts INSTANTLY if it senses anything that poses danger.

This ancient and primitive part of the brain plays a hugely significant role in influencing your child's daily behaviour. If they are hungry or too cold, or if they are anxious or afraid, or if their environment is too noisy, it is the lizard that drives the stress response and dictates how they react to external 'dangers'. This response can even be triggered just by thoughts our brains *perceive* to be threatening. If your child is worried about an upcoming spelling test, or if another child runs up behind them screaming, their lizard will react before they're even aware of it.

BRAIN BOX

'Even though we may not always be aware of danger on a cognitive level, on a neurophysiological level, our body has already started a sequence of neural processes that would facilitate adaptive defense behaviors such as fight, flight or freeze.'

— Dr Stephen W. Porges, Psychologist and Neuroscientist,

The Polyvagal Theory

The physiologist Walter Cannon was the first to describe our stress response as the 'fight or flight' response. Whenever your child appears aggressive, irritable, angry or 'on the offensive' you should consider whether they're actually in fight/flight.

The foot-stomp of the child who snarls 'I'M STARVING!' after a long day at school, or the howling and hitting that takes place if one sibling dares to take another's favourite toy should all be considered in context of their stress response too.

Consider how quick you are to stomp or shout if you've had too many late nights, or the irritability or 'hanger' you'll experience if you've skipped one too many meals. Our brains are constantly monitoring our welfare too and will drive us to act if it appears we might be in danger of 'starving' or vulnerable if we haven't had enough sleep.

Our FLIGHT response helps us to escape danger rather than tackle it head-on. You might see it in your children if you take them somewhere new and unfamiliar, such as:

A birthday party.
A noisy restaurant.
A new friend's house.
A new school on their first day.

When the flight response is triggered, a child might run around in circles or run away from you. We often see a child in flight when they are nervous or afraid. It can be easy to dismiss this behaviour as 'naughty', but it's a sign of a child whose brain senses danger and is compelling them to act. Big emotions like excitement, fear, shame, embarrassment, anger or boredom can all trigger fight or flight responses. If children feel threatened but their brain detects they cannot fight and they cannot flee, they might adopt the stress responses of freeze, faint or flop instead.

FREEZE. If a child is feeling overwhelmed in class, faced with a question they can't answer, they might freeze, staring blankly ahead. Or, if they're shouted at, they might go mute. Just as a lizard in the wild might stay stock-still if confronted by something it cannot fight or run away from, freeze offers a child a way to 'escape' the situation without physically removing their bodies. We might see a child seeking refuge, hiding beneath a table or refusing to move. Freeze is a form of dissociation, and we'll often see it in children who have experienced trauma – and in us as adults, too.

FAINT or FLOP can occur if a child is totally overcome by fear or even if they experience an overwhelming emotion like guilt, embarrassment or shame. Again, if the options of flee and fight are unavailable, we might see a child flop to the floor in a heap. A child who appears physically or mentally unresponsive is often mistaken as obstructive or, again, 'naughty'. I have seen teachers and parents trying desperately to scoop children up when they have collapsed on the floor, telling them to stop being 'silly'. But the child's brain stem and nervous system are doing precisely what they're designed to do. Again, the response is entirely automatic. The child has no conscious control, just as in the same way an adult has no control over whether they'll faint at the sight of blood. Fainting is another example of the flop response.

BRAIN BOX

'When threatened or injured, all animals draw from a "library" of possible responses. We orient, dodge, duck, stiffen, brace, retract, fight, flee, freeze, collapse, etc. All of these coordinated responses are somatically based – they are things that the body does to protect and defend itself.'

— Dr Peter Levine, author of *Waking the Tiger*

Unless we've had lessons in neurophysiology and been taught how the nervous system reacts to threat (and how many of us have?!), it's understandable why we, and certainly previous generations, have jumped to the conclusion that we are seeing 'naughty' (or even disordered) behaviour when we see a child acting in ways we don't immediately understand. Appreciating how a child's brain drives their behaviour when they're feeling threatened helps to put their actions into a more accurate context.

In Part Two of this book, you'll find numerous practical ways to not only help you translate what can often be mystifying (and sometimes mortifying) behaviour, but I'll also show you how to support your children therapeutically in these moments and quickly bring them back to calm.

We will also reflect on children who adopt a survival mechanism that we might refer to as 'people-pleasing' and has more recently been identified by psychotherapist Pete Walker as FAWN. Again, this reaction tends to happen in situations or with people who a child perceives as threatening. Children whose brain opts for fawning as a survival response can often be overlooked at home or in class because their behaviour is always so 'good'. But FAWN can be a defence mechanism for children who have learned to appease those around them, whether siblings, friends, parents or teachers, to avoid the threat of their displeasure – or worse. The overly compliant child puts others' needs before their own and this can deeply impact their wellbeing. Again, this mechanism is typically deployed if a child's brain determines that no other options are likely to work in ensuring their survival, i.e. that they cannot fight, flee or flop. We often see it in children who have experienced trauma and abuse.

Understanding the role of the brain in influencing a child's behaviour can change everything about how we view children and childcare. A child with a 'lizard on the loose' is not 'naughty'. It's a child unable to even stop to THINK.

The parts of the brain that take charge in an emergency have effectively evolved over millions of years. They're not designed to stop to consider the consequences of their actions because, when survival is at stake, there's no time for that. Your child does not seek to embarrass you if they flop and have a meltdown in the middle of the supermarket aisle – and they find it just as difficult to control the impulse to lash out at a sibling who snatches the last piece of cake, or at another child who has tackled them rather over-enthusiastically on the football field. This is not to say that we should encourage or ignore unsafe behaviour that can see a child hurting themselves or those around them. In fact, I'll explain why it's so important to lay boundaries around behaviour and have clear expectations of our children's conduct. But if we want to help our children understand and work with this very reactive, very primitive part of their brain, we must model the reflective, compassionate and calm behaviour that we want to see in turn.

I have also mentioned anxiety. Our brains have not evolved to distinguish between physical threats and emotional ones. It's why our children's worries and fears can feel like real dangers and why a friendship fallout, an upcoming exam or the anticipation of their performance in the school play can all trigger a fight/flight response in the same way a snarling dog lunging at your child in the park would.

Learning about the brain and helping our children to understand it too will help them to regulate their behaviour. I'll show you how to soothe your child's lizard when it's skittish and how to help your child to overcome challenges, build resilience and conquer future worries and anxieties too.

Now, though, let's look at the next area of your child's brain to fully develop. This part is represented in my metaphor as a baboon.

THE BABOON

This is what scientists often refer to as our limbic brain. It experiences its fastest and most significant growth during your child's first few years. I think of it as a baboon because it is the same mammalian brain that other mammals have, such as your dog or cat. The lizard and baboon areas of the brain work together and influence our children's more primitive behaviours, given both are heavily focused on survival.

Our baboon sits on a branch higher up the tree, above the lizard. He is rather more sophisticated in his skillset given that, unlike the lonesome lizard, he's all about relationships and connecting with others.

When your children were toddlers, it was the baboon who drove them to take their first steps, speak their first words and flash you their first gorgeous smile. What were beautiful moments for us were important rites of passage for the baboon. He knows a child cannot survive on its own. It's why he encourages a child to make a psychological connection with their primary carers (us). It's something we call our 'attachment'. All those early gurgles and smiles were designed to ensure you wouldn't easily forget him if there was a predator around!

Your child's baboon needs consistent care and a sense of security and safety for his healthy development in the first years of life. Having reliable, loving relationships enables him to build trust and develop healthy coping mechanisms for future separations from his primary carers. This is important as it shapes his capacity for handling stress further down the line. It's why the care our children receive in their first three years is vital for helping them regulate their emotions and build resilience for the future.

Early separations from primary caregivers, perhaps with long periods away due to work, illness, hospital stays, bereavement and so on, can sometimes lead to issues with a child's anxiety and stress-related mental health issues in the future.

Having this information can help us put our children's, and indeed our own, behaviour into a much more compassionate context. We might worry that periods of absence, stress or issues with our own mental wellbeing have impacted our children, but I want to offer reassurance and I will offer guidance too. Because if you have any worries about your relationship with your children today, the story doesn't have to end there. As we say in psychotherapy, where there is rupture, there is always repair.

Each time we help our children manage their fears, anxiety and 'stress' today, we support them in learning how to do it for themselves in the future. This is how we build emotional resilience and it's never too late to start.

Many of your child's early experiences are stored as memories in this part of their brain. Memories, and the emotions and feelings associated with them, serve as an important guide for survival given that they enable a child to remember the activities and people they have enjoyed and felt safe around, and, equally, those they have not.

Our memories are processed and given emotional meaning by our amygdala (pronounced amig-dulla). Considered the brain's fear centre, the amygdala works closely with the brain stem to process incoming information that might relate to our survival.

BRAIN BOX

'As a key part of the limbic system, the amygdala receives input from all of the external senses and from the body and is able to detect a potential threat in less than 1/10 of a second, much faster than the time it takes for our brains to create a conscious thought or feeling.'

— Dr Daniel Hughes and Dr Jonathan Baylin,
authors of *Brain-Based Parenting*

The amygdala is involved in processing big emotions like anger, fear and joy. It's why my children experience an immediate sense of excitement when my mum comes to stay. Their baboon associates her with the positive feelings and memories of the games she plays (and likely the chocolate she brings!).

By contrast, if our children are told off at school or have a fallout with a friend in the playground, the amygdala likely processes the incidents negatively and the memories get 'tagged' with negative associations such as shame, embarrassment and fear. Negative incidents are more readily remembered because the brain gives priority to these experiences given they might be crucial lessons for survival. This means that even just the thought of going to school the next day can trigger the stress response, as school is now associated with a negative event.

As we will see in Chapter Two, this can lead to a WHOLE-BODY response that drives those defensive behaviours of fight, flight, freeze and flop. It's something that Jo, a parent who contacted me recently, can directly relate to.

PARENT PONDER

Jo, mother to Olive, 6, Mia, 3, and baby Matthew

I have three children and my eldest, Olive, began 'acting out' on the way to school, holding us up, insisting her socks weren't 'pulled up enough' and whining that I was walking too quickly. We had to stop numerous times and I got so frustrated, trying to juggle a pram and a toddler as well. It led to Olive having a massive 'tantrum' when we reached the school gate. When I contacted Kate, she asked me to take a moment to consider why I thought it might be. Was anything troubling Olive or potentially upsetting her at school? In my stressed-out state I had simply assumed Olive was being difficult!

The next day, I asked her, with genuine curiosity, 'What is it about the socks that feels so important?' Olive instantly burst into tears, wailing, 'When they're straight, I won't hurt my knee!' She'd fallen rather badly in the playground the week before and there had been a fair bit of blood. No wonder she wanted her socks properly up and 'straight' – she wanted to protect her knees! I talked to her about the fall, as Kate suggested, and we spoke about the 'hurt knee' and 'all the blood' and how it must have been painful and rather scary too. I realised the fall had left more than just a physical mark. Olive was frightened about falling and hurting herself again.

I felt so bad about getting so cross. I stopped walking and we all sat down on a wall and I gave her a cuddle. Never mind being late! Olive cried some more and then sank into my arms. I told her I could completely understand why it felt so important for her socks to be 'up'. Now that I was calm it seemed only natural to think about a solution rather than telling her off! I asked Olive if she thought that wearing tights might help to reassure her when she was running around. The happiness (and relief) on her face melted my heart. She now wears tights and the walk to school is a joy. It's as though I'm the best mummy ever – and all because I stopped to wonder why.

In this case, a combination of the event – the nasty fall – and the memory of the pain and hurt feelings associated with it would have triggered Olive's baboon. Getting hurt is a potential threat to survival, so the baboon would have been doing backflips the closer Olive got to school. His job is to protect Olive, so he'll have tried anything to resist going (flight), then, when Olive's mum insisted that they hurry up, he tried 'fight' by refusing to walk faster. This is where we can see our children insist, 'I WON'T do that!' Olive's lizard and baboon brain were driving her to pull up her socks, both a delaying tactic and to 'protect' her from another fall. Clever brain! Except the behaviour was pitting her baboon against her mum's, given Jo's baboon was also stressed about the embarrassment of being late at the gate.

Little wonder it all felt so difficult and Olive finally FLOPPED with a 'meltdown' at the gate. It was only when Jo helped her to process the event of the fall, acknowledged her pain and the anxiety about it happening again that Olive could release her pent-up emotions, have a good cry and do what I think of as 'exorcise' the energy of the stress response. Olive and her mum could walk to school with the emergency over, a solution to the problem and Olive's demeanour restored to its usual happy, calm state.

In Part Two, I'll show you how to help encourage your children to tell you how they're feeling rather than 'act out' their feelings instead. I'll also explain how you can help your child release the energy of the stress response in a much safer, more appropriate way.

We can do it when our 'wise owl' is in charge.

THE WISE OWL

Formally known as the prefrontal cortex, the wise owl represents the part of the human brain that sets us apart from most other animals. Known as our 'higher' or more sophisticated thinking brain, it only comes 'online' at around three years of age and doesn't reach maturity until adulthood. It's why our children are so vulnerable to stress when they are very young. Because it's this part of the brain that helps us to manage stress and regulate our big feelings and emotions – it's still developing. Our wise owl helps us to learn, to have empathy, to consider the world from someone else's perspective and to problem-solve. She enables us to learn from our mistakes, build resilience and have a strong sense of self. The wise owl part of our brain allows us to perceive time, consider the past and future, and understand concepts and nuanced thought.

BRAIN BOX

'Mentalisation allows us to see ourselves from the outside and others from the inside. It enables us to understand misunderstandings and to know ourselves subjectively. Those psychological skills allow us to spontaneously and, largely in an intuitive manner, make sense of our own actions and those of others by considering their beliefs, desires and feelings, their mental states.'
— Peter Fonagy, Professor of Contemporary Psychoanalysis and Developmental Science

Having a wise owl helps us to consider right from wrong, and to think about the consequences of our actions. With the benefit of her 'big picture view', sitting high up in the canopy of the tree, it's this part of our brain that helps us to put our experiences, and other people, into context, offering us a clear perspective.

If our lizard is getting skittish, or 'fizzy', as I think of it, or our baboon is beating his chest in alarm, our wise owl will swoop down to scoop them up in the warm comfort of her wings with a reassuring 'it's OK, we've got this'. As we'll see, this is how we all successfully regulate our emotions and what gives us solid foundations for good mental health. It's what neuropsychiatrist Dr Daniel Siegel terms as having good 'vertical integration'.

Equally, if a threat is real, our strong wise owl helps the baboon and lizard, joining forces to defend us, making a formidable team! In short, having a wise owl allows us to navigate life happily, enjoying the emotional highs as well as experiencing any lows, without getting overwhelmed in between.

BUT …

Your child doesn't have a wise owl yet! What they have is more 'little owl', and remember, she's a little owl with learner plates on.

Sure, your child's prefrontal cortex is more developed than when they were very little, which explains why they can now sit still and concentrate for longer periods at school and why their emotional meltdowns are (hopefully) fewer and further between. But if your child has a worry, if they're ill, tired or feeling challenged, if they've had a difficult day, if someone's said something to upset them or their team lost at football, you can generally guarantee their lizard and baboon will jump into the driving seat.

Even at age 11, a child's little owl doesn't have the life experience, the wisdom or the wingspan to confidently swoop down to reassure.

But *your* wise owl does.

Whenever your child is in distress, for whatever reason (however irrational that reason might appear to you), sending in your wise owl is the quickest – and healthiest – route to calm.

In short, with your warmth, love and understanding, you get to show the little owl how to drive. It might feel counterintuitive, especially if, like my husband, you weren't raised that way as a child yourself.

MAN-OEUVRES WITH MIKE

As someone who grew up on a hard-bitten council estate in the North East of England, with a family that rarely, if ever, spoke about feelings, I'll admit my wife Kate's 'wise owl 'way of parenting initially seemed alien. I worried it would have us 'indulging' behaviour at home that was – let's just say it – 'naughty'!

Behaviour such as our seven-year-old son using our bed for a trampoline. Wilbur was doing it in the morning, when, not only would it mess up the bed, it was making us late for school. I'd bark 'stop it!' and chase him from our room.

One morning, frustrated and given my own parenting style clearly wasn't working, I considered what Kate would say. In her first book, she advised something she calls SAS, where you 'say what you see' and name the behaviour, then acknowledge the potential emotion associated with it, such as whether your child seems upset, cross, angry or disappointed. Then you soothe any upset.

I turned to Wilbur, who was mid-jump, and said as calmly as I could, 'Wilbur, I see you are jumping on our bed.' I paused for effect then followed up with, 'You seem a bit fizzy? Do you want to tell me about it?'

'Fizzy' is one of the words Kate uses to describe behaviour that appears more erratic. It felt very accurate given what Wilbur was doing. As if by magic, he immediately stopped jumping and blurted, 'I've got a playdate later with Ishaan, and I'm really worried!'

I was totally taken aback. Suddenly it made sense. Wilbur had just started at a new school and he was having his first playdate at his new friend's house. He wasn't being 'naughty'. He was just anxious!

I thought about it. The 'jumping' had only begun recently, around the same time he'd started at the new school. Had Wilbur been using it to work through the inevitable nerves that had likely arisen given the big transition of changing school and making new friends?

I thought about the symbolism of him jumping on our bed instead of his own. Had it been his way of trying to show me what he was feeling inside? Kate often says that what children are feeling on the inside is projected in their actions on the outside. My instant assumption of 'naughty' meant I'd missed Wilbur's behavioural Morse code entirely.

Asking my son a question in a way that suggested I wanted to help, rather than tell him off, was all he'd needed to open up. He could use his words to tell me what he was feeling, rather than jump them out on a freshly made bed instead.

When we're curious about what is going on with our children on the inside, we'll understand everything we see in their behaviour on the outside. In the next chapter, I reveal the significant role your child's nervous system plays in their behaviour. Because, what goes on in a child's brain doesn't stay there; it 'goes on' in their bodies too.

Wise Owl Wisdoms

- Your child behaves differently from you because they have a brain that is different to yours.

- When we understand the brain, we can better understand our children's behaviour.

- Symbolically, it can help to think of our brains using the analogy of the baobab tree. The tree is home to the metaphorical lizard, baboon and wise owl. They represent the parts of our brain that influence different aspects of our behaviour and what we feel inside.

- Our wise owl helps us to regulate our big emotions and consider the world from another's perspective.

- Our children don't have a fully developed wise owl brain yet. They have a little owl – and she's got her learner plates on.

- Using our wise owl wisdom, we teach the little owl how to drive. This is how we support our children's healthy brain development and their future mental health.

Chapter Two

CONSTRUCTION – The Role of the Nervous System in 'naughty'

*What happens in Vagus doesn't
stay in Vagus.*

Whether Wilbur is using our bed as a trampoline or waking us at 3am, yelling, 'a monster's in my room going BLEURGH!', it's not just his brain that's driving his behaviour, it's his nervous system too.

Our nervous system is our body's command centre; it includes our brain, spinal cord and a complex network of nerves. It connects all parts of the body, allowing them to communicate with each other, creating a superhighway for information. In the analogy, I imagine the baobab's long roots relaying information back and forth between our body and brain.

Our nervous system guides everything we do, say, think and feel. A crucial part of it is called the autonomic nervous system, named so because it functions automatically. It's constantly monitoring whether we are healthy and in balance. It's active whether we are awake or asleep, which explains why our children

are instantly up and running into our room if something goes bump (or bleurgh, as Wilbur would have it) in the night. Our nervous system ensures our survival and helps us make sense of the world and what we feel inside.

BRAIN BOX

'While we may think our brains are in charge, the heart of our daily experience and the way we navigate the world begins in our bodies with the autonomic nervous system. This is the place where the stories emerge about who we are and how the world works, what we do and how we feel. It is our biology that shapes our experiences of safety and connection.'

— Deb Dana, Therapist and Trauma Consultant, author of *Anchored*

To understand your child's behaviour, you'll need to understand their nervous system, because if it's out of kilter, so are they.

If a child feels unsafe (and remember, thoughts can feel as

threatening as physical events), stress hormones and chemicals are released into their body, priming them to act: this is our stress response. It is automatic and instant. We have already seen how Wilbur's worries about a future playdate triggered *his* stress response, as much as Olive's tumble in the playground triggered *hers*.

Our stress response is generally considered a positive evolutionary adaptation. It's our brain and body's automatic reaction to fear. Short bursts of adrenaline and cortisol allow us to escape or confront whatever it is that stands in our way. It allows us to take on challenges and get things done, whether walking into a room full of strangers, giving a speech, doing a workout, navigating the traffic or even falling in love!

The stress response is positive for our children, too. It helps them learn to ride a bike, climb a tree, make new friends and leave you at the gate on the first day of school. A little stress is a good thing. If we want our children to have resilience and confidence in life, we need to help them befriend their nervous system and positively harness the energy of the stress response. But they don't get there without our help. The stress response involves a WHOLE-BODY response and the symptoms can sometimes feel overwhelming.

The sympathetic nervous system is the part of the nervous system involved in activating the stress response. I remember 's' for sympathetic by visualising a skydiver.

The skydive analogy helps us understand what happens if we, or our children, face something that frightens or challenges us.

Let's imagine that you find yourself in a skydiving suit, about to climb into a small Cessna 182 aeroplane. For reasons now entirely unknown, you've agreed to do a charity skydive. Even the anticipation of throwing yourself out of a moving object at 10,000 feet has your lizard and baboon going wild. They (accurately) detect a potential threat to life and, before you know it, your baboon is bounding across his branch to hit what I think of as a 'big red fire alarm' to frantically alert you to danger. This alarm is your amygdala, and if the amygdala decides that yes, there is a threat to life, it sends a distress signal to a structure in your brain called the hypothalamus. The hypothalamus then 'speaks' with the rest of your body via your nervous system, triggering a whole chain of events.

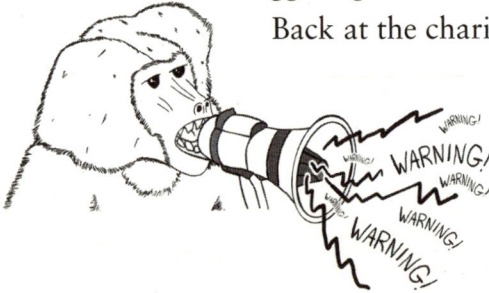

Back at the charity skydive, with your family and friends watching, you somehow manage to suppress your sense of dread and head for the runway and get bundled into the plane.

At this point, your system is on overdrive. Your adrenal glands furiously pump adrenaline and cortisol into your bloodstream, making your heart beat faster, sending blood out to your limbs, lungs and brain – preparing you to ACT. The plane takes off, your breathing quickens and more oxygen is sent to your brain, making your senses super sharp. Time seems to slow down and an increase in your blood sugar gives you extra energy to either FIGHT or in this case, quite literally, take FLIGHT!

It's worth repeating that this process is automatic and involuntary. You have no conscious control and it's just the same for your child.

The plane door opens and your hypothalamic-pituitary-adrenal (HPA) axis (you can see why I like using the metaphor) kicks in, adding even more stress hormones to the neurochemical wildfire now raging within. Sitting on the ledge, looking out at green fields thousands of feet below, you have head fog, your chest is tight, you find it hard to swallow, your heart pounds and your stomach churns.

Your wise owl – your prefrontal cortex – grabs the opportunity to offer some crumbs of comfort. She reassures you that it's natural to be frightened (no kidding) but, she adds, you have had some training (we'd hope) and you won't be jumping alone. At that point, your instructor gives you the nod, you gulp down some air and bottom-shuffle to the edge. Then it's off, out and away you go!

In free fall, your instructor's calm, steady presence helps you to remain calm too. The wind might be buffeting but your training kicks in and you manage to find your balance. Heck, you even start to enjoy the adrenaline rush and the view! Your instructor pulls your ripcord and up goes the parachute, breaking your fall. It slows your descent, allowing you to float gently and safely back to earth.

What Goes Up, Must Come Down: The Parasympathetic Nervous System – Our 'Parachute'

This is, in essence, how our nervous system works.

While not every challenge we face will be as extreme and

prolonged as a skydive, our brain and
body still respond the same way. We just
might experience the symptoms more
briefly. For example, the short shock
of energy and the pounding of your heart
if your child runs towards a busy road, the
sweaty palms and shortness of breath before a
big job interview, or the massive surge of energy and the trembling
hands you'd experience after a near miss on the motorway.

As soon as the 'danger' has passed, our nervous system
brings us back to balance. It's designed this way because having
equilibrium – being in balance – is essential for our wellbeing. We
cannot stay in a heightened state of emergency for too long; the
symptoms would be too overwhelming, and sitting with prolonged
and heightened adrenaline and cortisol levels is very harmful
to our health.

Just as the parachute slows our descent on a skydive, so the
part of our nervous system, called the parasympathetic nervous
system (we can remember 'p' for parachute), brings our body back
to calm after we've been in fight or flight. It actions the release
of anti-anxiety chemicals that bring our system safely back to
homeostasis – that is, back to stability.

This is how we keep our mind and body in balance as we
navigate the many trials and tribulations of parenting life, whether
we're running late for school or juggling work calls while making
supper. Our nervous system essentially ensures that what goes
up, must come down, and something called our vagus nerve is
central to it all.

'What Happens in Vagus Doesn't Stay in Vagus'

The longest nerve in the body, the vagus nerve represents the main component of the parasympathetic nervous system. It is responsible for calming our organs after the stress response has been activated. Most of the individual neurons that make up the vagus nerve are sensory ones. They pass messages from our organs to the brain and are activated by sensory input from the environment. It explains the 'gut reaction' we get about certain people or situations and why we can walk into a room and feel the tension if the people in there have been arguing, or 'sense' someone is following us before we've even turned around.

The vagus nerve plays an incredibly important role in our physical and mental health. Evidence suggests it plays a large part in governing inflammation and the immune responses that are involved in conditions such as heart disease, Crohn's disease, rheumatoid arthritis and Parkinson's. Stimulating the vagus nerve has been found to help people with epilepsy, diabetes, depression and post-traumatic stress. In short, a healthy vagus nerve is fundamental for our physical and mental health. Chiropractor and functional medicine practitioner Dr Navaz Habib, in his book *Activate Your Vagus Nerve*, describes the vagus nerve as 'the conductor of the human body symphony orchestra'. Meaning, if it is out of tune, then so are we.

How each of us responds to stress will depend on how easily we can tolerate the symptoms and how quickly we can bring ourselves back to calm. In Chapter Three, I share some easy ways you can activate your vagus nerve and ensure you get your parachute up quickly if you've been in fight/flight – and I'll help you to teach your children how to do the same. Having good vagal tone is key for our parenting because as well as supporting our children's health, it will lead to more balanced behaviour and less loss of control.

Think of the parenting programmes when cameras capture the child who is trashing their room with the adults outside looking on. This is a child in fight or flight – but without an instructor by their side. In Chapter Four and Chapter Ten, I'll show you how to help your children experience the 'full throttle' of a whole-body stress response – but to experience and express it safely. It means we'll see much less of the big, erratic behaviour we can see when our children are in danger of 'spinning out'.

A key part of having good mental health is in our stress management – how we cope with stress and how we bring ourselves back to calm. It's not something we are born with: it's something we have to learn.

Therefore, how we respond when our children are frightened or feeling challenged is instrumental in helping our children to regulate their physical and emotional responses to stress. This role begins at birth because our babies are incapable of self-regulation and need help managing stress. Every time your baby was afraid, they experienced that same burst of cortisol. Each time you instinctively responded, picking your baby up to comfort and reassure them, triggered a release of the beautiful 'love' hormone oxytocin and powerful endorphins that helped soothe and calm them down. With your loving, reassuring and reliable presence, you were already 'programming' resilience. As toddlers our children still needed our help – in fact, research suggests children under four need help with emotional regulation every 20 seconds! And your child still needs your help today as illustrated beautifully in the following parent ponder from a mother who read my first book and shares her family's experience here.

PARENT PONDER
Ami, mother to Leo, 6

My husband's work led to a six-month relocation to Austria. None of us could ski and we thought it would be a good opportunity for our son, Leo, to learn. Initially, he found it tricky and after a few days his instructor wanted to give him the chance to take part in a race, to show him how much progress he'd made. He told Leo about it right at the last minute, however, when a large crowd of children were watching. As the instructor explained the rules and what poles Leo had to go round, adding that the race would be timed, Leo burst into tears.

In front of everyone, he began shouting and screaming at my husband and me, and tried furiously to kick off his skis. He then dropped to the ground, sitting in the snow, 'refusing' to get up. I was so embarrassed, and I'll admit my big baboon took over. I stormed over, put my arms under his armpits and tried desperately to lift him up. My wise owl instinctively wanted to stop and give him a hug, but my embarrassment and my baboon were overriding her and, instead, I loudly told him off for 'being silly'.

Leo completely lost it with me and pushed me away. I could sense all the other parents and their kids watching me. I was mortified. Then, something clicked. I had read *There's No Such Thing as 'naughty'* and I suddenly thought, Leo's not being silly, he's just stressed! I felt such a rush of compassion for my son and I felt cross with myself for being embarrassed about his behaviour. Expecting a six-year-old to compete in a race without warning on his first time skiing might be too much. Ignoring everyone around me, I sat down in the snow and told Leo I was sorry it had come as a surprise, and I followed what I had learned in the book. SAS: Say what you see, Acknowledge and Soothe.

I said, 'I can see how cross you are' and 'I understand'. I said I realised we should have given him more warning about the race and that I was sorry. His rigid little body relaxed against mine and I rocked him just like I used to do when he was young. I went into soothe – 'it's OK, Mummy's here'. It took a few minutes as his baboon was really up and out the gates, but I kept going! It wasn't long before he calmed down, however, and I tentatively suggested we take a walk over to see how the other kids were doing it. I said then he could decide if he wanted to race. I was amazed when Leo instantly took my hand and, like a little wobbly giraffe on his skis, came with me to look! When we watched a few of the other kids race, I gently whispered to him that I reckoned he would be proud of himself if he did have a go. My husband and I promised to be there to watch him and that we'd walk down to greet him at the end of the race. I could have burst with pride (and relief) when he went over to the starting line by himself and finished the race!

How about that for some wise owl parenting?!

Leo went into the classic FLOP because his nervous system was overwhelmed. His sympathetic nervous system would already have been firing, given that skiing for the first time is a new skill, and it's pretty scary to be strapped to skis going downhill fast!

When Leo is suddenly told to race against other kids and do it immediately, without any preparation, his baboon goes bananas. He's angry at being put in what he perceives is a 'dangerous' – and potentially embarrassing – situation. Embarrassment is a big trigger for the baboon and, therefore, our stress response because the risk of humiliation is high stakes in evolutionary terms. If we humiliate ourselves, it could mean we are not accepted and perhaps even expelled from the 'troop', which spells certain death in the wild. Humiliation or embarrassment in public is a significant threat – whether for us or our children. It will almost always lead to a baboon response. Leo's baboon can't fight; he tries to kick off his skis to escape, but he can't flee either. What other option did he have to avoid doing something that his brain and body perceived as emotionally and physically threatening?

He COLLAPSES.
He FLOPS.

Leo was not 'naughty', he was not a 'wimp', he's just a six-year-old whose stress response is in charge.

Luckily, he had a mum who could override her own initial (and understandable) baboon response. Her soothing words and the rocking back and forth would see the release of all the wonderful anti-anxiety chemicals, including oxytocin, which would help his lizard and baboon stand down, and his little owl lean in. Sitting alongside him, Leo's mum ensured he first felt SAFE, which enabled him to CONTAIN the stress response and go on to HARNESS its energy. It gave him the confidence to choose to race himself.

THIS is where the roots of resilience grow.

Child psychiatrist and trauma expert Dr Bruce Perry's research reveals that when our children are in distress, anything that we do that is patterned, repetitive and rhythmic, like rocking our children gently, making shushing or soothing noises, will restore the brain and nervous system to calm. He explains: 'One of the most powerful sets of associations created in utero is the association between patterned, repetitive rhythmic activity from maternal heart rate and all the neural patterns of activity associated with not being hungry, not being thirsty, and feeling "safe".' In other words, rhythm, as he says, is regulating.

With her wise owl in the driving seat, Ami instinctively knew how to soothe and regulate her son, even mid public meltdown. You can too. I know it's not always easy to do and very often we'll need to override our own baboon responses when our children resist, cry or 'won't try'. But it's important. Because your child's ability to cope with future stress and their capacity for resilience is highly influenced by their relationship with you.

Whether it's the first day of school or learning a new skill, if our children are attempting to do anything for the first time that they find challenging, we help them most when we first support them 'alongside'.

There has been, and perhaps still is, a popular misconception that children need to 'buckle up' or that we should 'drop and go' when they're afraid, in the belief that resilience is born when a child is left to sink or swim. Sadly, as evidence shows, the opposite is true. Even for children who have experienced significant hardship, we now know it's in having a supportive relationship with someone who helps them to come through that they build solid foundations for future resilience and good mental health.

BRAIN BOX

'Despite the widespread belief that individual grit, extraordinary self-reliance, or some in-born, heroic strength of character can triumph over calamity, science now tells us that it is the reliable presence of at least one supportive relationship and multiple opportunities for developing effective coping skills that are essential building blocks for the capacity to do well in the face of significant adversity.'

— Center on the Developing Child, Harvard University

When we can be the calm, steady 'instructor' to our children's skydivers, when they're feeling overwhelmed, the sooner they'll make their 'skydives' alone.

It is now much more likely that Leo will go on to embrace any future sporting challenges because his baboon has banked a positive memory this time. It doesn't mean he found it easy but having an adult he trusted to first be 'alongside' enabled him to overcome that initial discomfort and feel empowered to make the decision to race for himself.

If Ami had continued to urge her son not to be silly or forced him against his will, it would likely have led to simmering resentment between mother and son. In turn, there would also likely be a loss of trust with the baboon banking a negative memory and association, leaving him much less likely to attempt anything similar in the future. If Ami had given up and walked away in embarrassment, it would have left everyone feeling bad and a valuable opportunity to build resilience would have been missed.

Please don't worry if you are now thinking back to a time

when this has happened to you. We've all been there! I know from experience how big blowouts in public can trigger our own adult stress response. I, too, have had occasions when my baboon has stepped in with my children, rather than me using my wise owl. We won't always get it right. But we can always repair, we can always effect change, and we can always do things differently.

It's important that we do.

BRAIN BOX

'Resilience results in healthy development because it protects the developing brain and other organs produced by excessive activation of stress response systems.'
— Center on the Developing Child, Harvard University

Our children's stress response will be triggered numerous times each day, very often when we're not there; whether they feel ill, fall out with a friend, fail a test or fluff their lines in the school play. With our help, our children learn to experience and manage stress, and are able to 'pull the ripcord' themselves, with a little owl who can stretch her wings and get them back to earth safely.

Most of the time, the nervous system does a brilliant job. Too much stress, or stress that is unresolved, can, however, tip us, and our children, into overwhelm. We're not designed to have high levels of cortisol and adrenaline constantly coursing through our system with not enough moments to pull the ripcord and relax. If we, or our children, are forced to sit with persistent and unresolved fear, it can have deeply negative consequences, because it is then that our stress can become chronic or 'toxic'.

Overactivation of the stress response in young children can

lead to a path of dysfunction, as the research of developmental psychologists like Dr Suzanne Zeedyk and paediatricians like Dr Nadine Burke Harris shows.

BRAIN BOX

'We might describe the stress system as "over-activated" when it is called on so often that it ceases to function well. It has to cope with so much unpredictability or uncertainty or fear that it doesn't have time to recover in between. This leads to a dysfunctional stress system. It doesn't have the capacity to calm down or spend time relaxing. It "learns" that it must be constantly vigilant, on guard against the threats in the environment. This can lead to physical problems, such as breathing too fast or a heart that beats too fast or cells that don't replicate properly. Over time, that can turn into heart problems or cancer. While this is uncomfortable to think about, it makes sense once we understand how the stress system functions. It can also lead to emotional or mental problems, such as poor concentration, because your stress system has learned to always keep an eye out for threats, or anxiety, because you have to cope with too much uncertainty, or lack of trust, because no adult ever came to help.'

— Dr Suzanne Zeedyk, Developmental Psychologist

As we will see in Chapter Fifteen (on difficulty / trauma) the study of childhood trauma has been uncovering the evidence of links between childhood distress and adult health. The links have surprised many people and Dr Zeedyk says it has taken courage to contemplate what the data is revealing. It's important because it helps us to appreciate the significance of relationships in our children's lives. What matters most is whether a child has to handle their fear alone or whether they have someone to help them.

If you or your child experienced stress that was not manageable, if you did not have someone to support you, or if you were not able to support your child for any reason, please don't worry. I say this with both clinical and personal experience. I am going to share plenty of evidence-based methods and resources for helping you and your children to safely release your stress, whether in the moment of the stress response, or with stress energy that has been long held.

Stress, as Dr Nadine Burke Harris says, 'lives in the body'. If we don't learn how to harness its positive effects, and help our children to release their stress energy healthily, it can get 'exorcised' in less beneficial ways – whether it's jumping on the bed, bouncing a ball around a room, fidgeting or fighting. If we feel 'stress' from within and we aren't encouraged and enabled to release it safely, our body will find other ways to release it, because our nervous system always wants to bring us back to balance.

FLOP/FREEZE

The flop or freeze response can see us immobile, shut down, even our mind shutting off to make a distressing event seem less real. Fainting, as I have said, is an example of the flop response and to stretch the skydive analogy further, I imagine the parachute falling over us on the ground, covering us, trapping us beneath. Just as we'd find it hard to make our way out from beneath the material, we now know, as the work of Dr Stephen Porges has shown, that our body doesn't easily transition out of the freeze, or faint, state. As he says, 'When the body is in that state, that body is in the state of profound autonomic defense.'

I'm going to show you how we can help our children to move out of those defensive states and regain physiological balance. Once we can read our children's cues, our job becomes much easier and their behaviour makes much more sense.

There will be times when we all realise that we have missed the mark, done the 'wrong thing' and our children have been angry with us because, just like Leo, they felt unsafe and we didn't read the signs. It can be hard to look back and think about times when we might have missed our children's behavioural Morse code. Again, it's OK; that's why we're here.

We have seen that the nervous system drives all the big fight or flight behaviour, from foot stomping to fighting. If we are to help our children to CONTAIN their big emotions and the energy of the stress response, we need to manage our own. We'll start the next chapter with easy and practical ways to activate your vagus nerve, support your health and find balance, leaving you calmer and more contained, which will support your children's calm, contained behaviour too. To help our children achieve CALM and not add to their chaos, we'll need a full cup of calm ourselves. It's something any busy parent knows is not always easy to achieve.

WISE OWL WISDOMS

- The stress response is an evolutionary adaptation designed to help us respond to stressful situations.

- Its job is to keep us alive, which means it takes charge if it's triggered.

- It involves a whole-body response – with symptoms that can feel odd or even overwhelming, especially to a young child.

- When the stress response is triggered, our children have little to no control over how their brain chooses to react.

- Our children need help in returning to calm – they can't always do it alone.

- The more we respond and soothe our children when they're experiencing 'stress', the more we programme for resilience.

- Resilience is vital for future mental health.

- Without our help, our children can offload and discharge the energy of fight or flight in ways that are not always safe.

- When we understand the nervous system, we can support our children and bring them back to calm.

Chapter Three

CALM – Addressing Our Parental Stress

We cannot always change the circumstances in which we find ourselves, but we can change how we respond.

I'm by the door, ready to leave for school, when Wilbur runs downstairs, proclaiming triumphantly.

'I'm wearing my red camouflage socks today!'

I'm already on high alert, given we're on the verge of being late. The prospect of turning up at school just as the gates are closing on top of the additional embarrassment of sending my child to school in the wrong socks sees my baboon lose his rag.

'Oh no, you're not! Quick, go back upstairs and put your grey school socks on!'

On another day, I might have smiled conspiratorially and waved Wilbur over to the shoe cupboard. I rather like his cheeky non-conformism. But today, I am tired. Mike is abroad and my wise owl is only just hanging in there. The last time Wilbur wore his red socks, the school called me at home to remind me about school uniform policy. It means my lizard is now 'fizzy', and my baboon beats his chest in expectation of the shame of, once again, being called out by the uniform police.

While all this flashes through my brain, Clemency dashes past me on the hunt for the water bottle she swore she'd packed last night. Then Gatsby, our puppy, emerges from the garden with something limp and grey in his mouth. It's rubbish collection day, and I suspect it's fox leftovers, judging by the smell.

I imagine my wise owl frantically flicking through her Little Book of Calm to offer a regulating thought …

STRESS. I think it's the most significant barrier to us being the parents we always hope to be and the fun-sponge parent we fear we have become.

Stress can be so much a part of everyday life we are forgiven for accepting it as 'normal'. Whether we're late for pick up, concerned about childcare, have a relationship on the rocks or are worried about work or wider world events, stress impacts us all.

BRAIN BOX

'For the vast majority of beasts on this planet, stress is about a short-term crisis, after which it's either over with or you're over with. When we sit around and worry about stressful things, we turn on the same physiological responses, but they are potentially a disaster when provoked chronically.'

— Dr Robert M. Sapolsky, *Why Zebras Don't Get Ulcers*

Parenting is messy, it's chaotic and I know of no greater test to human patience. Most of the time, our brilliant stress response kicks in and allows us to navigate our short-term crises (relatively) smoothly. However, as we've seen, the stress response can involve intense bodily arousal and we cannot stay in that heightened state for long.

Research has identified three factors that universally lead to stress: uncertainty, a lack of information and a loss of control.

Parenting, anyone?! Stress is part of our everyday package.

From the moment we wake (or are woken) to the time we clock off (which, let's face it, is never), *our* stress response will get triggered numerous times a day. If we don't learn how to release it healthily, it not only impacts our health, but also our children's.

Why?

Because stress can create what clinical psychologists Dr Dan Hughes and Dr Jonathan Baylin call 'blocked care'.

BRAIN BOX

'When we're in a state of parental frustration or stress, the deep parts of our brain that are tightly connected to our bodies are strongly activated, briefly suppressing our higher cognitive capacities for self-regulation, self-awareness and empathy.'

— Dr Dan Hughes and Dr Jonathan Baylin,
authors of *Brain-Based Parenting*

Even the best and most well-meaning parent will struggle with calm and compassion when they're under pressure. As Dan Hughes and Jonathan Baylin put it, 'While we're in this state of mind and body we are essentially "mindless" not "mindful".'

It means we can do or say things that we later regret. It means we see fear in our children's eyes when we shout and sense their simmering resentment when we insist 'because I said so!', rather than stopping to patiently explain why.

We will all lose our rag sometimes. I know of no parent who hasn't, nor who enjoys yelling or the sense of shame and regret that usually follow. It's important to forgive ourselves in these moments, because unless our parents were schooled by grandmaster Buddhists, it's likely we weren't taught the all-important art of emotional regulation when we were young. Few people are.

But learning how to manage our stress better is one of the greatest gifts we can give ourselves as well as our children. Stress doesn't just 'live' in us, it leaks into our environment too. In the wild, a baboon who barks and beats his chest in alarm when he spies a leopard in the undergrowth will trigger the other baboons in his troop to start beating their chests and barking too. It's something called 'stress contagion'. When we learn the art of emotional regulation, we get to break the cycle of shouting baboons and engage wise owl to little owl instead.

PARENT PONDER
Joe Wicks (speaking on the BBC's Joe Wicks Podcast)

As a kid growing up, I was in a very chaotic household. There was a lot of shouting and swearing and doors being slammed – and that, in a way, is my default setting. So to read Kate's book and understand how a child's brain works and how I can react differently, it's almost like a muscle that I'm training so that every time I'm in a stressful situation I'm being different ... by understanding and visualising the little owl who doesn't have the wisdom and the understanding of what's going on, it's really fundamentally changed the way I am parenting.

Our children learn what they live. If we shout, it scares them and triggers their stress response. Given that they're smaller than us, their brain might opt to flee, freeze, fawn or flop; but consider the fast-approaching hormone-driven teenage years, and your child might well learn how to shout back.

MAN-OEUVRES WITH MIKE

I think it's crucial that Kate shares personal stories in this book about stress and how it impacts our parenting. I work away a lot. When I come home, I can find myself out of kilter and disconnected and it can lead to less than calm behaviour on my part.

Once, when I was overseeing bedtime and watching the kids brushing their teeth, Wilbur, then seven, accidentally dropped his toothbrush down the loo. Clemency and I instantly laughed because we could see the funny side. Wilbur clearly did not. Yelling, he turned on Clemency, in full-on baboon, angry at being ridiculed. He had her in a headlock before I had a chance to step in. It immediately triggered my baboon and I flew at him, pulling him off her, shouting, 'WHY can't you CONTROL your temper?!'

The irony of my question was not lost on me.

From friends I speak to, few fathers can be Zen masters when their children are fighting. For me, the worry that my kids might get hurt is when I lose my cool. But I realise if I am going to help my son regulate his emotions and keep his temper, I need to work harder at regulating mine.

Acknowledging and talking about it helps me to be the father I want to be and to model the behaviour I want to see in my children. I still don't get it right when I'm tired or jet-lagged. These are the days when my baboon is more likely to hijack my brain and override my wise owl. Being more aware of it helps me to ensure I can more easily keep my temper in check. I now make sure I go for a run when I get home and don't make any important decisions or look at my phone in case work emails trigger my stress response. I can be the dad I want to be and help my children learn the essential lessons I was unfortunately never taught when I was young.

To use another flight analogy, we can't help our children with their oxygen mask until we've fixed our own. There are many ways we can support our mental and physical wellbeing and I list numerous resources at the back of this book. But I thought it might be useful to include some of the exercises and therapeutic practices that I find helpful, to support your wellbeing and activate your vagus nerve, allowing you to get your parachute up quickly, even when your little baboons are running riot.

We'll get to their behaviour – don't worry! – but let's get ourselves firmly on the ground first.

Do the Shake It Out (Not the Scream and Shout)

Clinical psychologist Dr Peter Levine observed that prey animals like deer or gazelles physically shake or tremble if they have been chased by a predator but then escaped. He noticed that the animals would shake uncontrollably for a few minutes as though literally shaking the stress out of their bodies. Once it was done, the impala or deer would return to grazing. He concluded it was the animals' innate way of releasing excess energy after a stress response. His research and his concept of 'somatic experiencing' is something I use for myself and in my clinical work. It offers a natural and gentle way to release our stress energy, every day as well as the energy of events that might be longer held.

Dr Levine observed that all animals, other than humans and animals in captivity, will discharge excess stress energy this way. Given that he also observed that animals in the natural world don't experience post-traumatic stress, this is something to consider for our own mental and physical health. I think it's time for us to re-learn how to do it, too.

You can try it for yourself. Stand up and do a gentle shimmy, shaking out your arms and legs as though you are shivering. You might stomp your feet, or run your hands up and down your arms and legs, allowing your limbs to move and stretch. Follow your body's lead. Perhaps put on some music and dance if you feel like it, anything to facilitate a gentle release and discharge of any energy that's built up inside over the day.

I encourage the children in my therapy room to do similar exercises, especially if we have had a deep session. We might stomp around, put on music, bang some drums, sing loudly or even shout! It proves a wonderful release and is often met with much laughter, too – laughter providing another lovely stress reliever with the release of wonderfully healing endorphins to boot!

Many ancient practices, including all forms of yoga, qigong, and tai chi, have much to contribute to somatic exercises and therapy and I'd encourage you to explore classes with qualified teachers, given the effectiveness and relief they can bring if we've been holding on to our stress. The ancients clearly knew what we appear to have forgotten: that our stress 'needs a release' if we're going to achieve inner calm and peace within.

Butterfly Hug

Another gentle approach for calming a 'fizzy' system can be found in the butterfly hug. Developed by Lucina Artigas, a therapist who worked with children in the aftermath of a natural disaster in Mexico City, this can be extremely effective in our day-to-day lives.

Cross your arms over your chest so the tip of your middle finger on each hand is placed below your collarbone. Your hands must be as vertical as possible, so that your fingers point towards the neck, not towards the arms. Raise your elbows to create the butterfly wings. Your eyes can be closed, or partially closed, looking towards the tip of your nose.

Next, you slowly tap your hands on your chest, alternating left and right. Breathe slowly and deeply in and out through your nose until you start to feel some relief.

A 'self-hug' can help too. Wrapping your arms around your body, with your hands under your armpits, you can hold yourself tight. I sometimes use a yoga bolster cushion and wrap my arms around that. It's something to consider when working with children for whom physical contact is not appropriate or who might not be ready to receive a hug: offering them the chance to wrap their arms around something firm yet soft can be very comforting.

Why Rhythm Rocks

As Dr Bruce Perry explained in the previous chapter, exercises that are patterned, repetitive and rhythmic can take our brain back to a time when it was in perfect 'balance', in the womb, when our world was in harmony, when we were not hungry or thirsty, when we felt safe and warm. It explains why anything we do that replicates those feelings can see us instantly feeling soothed. If you love the idea of having the sun on your face, rocking in a hammock while listening to the swooshing sound of the waves breaking on the ocean, it puts into clear context why! Anything we do that is patterned, repetitive and rhythmic can have enormous value in returning our nervous system back to balance. Psychiatrist Dr Bessel van der Kolk and Psychotherapist Dr Pat Ogden's work highlights many helpful activities, from walking, running, swinging, trampoline work, drumming, chanting, amateur dramatics, animal assisted therapy, massage and even skateboarding. In short, anything that takes our body and brain state back to a time in the womb, when 'all was well'.

Breath

Another powerful resource that's free and at our immediate disposal is our breath.

Our breath regulates everything.

Controlling and changing the way we breathe can take us a long way towards achieving parenting Zen. As yogis have known for centuries, how we breathe helps to calm an over-activated nervous system. Sit in a chair or lie on your bed. Feel the support offered by the back of the chair or the mattress. If you're sitting, notice the connection between the ground and the soles of your feet. Close your eyes if it feels safe to do so and take a deep breath.

How did it feel?

Did your shoulders rise as you took in a massive gulp of air? Did the breath feel high and tight in your chest? Or did you breathe slowly and deep into your belly?

Did it feel irritating to be asked to stop reading and breathe? Or did you get a sense of permission to pause and relax?

Try again. This time, breathe in slowly through your nose for four seconds, hold the breath for four seconds, then allow the air to release slowly for another four, out through your nostrils again. Pause for four, then repeat. This is called box breathing. US Navy SEALs highly endorse this method to calm their own stress response ahead of challenging missions. (Mike wryly observes they'd need it just getting Wilbur out of the door to school on time.)

Our stress is often unavoidable, but when we breathe intentionally, when we give our chance to pause, we help our nervous system to do its job. Using our breath is the quickest, most straightforward way to press pause when our children appear intent on pushing our every button.

BRAIN BOX

'Whenever you inhale, you turn on the sympathetic nervous system slightly, minutely speeding up your heart. And when you exhale, the parasympathetic half turns on, activating your vagus nerve in order to slow things down (this is why many forms of meditation are built around extended exhalations).'

— Dr Robert M. Sapolsky, *Why Zebras Don't Get Ulcers*

Journalist James Nestor has dedicated an entire, and brilliant, book to raising awareness about the importance of the 'lost art of breathing' for our health and I thoroughly recommend it if you would like to delve a little deeper. He has highlighted research suggesting asthma, anxiety, ADHD, psoriasis and a whole host of illnesses and what he calls 'modern maladies' could be 'reduced or reversed simply by changing the way we inhale and exhale'.

There are many other ways to breathe, and with some research, you will likely find a method that appeals and works specifically for you. For me, filling my lungs, focusing on breathing into my belly rather than my chest, inhaling and exhaling slowly, and rolling the air up as a wave helps calm me when I'm stressed. I also use a technique called nostril breathing. Yogic breathing has been shown to relieve stress, improve concentration and helps us to breathe better generally. Essentially, you isolate each nostril, breathing in through only one of them at a time and then exhaling through the other.

Integrative medicine specialist Dr Melissa Young explains:

Start by exhaling through your mouth, making a big 'whooshing' sound.

Bring your right hand up to your nose, with your index finger hovering over your left nostril and your thumb hovering over your right nostril.

Use your thumb to block your right nostril and inhale through your left.

Then use your index finger to block your left nostril – so both nostrils are now blocked – and hold your breath, for a beat of a second or two.

Release your thumb to unblock your right nostril and exhale.

Pause at the bottom of the exhale.

Keeping your left nostril closed, inhale through the right nostril.

Use your thumb to block off your right nostril. With both nostrils held closed, again, hold your breath for a beat or two.

Release your index finger to unblock your left nostril and exhale.

In summary, that's in through your left, out through your right; in through your right, out through your left. Whenever a nostril isn't in use for an inhale or an exhale, it should be held shut with your finger or thumb.

Repeat the process for as long as you like. Dr Young recommends five minutes at a time.

It's understood that breathing through the right nostril speeds up our circulation and heart rate. It essentially activates our sympathetic nervous system, to put our body in a more elevated state of alertness. It's a good tip to give your children perhaps ahead of exams or any time they are called to have more focus, given breathing through the right nostril has been found to feed more blood to our prefrontal cortex, our wise owl, helping us to make more logical decisions and problem-solve! Inhaling through the left nostril has the opposite effect:

BRAIN BOX

'Inhaling through the left nostril has the opposite effect: it works as a kind of brake system to the right nostril's accelerator. The left nostril is more deeply connected to the parasympathetic nervous system, the rest-and-relax side that lowers blood pressure, cools the body and reduces anxiety. Left nostril breathing shifts blood flow to the opposite side of the prefrontal cortex, to the area that influences creative thought and plays a role in the formation of mental abstractions and the production of negative emotions.'

— James Nestor, author of *Breathe*

Improve Your 'Vagal Tone'

Exercises that specifically activate our vagus nerve will enhance our sense of wellbeing and feeling of safety. The vagus nerve is connected to your vocal cords and the muscles at the back of your throat, which explains why singing, humming, chanting and gargling can all help to improve vagal tone. The vibrations caused by making these sounds stimulate the vagus nerve, regulating our immune system and lowering our stress, as well as triggering all the other benefits that come with activating our parasympathetic nervous system.

If you are a yoga devotee, you will recognise these as the same principles of when chanting om. If the idea of joining a choir or yoga class appeals, at least you can do so knowing there's a science to the wellbeing you will experience, as well as the benefits of being part of a wider community – something that is also incredibly positive for wellbeing.

The Power of the Pause

This is one of my personal favourites. I use it at home during the nights I feel my baboon rising up – when the traffic home has been hideous, the children are quarrelling, and I still have supper to sort, homework to supervise and showers to oversee.

For example, one evening, Clemency defiantly told me she didn't need to take a shower that night – despite being covered in mud after post-school football! Rather than engage baboon to baboon, I asked her to wait for a second using a playful 'hold that thought caller!' and pretended I quickly needed the loo. Once outside the room, I put my palms over my eyes and slowly and deeply inhaled before releasing a long, slow exhale of my breath.

The dark soothed my lizard. The brief pause gave my wise owl time to swoop down and switch off the baboon's clanging fire alarm. With the sweet release into my body of those all-important anti-anxiety hormones, I went back into the room and said soothingly, 'Mummy gets it, sweetheart: it's late, and I know you have homework still to do. I understand why you hate the idea of having to take a shower. Shall I come and help you?'

The calm and warmth in my voice and my understanding were enough to calm Clemency's baboon and her little owl could lean in. A smile spread across her face and she nodded, allowing me to steer her gently towards the bathroom.

My 'PALM PAUSE' bought just enough time for my wise owl to reflect that the argument wasn't about the shower. Clemency probably had a fizzy lizard and bounding baboon, given that it was late. She had a melee of thoughts in her head: the homework she still had to do, her annoying brother, and she was hungry! Stress response, anyone?!

When our children feel understood and heard, they are far

more likely to lean in than push us away. We get the result we want – Clemency had her shower – but taking time to pause and breathe also helps to fill my own cup of calm, which helps me fill my daughter's cup in turn.

Sleep

My former psychotherapist Liza Elle liked to say: 'The Devil does his best work when we're tired.'

And it's true. When it comes to keeping our stress response under control, sleep is a priority.

Too little sleep and my world can feel it's been turned upside down. Get enough and everything sets itself the right way up again.

As a busy parent I know the objection that getting to bed early just isn't possible given 'there aren't enough hours in the day'. I always used to view sleep as a bit of a luxury, but I've changed my tune since recognising how difficult it is to contain my baboon when he's sleep-deprived.

If I get to bed between 9 and 10pm, I know I'll wake up bright and early with time to make lunches, pack bags and fill water bottles. It leaves me with much more capacity to remain calm while Wilbur engages in every activity known to man, apart from what he needs to do, like brush his teeth and get his shoes and coat on. If I've had enough sleep, I can even turn on 'fun mum' and suggest a game that means we get to do it all together, in record time and with a lot of laughter thrown in for good measure.

In contrast, if I give in to a binge-watch on Netflix, I'll inevitably crawl from the bedroom having pressed snooze too many times, with my baboon already on the brink. The days when I turn from fun mum to fun sponge correspond directly to the previous night's bedtime.

So, I've learned not to beat myself up if the house is a mess, comforting myself that with an early night, a bedroom that feels impossible to tidy now will sort itself in minutes in the morning. My wise owl turns again to her *Little Book of Calm*, reminding me of Nelson Mandela's quote: 'It always seems impossible until it's done.' She then winks and offers a quote of her own: 'It always seems impossible until we've had an early night.'

Time for You

There was a time when I considered taking time for me to be selfish. It seems ridiculous to say when I look back on it, but when chatting with other parents, I have learned I am not alone. When we reframe selfishness as self-care, we give ourselves something fundamental: permission to rest.

It's enormously important to find time just for you. Time 'off the clock' allows us to reconnect with our inner selves and refill our depleted cups of calm. Again, we cannot help our children if we cannot help ourselves, so we must practise this where we can.

Meditative music is therapeutic, perhaps while preparing supper or tidying up. Type in 'healing sounds' or 'music to calm the nervous system' and you will find numerous options to try. I have also become interested in yoga and stretching. I now prefer less strenuous exercise as it suits my nervous system and body more than the vigorous exercise I enjoyed when I was younger. But if you prefer a high-energy exercise class or a run, go for it. What's important is finding something that is yours, whether walking the dog, having a long bath with candles and soft music, taking a dance, art, or other creative class or catching up with friends or family. One of my favourite quotes is: 'If you don't have time to spend ten minutes in nature, take an hour.'

Finally, Therapy

As you might expect, I am an enormous advocate of counselling and personal therapy. Having someone to yourself for one hour a week, someone who will really 'hear' you and support you unconditionally, really can transform your life. We all need to feel heard and understood and therapy can help us to work through some of those deeper stresses or traumas that we might have held on to for too long.

Therapy can be expensive and may not be for you right now for many reasons. I share more resources in the back of the book to help you find support if you want to explore it further, with the names of organisations and charities that can offer means-tested services and free online resources. Looking for parenting groups in your local area or through your child's school is another way to connect with other parents. Again, many charities, organisations and online networks can provide a great wealth of experience, advice and support. I share more general advice for parents in my own online community. I am passionate that no parent or child should ever feel alone.

Depending on our circumstances, our friends, family, partners, faith and social community can prove a tremendous buffer if we find things challenging. We need each other; human beings are social beings and we should not have to suffer our stresses alone.

Our bodies and brains don't like being out of kilter, out of balance.

Prolonged and chronic stress is not conducive to our good health. It impacts us physically and psychologically and it impacts our children too.

Doing all that we can to ensure that in any given day we give ourselves and our children some time, compassion and understanding will go a long way to keeping us ticking over, during the busy working week.

I have shared exercises that are, in the main, free and easy to implement. You can carry them wherever you are, allowing you to ground yourself in the car before pick up, or at night before you go to bed.

My list for self-health is personal. Talking to your friends and colleagues about 'what works for them' can prove a rich source of information and advice. We all need help and support sometimes. I know I do.

Your wellbeing is vital, because when your own cup is full, you'll have enough love to pour for your child.

When we achieve our own inner calm, it is then we can help our children to achieve it too.

WISE OWL WISDOMS

- We cannot expect better behaviour from our children if we are not modelling it ourselves.

- Stress creates 'blocked care' and can leave us struggling to parent with compassion.

- If our children are to learn the art of emotional regulation, we must first learn it ourselves.

- Stress is natural, and so are stress relievers. We can learn to 'pull our parachute' and bring our nervous system back to balance.

- Finally: sleep. Make it your number one priority. Without good-quality sleep, you can kiss everything else goodbye.

Chapter Four

CALM(ER) KIDS – How to De-Stress our Children Too

When we can quiet our own storms, we can help our children to quiet theirs.

Okay, so now *we're* calm, what about the kids?!

In the words of clinical psychologist Rachel Samson: 'Children don't calm down by being told to calm down. They develop the capacity for calmness by being supported to experience it.'

Over the following few chapters, I'll show you how to help your child when they are in the middle of a meltdown.

The first step is to start a conversation with our children about what stress is and why we behave the way we do when our stress response has been triggered. Typically I talk to my children about their nervous system and how it connects all parts of their body and our brain. I talk about the body's stress response that gets triggered if we feel threatened. I say I imagine it like the roots of a tree, sending messages up to our little lizard, telling it what to do. In this way I can explain that if the lizard gets 'fizzy' and starts jumping around because he's anxious or scared, it can make us want to jump up and down or run around too.

However you explain the science to your child, you'll want to make your language age-appropriate and convey these essential points:

- Our body's stress response is normal
- It is there to keep us safe
- It can get triggered by emotions like fear, excitement and even shame or embarrassment.

I explain that even our thoughts can make our lizard feel fizzy, having him worrying about what might happen in the future, as well as what's happening to us today.

You might think of some examples of when your child's lizard might get fizzy:

- If we're playing football and we have the ball and everyone runs towards us!
- If someone tells us off or shouts at us in class
- If we're hungry/thirsty, if we are too hot or cold or if we need the loo!
- If we get stranded on the high ropes at Go Ape
- If we're worrying about a test, or a fall out with a friend.

We want our children to know that their stress response is normal – it's their brain and body's way of responding to something it finds scary or embarrassing.

You'll want to explain that how we feel inside can sometimes feel a bit fizzy too and if we don't use our words to tell an adult about our big feelings, we might 'act them out' instead.

Again, giving an everyday example is helpful. So you might say, 'If we feel "fizzy", we might jump on the bed. Or if we feel frightened, we might lash out without thinking.'

When I speak to my own children and the children in my clinical care, I keep my language simple and my sentences short. I explain that our brain is brilliant, that it has lots of different parts and each part has an important job. I explain that some parts tell us when we are hungry, if we are thirsty, ill, or tired. With my children I might use gentle humour and throw in examples like Clemency's grouchiness if supper's taking a while, or Wilbur's fizziness if he's not had enough sleep. We don't do this to shame or embarrass our children. We want to show them that we get it, which translated means we 'get' them.

We might even use the opportunity to throw in an apology if we look back and realise that we had missed our child's 'behavioural Morse code'!

When children feel understood, when they realise that we understand their behaviour (especially when they so often don't!) – or at least we are TRYING to understand – they're much more likely to turn to us for help the next time they're struggling, rather than pushing us away. They're also much more likely to temper their behaviour.

Why?

Because the behaviour *we* model is the behaviour our children tend to model in turn. It can take time and practice (for us both) but the more we can help our children to reflect on their behaviour – BEFORE they're in a frightening free fall – the more we help their little owls grow.

Children don't LIKE feeling like they're in the equivalent of a skydive without having someone alongside – just as neither would we. When our children trust that we 'have their back', that we want to help and understand them, the more likely they'll come to us for comfort rather than rebel.

If this feels awkward at first, you can try sharing examples of situations when you've felt scared or fizzy. Watch the expression on your child's face when you 'confess' that you also get scared about taking tests, that you also feel grumpy when you're hungry and irritable when you're tired. When I explain to my clients in the therapy room that even adults feel butterflies and get tingly fingers if they're nervous, the look of relief on their face is priceless.

Sometimes, and you could try this too, I'll take a blank sheet of paper and draw the animals, naming them the 'lizard, baboon and wise owl'. Or, given that I'm never going to give Picasso a run for his money, I might just draw a circle to represent our heads, an oval for our bodies and invite the child to create a colour code to represent the different animals/parts of the brain themselves.

If your children are older, you could pull up a scientific illustration of the brain. It's a good exercise to teach a child about their anatomy. You might reference the brain stem when speaking about the lizard, or the amygdala when speaking about the baboon. Who knows? It might see you encourage a budding neuroscientist!

I emphasise that the different parts of the brain have an important job: they are there to keep us safe. I explain that if the lizard part of our brain is scared, he might make us want to run around or even run away.

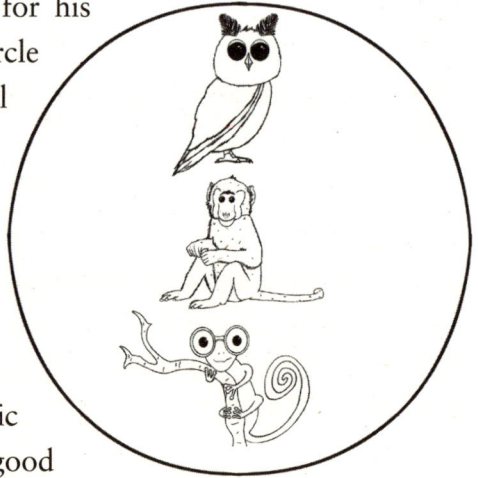

'Sometimes he might freeze and not move because he's so scared. Or he might fall to the floor or make us feel we want to find somewhere to hide.'

It can help to reference a few examples from your child's everyday behaviour – again, without shame or blame – because it can help them to remember and reflect on their actions in future. I might gently reassure that, 'It's why we might feel shy or forget what to say if we meet someone new.' Or, 'Remember at the train station yesterday and you put your hands over your ears because you found it NOISY? That was just the "lizard" part of your brain getting a bit fizzy because sometimes loud noises can sometimes make him feel anxious and want to run away!'

Any conversations where you can reassure your child and normalise the nervous system and stress response in a way that you feel is appropriate to them can be hugely comforting, especially for children who are more sensitive or struggle with environmental changes or novel situations. We want to emphasise that what some children find stressful, others might not, and vice versa. The only focus should be befriending our nervous system and our lizard and baboon, because when we help them to find calm, it helps us feel calm, too.

The child who has difficulty getting up on the high ropes at Go Ape can give themselves a hard time. They can even conclude they've got something 'wrong' with them because their friends found it such fun. It's empowering to learn that everyone's lizard works differently. I explain that some children's lizards might feel fizzy in the dark, and others won't like heights; for others, it might be feeling vulnerable in small spaces, hearing loud noises, bright lights, the taste of a particular food or wearing 'itchy' scratchy clothes.

As I type, my children have just come to see me in the garden office. Clemency, now 11, readily points out that her lizard gets fizzy if we're on a train or at the shops and she sees someone 'acting strangely'. Wilbur, now nine, asks me to write that if his lizard gets fizzy, playing football helps!

Normalising the nervous system and having an easily accessible visual reference like the lizard, baboon and wise owl can be enormously helpful for us and our children when exploring our mental health.

When I talk about the baboon part of our brain, I describe it as the part of us that loves to have fun and can get super excited (or scared) about going to school trips, parties and playdates – delete or add emotions as appropriate for your child! I explain that the baboon has really BIG emotions! He can make us feel super HAPPY and sometimes very CROSS. 'He might want you to stomp your feet and shout. It's not that he's bad, he's often afraid and trying to protect you.' (The next chapter will look at emotions like anger in detail.)

You can even add for reassurance, that, 'Mummy/Daddy loves your baboon regardless and I always want to help him, even if he's cross. I can help him to take a breath and use calm words to tell me what he needs, rather than shouting them at me instead!'

Using everyday examples in a light and breezy way can set this new information into much clearer context. We are letting our children know that we understand why they might behave the way they do sometimes, and that our children (or, more accurately, their baboon) can sometimes make mistakes and it's why he might need some adult wise owl help.

I might remind Wilbur: 'Remember when you got cross with Clemency when your toothbrush fell down the loo? I get that your baboon got really MAD! Because he doesn't like being laughed at – but Clemency was laughing at the situation – not you. Your baboon got MAD and he tried to stop her from laughing. But can you see why that wasn't OK? Our baboon shouldn't hurt others or you. We have to help him to find another way to show he's cross. I can show you how.'

Or:

'Remember when Ollie pushed you in the playground by accident? He never meant to bump into you, but your baboon didn't know that and because his job is to keep you safe, he reacted REALLY quickly and shouted at him because he thinks he has to defend you. But we have to help our baboon to use his words kindly. It can be really hard, I know, and even Mummy and Daddy don't always get it right, but the more we practise, the more we can help our baboon to keep control and use a strong voice instead.'

Referencing 'the baboon' and thereby using the third person, rather than using the word 'you', can help to reduce any shame a child might experience if they get things wrong. If we shout, discipline or shame a child, their baboon will always jump in the driving seat. Engaging your child's prefrontal cortex allows them to learn from their mistakes and better regulate their stress response in future. We need the little owl on board given she represents the only part of the brain that can 'mentalise' and consider 'right from wrong'.

These conversations are therefore best to have when your child's lizard and baboon are relaxed and not feeling pressured. Bedtimes, walking home from school and car journeys are often good opportunities in this regard.

In the therapy room, I work gently and slowly, given some of my clients have had to overcome significant trauma and difficulties. It's important to work within a child's 'window of emotional tolerance'. If your child gets defensive or appears to switch off or disengage, you might say to them that 'I am wondering if I am talking too much? That's OK, shall we play a game instead?'.

We don't want to trigger a stress response or go beyond what a child feels comfortable with. We can layer these conversations over time.

Where a therapeutic relationship is established and a child is calm, I might gently ask my clients where they feel it in their bodies when they are frightened. Typically, they'll point to the areas of their body influenced by the stress response, usually their stomach, chest, hands, feet or head.

They might tell me they feel tingling in their arms, legs, fingers or toes.

When I ask how worry feels, they might say 'foggy' or 'fuzzy in my head'. It's often a huge relief for a child to learn that this is normal; that it is just their stress response doing what it's designed to do.

I think the lack of conversation around emotions and stress and how they are 'felt' in the body has led to some confusion around anxiety and aspects of mental health. As psychoanalyst Professor Peter Fonagy explains, the sensations we experience when we are worried or anxious are normal. It's how we handle them that counts.

BRAIN BOX

'Stress and difficulty are common and normal. Low mood and anxiety are not an "illness" but signals the mind created for certain types of action (for example 'lie low while in danger'). Our increasing willingness to talk about mental health has led more people to disclose symptoms, which is a good thing, but we must be mindful not to conflate our response to stress with having mental health problems.'

— Professor Peter Fonagy, Professor of Contemporary Psychoanalysis and Developmental Science

Having this information can help set our own mental health into better context too. A mum reached out to me recently and told me she had always thought she was 'weird' because her toes curled up when she was nervous. She only made the connection with the lizard after hearing me speak online. She said her newfound understanding of her nervous system had helped her reassure her son about his symptoms when he was feeling anxious ahead of the first day of school.

For me, having a greater awareness of the feelings that arise within me when I am stressed, and the fight or flight response I can fall into, means I can treat myself with compassion rather than judgement and use my wise owl to consider what might help: I might take a bath, go for a bike ride, do some gentle yoga or even just get an early night.

Exploring the stress response, its symptoms, and how they can get the better of us, can be very helpful for children who have experienced trauma or who are considered neurodivergent (a non-medical term to describe someone who thinks, learns or behaves differently from what is considered 'typical' in a particular context). The more aware our children are of what's going on in the inside, the more it will help them to regulate and achieve calm, with more contained behaviour on the outside. It's something we call having good interoception. It's a vital skill for achieving good and robust mental health.

BRAIN BOX

'Neuroscience research shows that the only way we can change the way we feel is by becoming aware of our inner experience and learning to befriend what is going inside ourselves.'

— Dr Bessel van der Kolk, *The Body Keeps the Score*

I believe the more we understand the nervous system, the better we can support children with nervous behaviours including nervous tics, repetitive behaviours like head-banging, nervous stutters and specific sensory sensitivities, such as to noise, taste and how things feel to the touch. We will always want to seek professional and specialist advice if our children display behaviours that give us cause for concern, but I have found, from personal experience and in my clinical work, that when we help a child to feel safer, and when they feel reassured there's nothing 'wrong' or 'bad' in them, many nervous system related behaviours can diminish or even disappear.

PARENT PONDER

Tara, mother to Jacob, 9, and Jade, 6

My eldest was referred to therapy, given there had been violence in the home. It was a really difficult time, and he had become very anxious and wouldn't leave my side. He also had nervous tics, which got worse whenever he was stressed. He barely spoke in class but then he was getting into trouble in the playground and having lots of fights. Having therapy has completely transformed him. I can't believe how much it has helped. I'm so grateful. The tics have gone, the fighting has stopped, and even the school say he's like a different boy. It's honestly changed our lives.

Organisations and charities like Unlocking Potential (UP) and Place2Be (P2Be) can offer tremendous support to families in school settings in this regard and I have been privileged to work with both. Do always speak to your child's school if you are concerned about their behaviour and ask if there are any provisions for counselling or parenting groups (which can often prove a valuable support).

Encouraging all children to think about, and embrace their feelings, puts them on a path towards healthier self-regulation and the ability to work with the energy of their stress release in the future. When we engage their little owl, we help her 'stretch her wings'.

Children who have experienced trauma, are neurodivergent or have different educational needs might struggle more with self-regulation. We should always be mindful of a child's circumstances, given research shows the HPA axis is much more reactive for some children than others. The art of self-regulation requires practise and regular reflection and needs our patience and calm. As Mike highlights here, managing our own baboons in 'emergency' situations is something even we can still find difficult in adulthood!

MAN-OEUVRES WITH MIKE

I work in security and I'll often hear stories from people who've been mugged or robbed on the street. Many times, they'll tell me they instinctively went into FIGHT rather than flight; refusing to give up their bag, even trying to wrestle with their assailant, without stopping to consider they might have a knife. Only once the danger passes (and I guess with their wise owl back in charge) do they reflect that they've just risked their life for a credit card that can be cancelled or a driving licence that's easily replaced. In the cold light of day, they recognise their behaviour made no sense – it's just the same instant FIGHT response that I see in my children if they quarrel over something that seems so irrelevant, but clearly feels REALLY important to them! The challenge for us as parents is to remember that their baboons are driven by primitive impulses and in certain situations they'll 'act first and think later', but then, as I know, very often so do we.

I'll still have days when my baboon takes charge. It might see me snap at Wilbur if he's kicking a ball around kitchen, rather than calmly asking him to take it outside. On that particular occasion, and when my wise owl was back at the helm, I wondered whether my eight-year-old might have been using the repetitive bouncing of the ball to 'release' his own stress or soothe residual nerves. I said to him, 'I was thinking about earlier and I'm sorry for getting cross.' Wilbur knew instantly what I was referring to and responded with an outraged 'Yes! You told me off for kicking the ball, but I was just nervous about my homework!'

Aha! Every day's a school day as they say – especially when it comes to parenting.

Again, our understanding of the stress response does NOT mean we can't lay boundaries around unwanted behaviours. I don't want my son kicking a ball in the kitchen when there is the potential for something to get broken. But I can remain calm when I tell him, rather than resorting to a cross word.

I apologised again, explaining that my own lizard had been a bit fizzy because I was trying to do too many things at the same time and my lizard found the noise of the ball distracting. I also explained that I didn't want anything to get broken. 'I am sorry I used my baboon to tell you, and not my wise owl.' The apology and my understanding immediately calmed Wilbur down. Once his baboon stands down, his little owl can re-engage. Now I can throw in a boundary, knowing that he's listening.

'And can you help me and try to remember to use your words to tell me next time you're nervous rather than kick a ball inside?' I also offered to help Wilbur with his homework the next time he felt anxious.

Wilbur (and his little owl) nodded happily.

The exchange allows me to re-engage my 'playful parent' and I enthusiastically offer, 'I'll tell you what; once I am done with dinner, shall we go out and have a kick about?'

Modelling the behaviour we want to see helps to build trust, strengthen our relationship, and ultimately get ahead of any potential 'big' stressed-out behaviour.

A few months on from the kitchen incident, Wilbur asked me, 'Mummy, can I tell you about something that goes on inside me? It's a bit weird.'

'Of course!' I said, eyebrow slightly raised, wondering what might come next.

'Well, just before I play football with my friends, I get this really big feeling inside.' Wilbur pointed to his head and chest.

'I feel really stressed before we start, because everyone chooses their team and then everyone starts shouting because they all want to be in the best team and there's only one team, we all want it, but it makes me really stressed and I get like this...' Wilbur threw himself on the bed with his hands over his ears.

It's a great illustration of the 'baboon stress contagion' that can take place when children get together. It's also a good example of how some children can become more sensitive to sound or other sensory input when their sympathetic nervous system is triggered.

As Wilbur's words tumbled out, I could feel in my own chest the fizzy sensation he'd described. This is something we call 'transference'. You might notice it when your own children talk to you about their anxiety or nerves, they might start speaking more quickly and breathlessly and it can make us feel slightly breathless too! The same of course can be experienced with anger or joy.

'Oh darling,' I said. 'Remember I told you about the stress response, and how it can make our lizard fizzy, and make our baboon throw himself around? Does it feel like that's what happened?'

I pointed to my chest and said I could feel the anxiety Wilbur described. It's a powerful way of showing him that I really do understand and can empathise with what he's telling me.

In educating children about stress and how it's felt not just in the head but throughout the body, we encourage what psychiatrist Dr Dan Siegel calls 'vertical integration'. In simple terms, this means the lizard, baboon and wise owl have all learned to speak to each other when and if they need help. Teaching our children how to pay attention to the sensations they experience inside means they can attune to what their nervous system is 'telling' them, rather than suppressing or ignoring important feelings instead.

BRAIN BOX

'By and large, anxiety is a defence against intense feelings which have been pushed underground. Address the frightened feelings beneath, whether they are intense grief or rage or despair and so on, and the anxiety dissipates. But this is not something you can just do on your own. You need to feel those frightening feelings in the presence of a very trusted emotionally regulating listening other person.'

— Dr Margot Sunderland, Child Psychotherapist,

Draw on Your Emotions

I suggested that if the other boys were shouting and getting anxious themselves, it was likely they were all feeling the same way. I explained that just as baboons in the wild spread stress to each other when they are excited or afraid, so do we.

Wilbur was quiet as I spoke, taking it all in.

'I just want us to decide our teams fairly,' he said. 'Everyone wants the best team and then everyone starts arguing and then we end up not playing!'

'So what do you think might help?'

'Well, I could say perhaps we can take turns? Or,' he added, 'we could pick straws?'

'They sound like great ideas, Wilbur. Well done!'

Encouraging our children to find solutions is great for building that 'stress management muscle' as well as creating a stronger little owl.

At this age, our children won't always know how to fix things, however, and it might see a child get stuck in the 'I DON'T KNOW WHAT TO DO!' state. If your child does get irritated or cross when you are trying to help them solve something they're struggling with, remember that it's likely their lizard and baboon are in charge. Our baboons often use anger as a defence against fear. Fear can make us feel vulnerable. In which case you might respond with an 'it's OK, I know these things can sometimes feel really difficult'.

It's not that our children won't have tough times or face friendship issues. That's life. But when you show your child that you can 'skydive' alongside them if they need you to, it forms a powerful glue.

You might wonder out loud. 'Hmm, would you like me to tell you what I did when this happened to me...?' (Clearly only if you had a positive outcome!)

Or:

'OK, I can see how difficult it must feel. Shall we think of some solutions together? I bet we'll find one.'

Together, you could draw images, perhaps using stick people with speech bubbles to practise what your child might like to say or how they'd like conversations or situations to play out. Be mindful to be guided by your child; this is an opportunity for their little owl to think hard and reflect. Remember, you are the instructor; your child is the one who needs to make the jump. If you do everything for them, they'll find it harder to make the leap themselves next time. While they are still learning the ropes, you just want to be there offering a steady presence, guiding them as they go.

The following morning, Wilbur woke up already 'game planning' the conversation he would have later with his friends. Managing a group of excited boys is a big deal for one eight-year-old to navigate, but I told him: 'I am very confident you will find the right words.'

It's important for our children to know we have faith in them and their ability to problem-solve. That's what builds resilience and a strong sense of self. This is what helps their little owl to grow.

Having these 'conversations that count' will put you and your child 'ahead of the game', allowing both of you to start recognising the early signs of stress. Rather than asking crossly, 'What's WRONG with you?!' when your child starts 'acting it out', you'll likely find yourself saying instead:

'Sweetheart, I am sensing that your lizard is fizzy today. How can I help?'

Asking these questions authentically, with a genuine interest in how your child is feeling, will help you to get ahead of any 'emotional explosion' that can happen if big feelings are left unchecked. Yes, it takes time, and we'll want all our Cs in place for the 'jump' to run smoothly. But when we stop seeing 'naughty' and understand our children's needs, we can have conversations that count, which leads to more collaboration, calmer kids and certainly a calmer you.

WISE OWL WISDOMS

- Teaching your child about their nervous system and their stress response in an age-appropriate way helps them to understand their behaviour, as much as it allows you to understand it too.

- Normalising the stress response gives your child permission to come to you as soon as they feel triggered or overwhelmed.

- Understanding the symptoms of the stress response will give your child good interoception – the ability to befriend their feelings, rather than resist, fear or suppress them.

- It takes time and practice, but when children can use their words to tell us how they feel, they're more likely to come to us for help, and much less likely to 'act out' their needs instead.

Chapter Five

CONTAIN – Anger Management and Big Emotional Outbursts

A child can learn to contain their big feelings, but they cannot learn to do it alone.

Anger is one of our most valid and essential emotions but as the child and adolescent psychotherapist Violet Oaklander said, it is also one of the most misunderstood. Anger acts as a defence. It tells us we feel wronged, and it helps us challenge injustice. Sadly, few of us are taught how to express it appropriately. This is a problem because, at its most extreme, anger has the potential to lead to violence and is one of the most common emotions parents will seek help in dealing with. In the US, a 2020 survey of 2,000 parents found more than a quarter admitted their six- to eight-year-olds displayed 'the most brutal meltdowns' with parents admitting their children had hit, kicked or bitten them when they did.

To see safer, more contained behaviour we must teach our children how to regulate and healthily express their emotions. In fact, the psychotherapist and clinical scientist

Dr Allan Schore asserts that 'enhancing self-regulation should be considered the whole of child development'.

Why?

Because, he says, 'just about every psychiatric disorder shows problems in emotional dysregulation'.

Most scientists agree there are at least five core emotions, and psychologist Dr Paul Ekman's research identifies seven: ANGER, CONTEMPT, DISGUST, SURPRISE, SADNESS, FEAR and ENJOYMENT. Our emotions can be complex, with one often serving as a cover for another; anger, for example, sits on top of fear.

PARENT PONDER
Dee, Kinship Carer to Donny, 9

I took Donny to the shops and asked him to stay outside with the dog while I nipped in for some bread. He refused, telling me angrily, 'No! I'm coming with you!' I got cross as it felt like it was just oppositional behaviour. I told him, 'Stay there and do as you are told!' But he still refused. It was only when I stopped to question why he was behaving this way that he said: 'Because someone might take me.'

Our emotions serve as a crucial guide in life, giving us 'real-time data' that helps us respond to important events. Fear, as with Dee's nephew, tells us to be on guard, whereas love tells us to dive right in. Emotions are an essential part of being human and one of the greatest gifts is to be able to experience all the highs and lows of life without getting overwhelmed in between. But if we are to support our children and indeed ourselves, we must learn how to express big emotions safely.

It is not OK for children to hit or hurt – just as it is not OK for adults to do it either. I understand the frustration and fear when children are enraged, and parents feel they're left with no other option but to smack, shout or send children to their rooms. But parenting, and childhood, don't have to be this way.

As the American congressional minister Lyman Abbott said, 'Do not teach your children never to be angry; teach them HOW to be angry.'

Which is what we're going to do. We must start by accepting that all our emotions are valid and welcome. I appreciate this might feel counter-intuitive! It often does to my clients when, in the very first session, I explain to them the 'rules' of our time together, of which there are only a few. I explain that 'in here there is no hitting or hurting'. I clarify that it means: 'I don't hurt you, and you don't hurt me.' But I go on to explain that 'all our emotions are welcome', at which point the children almost always ask me, eyes wide with surprise, 'What, even anger?!' To which I reply with a smile, 'ESPECIALLY anger!'

BRAIN BOX

'We tend to think of anger as distasteful and abhorrent, something that we would rather not experience. Actually, I believe that anger is an expression of the self. It is a protection of one's boundaries. When a young child says NO! in a loud voice, mobilising all the energy she has to express the dislike of something that offends her in some way, she is not angry as we have come to know it, she is expressing her very self.'

— Dr Violet Oaklander, Psychotherapist,
The Many Faces of Anger

Society has often viewed anger as something frightening to be repressed, dismissed or diminished. But it's not anger we should be afraid of, it's if our children grow up not being taught how to express it safely.

If we don't 'accept' anger, and we don't help our children to experience and express their feelings, in the words of child psychotherapist Dr Margot Sunderland, it can see them either 'shrinking from the world or doing battle with it'.

Extensive research reveals that children shamed or punished for expressing big emotions often become adults who have learned to suppress strong feelings, perhaps using food, work, sex, cigarettes, alcohol, drugs or anything else that might keep their 'bad' feelings at bay. Rather than using strong words to lay healthy boundaries, expressing righteous anger with a firm and clear 'no, that is not OK' or 'I was upset when you did that', suppressed anger often leaks out disguised as critical comments and putdowns, barbed humour, bitchiness and bullying.

Clinicians working in the field of what psychiatrist George Engel called the 'biopsychosocial' model ultimately conclude that repressing our emotions damages our health and happiness. The addiction specialist Dr Gabor Maté observes of his own patients: 'In over two decades of family medicine, including seven years of palliative care work, I was struck by how consistently the lives of people with chronic illness are characterised by emotional shut down: the paralysis of "negative" emotions in particular, the feeling and expression of anger.' Maté's clinical work and his own extensive research has led him to conclude that repressed anger plays 'a significant role in a wide range of diseases and less happy lives', given that 'people seemed incapable of considering their own emotional needs and were driven by a compulsive sense of responsibility for the needs of others. They all had difficulty saying no'.

We need to teach our children it's OK to say 'no' and tell someone their behaviour is 'not acceptable', whether that's a sibling or someone at school. We want them to be able to sit with sadness if they lose something or someone they care for, and to grieve those losses fully and healthily. If they feel disappointed, we want them to say so, rather than projecting big feelings on to others instead. Having what we call emotional literacy enables our children to endure frustration, form healthy relationships, get into fewer fights and less self-destructive behaviour.

Just yesterday, Wilbur came into my office and furiously kicked at a rug on the floor. One sideways look from me and his face crumpled, and he said, 'I'm sorry, it's just that Newcastle lost.' His favourite team lost out to a goal in the 89th minute. I can understand his disappointment. Far better to bring him in for a hug than admonish him for behaviour he's already realised was wrong. He's nine; he's still learning. Next time, he'll cut out the kick (which showed me how he felt) and use his words to tell me his feelings instead.

The notion that we should embrace our emotions is not new. In this beautiful poem by the thirteenth-century Sufi poet Jalāl al-Dīn Rūmī, he uses the metaphor of a guest house to invite all our feelings in.

> This being human is a guest house.
> Every morning a new arrival.
> A joy, a depression, a meanness,
> some momentary awareness comes
> as an unexpected visitor.
> Welcome and entertain them all!
> Even if they're a crowd of sorrows,
> who violently sweep your house

empty of its furniture,
still, treat each guest honorably.
He may be clearing you out
for some new delight.
The dark thought, the shame, the malice,
meet them at the door laughing,
and invite them in.
Be grateful for whoever comes,
because each has been sent
as a guide from beyond.

Rumi

When I give talks on mental health to adults, I will often ask how many of them were taught how to regulate their emotions when they were young. Few hands, if any, go up. We all need to talk about our emotions and become emotionally literate! Here are some exercises you might like to try with your child to get conversations about emotions underway.

Tools for Teaching Emotional Literacy

Emotions Wheel

An emotions wheel can be a very useful tool for teaching children emotional literacy. I use a version of psychologists Dr Paul Ekman and Dr Robert Plutchik's emotions wheel. You can make one with your child at home or print one online and stick it on the wall. Dr Plutchik believed that humans can experience over 34,000 unique emotions – it often comes as a shock for children to know there are so many! Needless to say, you can just stick to the typical seven or invite your child to identify as many as they can.

In therapy, I explain to children that all emotions are valid and they all deserve to be heard. I explain that if we find it hard to tell someone how we feel, we can point to a word on the wheel that might best explain it instead.

A quick breezy before school 'ooh, OK, so which emotion best sums up how we're feeling this morning?' can be a great way to start the day and allows you to discuss and hopefully alleviate your child of any worries or wobbles they might have. Your child might prefer to use the wheel once they get home to tell you which emotion best summed up their day. You might also use the wheel yourself. Use humour if it feels right to do so. You might make a face, sharing with your child that the emotion you felt that morning was 'DISGUSTED' when you had to pick up the puppy's warm poo.

If your child names an emotion like 'sad', 'disappointed' or 'lonely', you can respond with a simple reflection of: 'Ah, sad ... Well, hello, sadness. Can you tell me more?' Or, 'Hello, sadness, thank you for being brave and showing me you are here.'

If the emotion is a more positive one, like 'confident', 'excited' or 'happy', you can raise your tone and energy to match your child's and do the same: 'Ooh! Excited! Tell me more!'

Our children need to know that sadness has a 'seat at the table' in the same way happiness does.

Just as you did with the stress response, you can also talk to your children about how our emotions aren't just felt in our heads, they can be felt in our bodies too. You can explain that excitement, joy, pain and disappointment can all trigger the stress response in the same way fear can.

As neuroscientist Jaak Panksepp said, 'We are deeply feeling and deeply biological creatures … We must come to terms with the biological sources of the human spirit.'

Give Emotions A Physical Presence

Emotions can be a funny thing for children to grasp so anything that helps to give them a 'physical presence' will be helpful.

Invite your child to think of ways to bring their emotions to life – you might make sock puppets to represent each feeling, or have your child allocate different emotions to different toys, or just draw the names of the emotions as words or colours on different scraps of paper. The idea is to bring your child's feelings and emotions into the room. It reinforces the idea that ALL emotions are welcome and invited. NONE of them are wrong.

The movie *Inside Out* provides a lovely opportunity to see emotions brought to life. There are some wonderful books that I also find helpful to explore emotions with children in the therapy room. Some of my favourites include the therapeutic story series, written by child psychotherapist Dr Margot Sunderland, including *A Nifflenoo Called Nevermind* and *The Day the Sea Went Out and Never Came Back*. They are BRILLIANT resources for talking about emotions with wonderfully abstract titles and storylines that engage children and address important themes of loss, sadness, grief and bullying.

At home, you could take a blank piece of paper and draw a circle for a head and an oval for the body. Then, ask your child to see how many emotions you can think of and draw them on the paper, either as words, or colours or both. Encouraging your child to write the words or scribble the colours themselves gives them ownership over the exercise and is more powerful this way.

You can explain that if we try to keep our emotions quiet and stuff them down inside, especially big ones like sadness or anger, they can sometimes end up bursting out! In the therapy room, if a child has chosen yellow to represent sadness and red for anger, I might take the red and yellow crayons and draw 'fireworks' coming out from the top of the circle head. 'Just like this!'

Speak to your child in a way that feels comfortable for you. There's no need to rush and you'll want to keep your conversations light and breezy.

Your children are never too old to have these conversations. The more we normalise our emotions, the less reason to suppress them and the less likely they are to 'explode'.

Code Red

Another tool to encourage your children to more readily communicate how they're feeling is something I call Code Red. Ask your child to allocate a different colour to a few different emotions. They might choose black for bored, yellow for happy, gold for EXCITED! And possibly red for anger! My children came up with their own colour codes to enable them to quickly tell me what kind of a day they'd had at school.

Even now, Clemency and Wilbur might sometimes refer to

Code Red if they want to let me know they've had a difficult day, immediately telling me at the gate, 'I had a Code Red today.' I can then respond with, 'Ooh, OK. Do you want to talk about it now or later?' You might find your children are happy to discuss it straight away, or very often, just before they go to bed.

Some children prefer to colour in a red card and carry it with them, so if they're feeling wobbly they can discreetly show their teacher or you without the need for words. It's just a sign to say 'I need some help'.

Be More Columbo

When I was young, there was a very popular detective programme whose main character was played by the actor Peter Falk. It was called *Columbo*. Columbo wore a shabby raincoat and had a rather shambolic demeanour. He would amble into investigations and disarm all those around him, but beneath his slovenly appearance lay a fierce cunning. He'd ask some simple questions and then, just as he was walking away from the main suspect, he'd throw in 'just one more thing ...' and deliver the question that would have the criminal exactly where he wanted them.

If your child is proving more difficult to reach, sometimes we just need to be more Columbo with our kids. If your child is grumpy at the gate or niggling at their sister, you can guess how you think they're feeling, or venture a diplomatic: 'How're you doing? It feels to me like you might have had a difficult day?'

Be prepared for pushback if you 'guess wrong' – that's OK. In fact, if you are met with a snarl and a 'I AM NOT!' or a 'I'm FINE!' You can shrug, Columbo style, 'Oh, OK. So you're OK. I am so sorry, I must have got that wrong.'

You can follow up: 'If there WAS something you wanted to

share, can you can let me know which bit I got wrong so I get it right for next time?' Or: 'That's OK. I'm here if you need to talk, or if you want to tell me how you're feeling later – I might be able to help'.

The invitation to correct you might prove so tempting you'll find your child blurting out 'I'm just hungry' or 'I'm ANGRY because Mr Smith told me off for forgetting my gym shoes!' Which translated, means your child felt embarrassed, or ashamed, and quickly explains their baboon behaviour.

When given the space, children will also often open up the conversation voluntarily, typically at bedtime when they'll tell you, 'I was sad today.' Or blurt out, 'Dean laughed at me because I missed a goal,' allowing you to immediately join the dots on their behaviour after school.

I appreciate it can take a lot of patience and faith, but – hitting or hurting aside – I am going to ask you to overlook any difficult behaviour your child might display while you start putting your Cs into practice. If we get drawn into baboon battles about a grouchy mood or demand 'don't speak to me that way!', we stand to undermine the foundations we're carefully laying, and certainly undermine our assurances that all emotions are welcome! I promise the growls and grouches will disappear when your child trusts they can have open and honest conversations with you.

In the therapy room I can see some pretty big behaviour as emotions like anger and sadness get 'welcomed in', but I'll show you how we keep ourselves and our children safe when they arrive.

Give Emotions a Voice

If you have a child who still seems reticent to engage, you might try to have a conversation with the 'emotion' rather than the child. You can do this by directing your questions to a particular puppet or a toy.

My friend Francesca tried this with her own daughter, Raffy, who had a massive blow out in a bookshop one day after school. Back home, when her five-year-old still refused to tell her what was wrong, Francesca tried asking her daughter's teddy if he could tell her instead. 'Teddy' immediately 'replied': 'Laurel said she doesn't like me anymore!!!' followed by lots of tears from Raffy and lots of healing hugs from Mum.

The more creative you can be when having these conversations, the easier they become. A quick internet search will reveal lots of gorgeous resources for talking about emotions, from kit bags and 'dealing with feeling' cards. You can enjoy spending time making some with your children too.

I know all too often we just want to know what to say when, and what to do NOW and HOW! So here's a quick summary of questions that can help start up conversations about how our children are feeling on any given day.

How're you doing? Any Code Reds?

What emotion would you say best sums up school today?

You seem a bit cross today, can you show me where you feel it in your body?

Can you tell me more about how you are feeling?

And don't forget the simple things – Clemency's just reminded me that sometimes a simple thumbs up or down at the gate can be enough!

Truth Arrows and Emotional Boils

Difficult as it is to hear, our children will sometimes feel anger, infuriation and disappointment with us. It can lead to the 'I HATE YOU!' statements that can be so hurtful to hear. It's important to remember that it's not you your child hates, it's the feelings they have inside them. The more you can help to address those big feelings (which usually have their foundations in hurt or fear), the quicker the hurtful words will disappear. Again, I will share scripts in the chapters ahead to help you in this regard.

As an example from my own family, when Clemency was nine I collected her from school and she was rude to me. I had been looking forward to seeing her, so I had to swallow my own hurt and cross response (yes, I have had to do it, too!). I was able to put aside my personal feelings because I suspected it was her way of showing me that she was upset that I had missed a school performance that day.

At home, I sat beside her. In silence, taking a blank piece of paper, I drew a tall stick figure of me, then a smaller one of Clemency with a speech bubble coming out of her mouth. I drew the word 'hurt' inside it. Then I drew another bubble next to it that said 'cross'. I then drew a zigzag beneath the speech bubbles to really emphasise that sense of CROSS, and to show her I could really sense her hurt scratchy feelings and the upset she felt inside.

In a calm, warm voice, I said aloud, 'I am wondering if

Clemency is feeling cross with me and hurt, because I didn't come to watch her at school.' (Again, talking in the third person helps to alleviate some of the discomfort of 'naming a painful and direct truth'.)

Naming the truth of a 'hurt' can see a child shifting uncomfortably, but if you are speaking authentically and with compassion (rather than sounding like you are telling your child off), it's a good sign, because you will know your 'truth arrow' has hit home. *I* was upset to have missed the performance and deeply sorry that I couldn't be there. I had explained to Clemency why I couldn't go, but I was not going to try to remind her of that because then I would be distracting and potentially sounding as though I were dismissing Clemency's feelings. Though I felt her behaviour earlier had been rude (and unfair, given Mike <u>had</u> been able to go to watch Clemency), it's not important. All my daughter knew was that she really wanted me to be there and I wasn't. She likely felt disappointed, sad, let down and, beneath it all, there is usually fear. Fear that Mummy cares about something else more than me. It can feel difficult for us to hear, especially given it's clearly not the case at all. But our children still see the world through the eyes of a little owl with a lizard and baboon running the show. They don't have that big picture perspective just yet. They can't fully appreciate that it was a medical appointment that I couldn't miss. Just as our children can't fully appreciate we have to work to pay the bills, or that Grandma might need urgent help or that the dog has swallowed something he shouldn't and needs to go to the vet. Their lizard and baboon only know that we're not there when they need us to be. And that, above all else, can drive fear. Fear that 'I am not enough', fear that 'Mummy doesn't love me' or even, that 'she doesn't care'.

It's important we know these are the 'stories' our children can tell themselves.

In naming her hurt, I show Clemency I understand her crossness, and I can hold her upset. Her feelings have been heard. She doesn't need to sulk or shout.

Back in the bedroom, Clemency nodded and told me that yes, that's how she felt. When a truth arrow lands this way, you will often sense a shift in the energy between you. When you have named their most vulnerable thoughts and feelings, and your child feels understood and heard, you get to lance what I think of as an emotional boil.

I drew a speech bubble coming from the tall stick person's mouth. I wrote the word SORRY. I turned to Clemency and told my daughter how truly sorry I was to have missed the performance and how upset I had been too. Children need to hear that we want to spend time with them. They need to know we care. I could promise that I had the next date in the diary and that I would absolutely be there. I could also say again, I understood why she had felt cross, and, I added, sad.

Remember: ANGER SITS ON TOP OF FEAR.

All children unconsciously fear they'll 'get left behind' or that we might 'not love them as much' as we do their brother/sister. It's just our evolution in play. The lizard will always have a niggle of 'will she/he/they be there for me if I need them? Can I rely on them?' Can I trust them to keep me safe?'.

If your child is sitting on deep-rooted fears that you might not love them, or that you don't like them, or that they can't depend upon you in a time of need (and all children will have these feelings at one time or another), it will often manifest itself in anger. Because anger provides a protective armour.

This is where the 'I HATE YOU' comes from. It comes from

a place of hurt. It comes from a place of upset. And it comes from a place of fear. Remember, our children won't even be conscious of these deep, ancient feelings; or understand why they project them out in the form of hitting or cross words.

Consider reflecting on the times your children have behaved recently in ways you found hurtful and consider what might have been going on for them instead.

You might try drawing your own stick figures with speech bubbles and try to imagine what emotion was really beneath the 'HATE'.

'I HATE DADDY!' might become: 'I HATE that Daddy doesn't live here anymore.'

'I HATE YOU' might translate to: 'It frightens me when you shout / I'm scared that you're getting a divorce / I sometimes think you love my baby sister more than me / I hate that you don't understand me and you punish me when I am sad.'

'I HATE HER!' when talking about a best friend might translate to: 'I HATE how vulnerable and alone I feel when she won't play with me.' And again, there's that baboon fear beneath the anger of: 'I am frightened, because if I don't have a friend, I'm alone.'

'I HOPE HE DIES!' might translate to: 'One of the boys at school laughed at me and made fun of me in front of everyone and it felt so painful I just want the pain to go away.' In other words, if the person is not around, the pain won't be around either.

'I WON'T GO TO SCHOOL!' could mean: 'I'm too nervous about my spelling test.'

There are SO many emotions that sit beneath our children's cross words. Finding ways to name these feelings out loud on behalf of your child gives them permission to admit them to you. They receive the message that: 'It's OK to be you. It's OK to tell me if you are sad, nervous or scared.' These honest exchanges help your children to reflect and use their words rather than projecting, shouting or 'body slamming' their big emotions out instead.

Responding to big and painful statements

If your child says, 'I HATE you!' You might ask them: 'What is it about Mummy / Daddy that you hate?'

If your child says, 'I HOPE they DIE!' You can reply: 'Oh my love, what a big feeling! What is it that you want to stop?' Using terms of endearment like 'my love', or 'darling', or a pet name you have for your child can really work to soothe the baboon quickly.

If your child says they hate their brother, you might ask them, 'Any idea what that's about ?' or 'Have you felt that way for long?'

It's not often, but if children use strong statements like 'I want to die' it tells us they are truly and deeply unhappy and likely to be in a great deal of pain.

Being able to hold the space for your child when they are hurting is vital. Showing them that you can hold their pain, even, and especially, when they don't feel they can hold it themselves, is crucial, because they will likely feel more able to lean on you and tell you how they feel. It can lead to important conversations that can help to heal. When children are hurting, they can say painful things. We must always take their pain seriously. And we should always know we can help. Child psychiatrist Dr Bruce Perry says parents are more powerful than they know in this regard. Do always seek advice from your GP or a qualified mental health professional if you feel you need support and if your child says something that indicates they have an intention to hurt themselves or others. As mentioned previously, this book is a parenting guide and as much as it is designed to help parents to work with their children therapeutically, it should not be considered a replacement for therapy or other support that your child might require.

If your child tells you they are sad, angry or feeling 'bad', always thank them for sharing it with you, and tell them how brave they have been to do so. It takes courage to be vulnerable.

If these conversations feel too difficult to have alone, you might gently suggest that together you seek support. Never feel that you must go through difficult times alone given we all need help sometimes and it serves our children best when we seek help and advice early. It might even be that your school could run a parenting group where you can get together with other parents to discuss different ways to encourage all-important emotional literacy.

It's crucial that we do. Because, when we give our children the gift of emotional competence, we give them a gift for life. In 2013, the London School of Economics research paper 'What Predicts A Successful Life' concluded that the 'most important predictor of adult life satisfaction is the child's emotional health, followed by the child's conduct'. The study also found that 'the least powerful predictor is the child's intellectual development', which policymakers and schools do well to consider if we are serious about supporting our children's future mental health.

In fact, emotional regulation facilitates learning, given it allows children to sit comfortably and focus at school, to take turns in games and control their impulses. It allows them to make friends easily and engage with others appropriately in social settings. It ensures they make wise decisions independently when we are no longer by their side. Consider the fast-approaching teenage years and you'll see why addiction specialist Dr Gabor Maté describes emotional competence as the 'best preventative medicine'. It enables a child to understand and manage their behaviour, and to reflect on feelings that arise within them in response to external events.

When a child has good and healthy emotional regulation there's no need for time outs, punishments or sending to their rooms either. They simply become redundant.

As child psychotherapist Violet Oaklander poignantly explained, a child living in a household that does not allow the expression of anger might ultimately 'behave', but, she said, 'the good behaviour will often be driven by fear and the child's self becomes diminished due to lack of expression; his deep-felt feelings become buried inside of him.'

We want our children to be 'whole' and healthy, not 'versions' of themselves. They can only do that when we accept them as they are, and all the emotions they bring.

Our children thrive on our interactions with them. Finding these calm, more intimate and honest ways of discussing our emotions, how they feel inside, and what they really tell us, is a tremendously powerful way to connect with our children and facilitate the all-important conversations you and your children can have, not just today, but for the rest of your lives.

WISE OWL WISDOMS

- Our emotions serve as an important guide in life.

- All emotions are valid, but we must teach our children how to express them safely.

- Having good emotional regulation is vital for good mental health.

- Our emotions can be felt in our bodies.

- Big emotions like anger, fear, excitement and disappointment will often trigger the stress response.

- Give your child their voice and they won't need to shout.

- Through enabling our children to understand and articulate their feelings, we build emotional literacy and give them a gift for life.

PART TWO

BUILDING SECURE AND SUPPORTIVE RELATIONSHIPS

In Part Two I will show you how to build trust and deepen the relationship that you enjoy with your child. We will also look at the 'C's that form the pillars to support us in our parenting, and help our children to feel more secure in themselves.

Chapter Six

CONNECTION – Why We Must Connect Before We Can Command

Connection is a child's greatest need, and a parent's most powerful tool.

A seven-year-old boy runs into his bedroom, grabs his pyjamas and quickly puts them on, grinning happily at his mum, who stands smiling at the door. He jumps into bed and asks her if she'll read him his favourite story before they turn out the light. She sits beside him on the bed and they read together, before she smooths his hair, hugs him tight, then kisses him goodnight.

In another scenario, a seven-year-old runs around his bedroom with an exhausted parent trailing in his wake. Ignoring her calls to get into bed, he scrambles across it, flinging a pair of dirty pants behind him. Laughing wildly, the boy runs across the landing to his sister's bedroom and snatches her favourite toy. His sister chases him, yelling, 'Give it back!!!!' Exasperated, the boy's mother loses her patience – and her temper. She yells at her son to 'get into bed now'! He does as he's told but lies on his back with his feet up in a cycling motion. Literally climbing the walls.

What's the difference between the two boys?

The connection they have with their parent.

Who is their parent?

Me.

How closely connected our children feel to us has an enormous influence on their behaviour.

That's not a value judgement. It's a fundamental truth of what it is to be human.

We are born with a biological drive to 'attach' to others. Why? Because we cannot survive on our own. When our children feel secure in their connection with us, what we call our 'psychological attachment', they – or rather, their nervous system – can relax, trusting that we will be there, should anything terrible happen.

If our children feel disconnected, they'll feel less safe. It means we're likely to see more of the wild behaviour that I liken to a sail that has come loose from its mast and starts flapping wildly in the wind. As with Wilbur, it leads to behaviour that can cause havoc and can threaten to capsize the family boat. If our parenting's to be plain sailing, we need to secure the sail. It starts by reinforcing our connection.

In my therapy room, I have a lovely book called *The Invisible String* by Patrice Karst. It tells the story of a little boy and girl who run to their mother's room when they are frightened by an angry storm in the night. She soothes them with a story about the invisible red string that connects them to her, even when she's not in the room. It helps to reassure them that if ever she's not there, it doesn't mean they are not connected.

Our children are apart from us for extended periods now. They will increasingly be without us when their stress response gets tested. Working long hours, travelling abroad, or being absent due to a family or other emergency can all create a rupture in the connection, the sense of safety that our children depend upon in order to feel secure. Their ancient lizard and baboon know they still can't likely survive alone, so if we're poorly, have a hospital stay, if there are significant life changes such as a divorce, separation or bereavement, or even if we are just tired and overwhelmed, it can threaten our children's sense of security. It can lead to more anxious behaviour and to our children being more vulnerable to tipping into fight or flight.

I appreciate it can take all our resolve when dealing with 'flappy sail' behaviour. Especially if we're feeling disconnected, too. On the evening in question, when Wilbur was running wild, and I was exhausted from solo parenting, my wise owl really had her work cut out!

I stepped outside Wilbur's room and did a 'palm pause'. I took another breath and reminded myself that my son's behaviour was not personal, however bloody personal it felt! I had to get curious. I asked myself, 'What is this behaviour telling me?'

When I returned to his bedroom, Wilbur was still on the bed, a defiant look on his face, and still doing his upside-down cycling. I walked over to his bed and sat down, placing my palm gently on his chest, re-establishing a physical connection.

Wilbur turned to look at me. Likely he expected another telling off, but I met him with calm curiosity. 'I'm wondering, Wilbur, if you need a bit of help right now?' My voice was low and gentle, and, with my wise owl back in charge, it was steady and in command.

When using this grounding technique, you will need to decide intuitively what feels right and appropriate for you and your child. This is not about restraint or holding them down. But a gentle palm placed on an ankle, in the centre of the back or on the chest can help give a child the sense of being 'held', of being grounded by our touch.

If you try this and your child shrugs you away, as much as that might feel like a rejection, it might just be too much stimulus to have you near them. If so, still keep a calm presence and stay as close as your child will allow.

Softly, I asked my son, 'I wonder if you are showing me you need a bit more of Mummy?'

My curiosity was genuine. Clearly, my son was dysregulated and I knew my shouting at him had not helped. Equally, I suspected there was something else going on. Wilbur stopped cycling and with a pained look on his face he whimpered:

'When you get cross with me, I think you don't like me.'

I felt a pang of grief in my chest.

Then the words – and tears – spilled from him. 'And I miss Daddy! Why does he have to work away? Why can't he be at home like the other daddies? AND I got pushed over in football today!'

Wilbur was really crying now and he sat up in bed. All that pent-up stress energy – all the thoughts, worries and fears he had been holding in that day could finally find a healthier release. Rather than 'climbing the walls', my seven-year-old could communicate using his words instead.

'Oh, Wilbur. I am so sorry it's felt like that for you. How terrible it must feel if you think Mummy doesn't like you.'

Repeating our children's words, even when they tell us something this painful, is so important. As parents, we always want to make things better for our children. So when they say something painful, we might find ourselves falling into the trap of what I call the dastardly Ds.

TOOLKIT TIPS
Ditch the Ds

When our children tell us something that evokes emotions in us that make us feel uncomfortable or awkward, depending on the responses we received from our parents when we were young, we can often respond in one of the following ways:

Defend
We may seek to defend our parenting or our reaction to something that has happened:

'Don't make this about me; you were just being 'naughty'!'
'Don't shout at me. It's not MY fault!'
'If you WILL run around like that, of course I don't like you.'
'You MADE me shout!'

Dismiss
Rather than acknowledging and exploring our children's feelings, we may dismiss their concerns:

'Don't be silly! Of course I like you.'
'You're just imagining it.'
'I'm sure they didn't mean it.'

Diminish
We might even diminish our children, denying or invalidating their feelings:

'Oh, come on! You're too old to cry about that.'

'You're just being silly!'
'Stop it now – it's not that bad!'
'Why can't you be more like your brother? He wouldn't
do this!'

Deny

Denial is a psychological defence mechanism that we may
have inherited from our own parents. It can see us telling
our children:

'You are not upset, come on now'
'You are not homesick, you are just bored'
'You're ok, you can't feel that bad'

To achieve the ultimate CONNECTION with our children we
need to ditch the Ds and instead honour what they tell us in their
moments of distress. Consider how you would feel if you were
sad about something, and when you shared it with a friend or a
partner, they denied or dismissed your feelings with an 'oh, you'll
be fine' or 'oh, I had that; it's not an issue'. Or if they tried to
solve your problem for you, thereby diminishing the emotions
you felt inside.

How much more connected to them would you feel if they
responded with: 'Oh, I am so sorry. That sounds really painful/
difficult. Can you tell me more?'

If our children are telling themselves the story that 'Mummy/
Daddy doesn't like me', then little wonder it can lead to difficult,
unconsciously 'rebellious' behaviour. Our children conclude,
'Well, if they don't like me, I might as well behave this way!'
Delinquency has its roots here.

I can see this with the children in my therapy room. If they feel dislikeable, they unconsciously conclude that they might as well behave in a way that confirms it. Challenging or provocative behaviour can also be a way to evoke a response – better for a child to receive some attention than none at all. In the context of connection, their rationale is 'at least if I am SEEN, I am safe, because people at least know I am there'.

Using my curiosity rather than my Ds allows me to look beyond my son's exasperating behaviour, empathising with his feelings instead.

'Oh, how brave you are to tell me that, Wilbur. What a big, terrible thing to feel! I am so sorry it has felt that way. I love you so, so much. I always like you. I always love you. It's just the behaviour I didn't like, not you.'

It's so important to emphasise this point.

It's not our children we dislike, but their behaviour.

If we are not clear on this, our children can internalise the message, as Wilbur had done, that me getting cross with him meant I didn't LIKE him. And imagine feeling that your own parent DOESN'T LIKE YOU? That's the sort of internalisation that shapes a child's future sense of self. And, as you'll appreciate, that's definitely not something we want.

We can still address and boundary behaviour, but for now I need to help my son to exorcise the big fears and grief that were driving it.

Naming the fear, in this case 'Mummy doesn't like me and Daddy isn't here', allows me to make an all-important repair. I can correct the 'story' Wilbur has been telling himself and also apologise for losing my temper, acknowledging that I should have spoken to him more kindly. Later, when he's calm, I can also remind him why not listening is not great on his part and look at ways to 'use our words' next time.

In the bedroom, I told Wilbur how sorry I was to have shouted and how it must have set his baboon up and running. I also said, with warmth, repeating my son's words, 'And I am also hearing that you are really, really missing Daddy.'

Here I go, firing off those truth arrows.

'You miss him SO much, and you wish he were here.'

And another.

'I understand, sweetheart; it's hard when Daddy is away. Mummy misses him too.'

'I miss him too!' Clemency suddenly yelled. She had been waiting patiently for me at the doorway.

We gathered round, and Wilbur, his tears slowly abating, showed us his grazed knee. Then, he came onto my lap for a cuddle, and we talked about bedtimes and how together we could make it more fun.

With everyone calm, I could also wonder about my own dysregulated behaviour and how my crossness might be connected to me missing Mike, too. Reflecting on our behaviour with our children not only shows them that we are human, that we make mistakes as well, but that when we are able to own up to our failings, and want to learn from our mistakes, we show our children they can learn too.

Taking that all-important breath by Wilbur's bed, placing my hand on his chest and holding the space rather than telling him off again had opened up a really important conversation that now saw us cuddle and reconnect.

Rupture and Repair

In psychotherapy, we often talk about the value of what we refer to as 'rupture and repair'. This is when the mistakes we make as parents (or even as therapists in the therapy room) can provide a rich opportunity for healing, as well as modelling how to resolve situations when there is difficulty or conflict.

To ensure the repair, our children need to trust that when they open up and show their vulnerability, we will listen. They need to know we like them and accept them as they are. It does not mean we shouldn't set limits or boundaries around what we expect to happen at bedtime. It's just so much easier when we get there as a team. I could still remind Wilbur that it's difficult for Mummy when he's running around and that I am trying my very best when Daddy is away.

These 'rupture and repair' moments can help form a powerful glue for our relationship with our children. It's important because the strength of the connection they share with us forms a vital part of their emotional development. The British psychiatrist John Bowlby defined this connection as our 'attachment'. He described it as a 'lasting psychological connectedness between human beings'. Bowlby and the developmental psychologist Mary Ainsworth found that the 'attachments' we form in our earliest years are enormously influential over our future happiness and health. Mary Ainsworth even showed that the emotional connections we forge in our first year can determine our future relationships. Even the romantic ones!

BRAIN BOX

'The children who are most stable emotionally and who make use of their opportunities are those who have significant adults who encourage the child's independence yet are available and responsible when called upon. A child who has not been able to make satisfying attachments might be afraid to allow him or herself to become attached to anyone for fear of a further rejection, with all the associated agony, anxiety and danger. Such a child may have a defence against expressing, or feeling the desire for close, trusting relationships.'

— Paul Greenhalgh, author of *Emotional Growth and Learning*

Generally, many of us will sit somewhere on a spectrum of attachment. We might feel 'secure' in the attachment we have with our parents for the most part, but certain situations might trigger what are considered maladaptive 'anxious', 'avoidant' or 'disorganised' responses.

Just as Wilbur in the first situation at the start of this chapter would be considered a child 'secure' in his relationship with me, there was something very insecure about his behaviour in the second scenario.

The push–pull behaviour of ambivalence or disorganised attachment can often express itself as hyperactivity. I can see this in my son if I have been working long hours and my husband is away. When I focus my time and work on our connection, spending more one-on-one time in play, with lots of cuddles, hugs and conversations, the dysregulation disappears.

We can all appreciate how disruptive dysregulated behaviour can be, whether that's at home or in school. When we look beyond 'naughty' and wonder 'why' it might be, we can support the child and resolve the behaviour. And it's vital that we do. Pam Leo, author of *Connection Parenting*, puts it this way: 'Either we spend time meeting children's emotional needs by filling their cup with love or we spend time dealing with the behaviours caused from their unmet needs. Either way, we spend the time.'

You might wonder how to tell if your child feels securely connected to you. I asked my colleague Dr Gabor Maté this question when my children were very young. He replied, 'Does your child come to you if they're hurt, distressed or afraid?'

It was a profound moment when I reflected that my daughter, who was then five years old, mostly did – but not always. As a working parent who worked longer hours when my children were much younger, I acknowledged there might be some 'ruptures' in our relationship that needed some repair and I invested a lot of time and energy in doing so. Reflecting this way should not have parents lost in shame or guilt. We all do our best; every parent is bound by different circumstances. But it is beneficial – and crucial – for our relationship to apply the science and use what we know to ensure we and our children enjoy the most robust connection possible, not stay stuck where we are. Science shows us how the brain can 'heal' when we have an emotionally available adult whom we feel connected to and who we can trust. Just as adults can gain 'earned secure' attachment by having therapy, we can help our children do the same.

Achieving CONNECTION with our children is something we can practise daily. In my first book, I introduced the idea of 'TEN MINUTE TOP-UPS', where you commit to just ten minutes a day and one hour a week with each child. Ten minutes where we put the phone aside and focus on our children, chatting about their day or simply just in play. I have lost count of the parents who have written to me since, telling me that this simple daily intervention has seen their children's behaviour improve immeasurably. Not only do they tell me their children seem more connected, but *they* feel more connected too.

PARENT PONDER
Nadia, mother to Nico, 10, Kai, 8, and Leo, 5

In the craziness of daily cooking and cleaning, life-min and taxiing, the love can get lost. *I* know I love my children, but I have been wondering lately, do *they* know?

I have started offering each of them half an hour where they get to spend time with me. No phone, no outside influence. Just me, doing whatever they want. I have to be entirely present for them. I can only manage to do it once a week but that's a start. I have seen how much it filters through, and how they want to be even nearer to me for the next hour at least after that.

One of my sons chose just to watch something together. I felt instinctively that he craved the proximity, our bodies together on the sofa, co-regulating with a connected heart energy.

TOOLKIT TIPS

Ways to Connect

Download My Day

When I asked Wilbur and Clemency how we could make bedtimes 'better', they suggested a great ten-minute game called Download My Day.

The kids decided we had to 'meet' in the bedroom half an hour before bedtime and take turns to discuss the important things that had happened in our day. Conversations can range from: 'How did you deal with bullies when you were at school, Mummy?' through to: 'I have a crush – do you think I should tell?' It's a great way to reconnect, but it's also good for sibling bonding and problem-solving too.

The Readathon

My children came up with this one, too. The incentive for getting ready for bed quickly on nights when I am frazzled and keen to get to bed myself is that they get to jump into my bed with me and, rather than me reading out loud, we each bring our own book to read to ourselves. We lie side by side, snuggled up in silence, with little interruptions as we share plot lines or complicated words. On nights when I am too tired to think straight, bedtime becomes the best time.

Reading together, especially at bedtime, is a lovely and natural way to reconnect after a day of separation. I still enjoy reading to my children, but on days when I've been flat out from the get-go, a 'readathon' is a great 'game' and tool to have up your sleeve, and it can transform chaotic bedtimes to calm in an instant.

In these moments of connection, I'll often find myself leaning in to take a sniff of my children's heads as we snuggle up, taking in that delicious scent just as I did when they were little. The flush of oxytocin and dopamine sees my lizard lounging happily and my baboon in peaceful bliss. With my nervous system nicely down-regulated, I typically have a much-earlier night myself – often turning out the light and falling asleep with them!

Encouraging collaboration, where your children get to decide what makes the 'best bedtime', is great for bringing calm and it also helps their behaviour to remain within boundaries. Collaboration is a sure-fire route to successful parenting because when kids set the rules, they usually like to stick to them!

Touch

Research shows that physical touch in the context of a secure attachment relationship is as powerful as a drug in calming the baboon.

The importance of touch was highlighted in a famous experiment conducted in the 1950s by the primatologist and animal psychologist Harry Harlow. He separated baby rhesus monkeys from their mothers immediately after birth and gave them the choice of either a wire-mesh surrogate 'mother' with a soft cloth wrapped around her, or a wire-mesh mother without a cloth but with a bottle that dispensed warm milk. The monkeys spent most of their time with the cloth mother – even though she had no milk. They would only go to the wire mother when they were hungry. If a frightening object was placed in the cage, the infant took refuge with the cloth mother, hugging her tightly.

Touch and closeness are as important to our children as they were to Harlow's baby primates.

When he was younger, Wilbur would often ask me to do a 'pitter patter' of my fingers on his back before he went to sleep. Taking ten minutes to snuggle up with your children before bedtime can mean the world, in turn benefitting their behaviour and, all importantly, their health.

It's essential to recognise your own need for sensory soothing, too. On long winter nights when I've had a busy week, I love coming home from school, picking up and immediately changing into a soft white onesie. (Easily pleased, I know.) Stepping into it feels like a (friendly) polar bear hug. I'll head for bedtime, keen to reconnect. My children love the onesie. 'This is so soft and snuggly, Mummy.' And we'll cuddle up and talk about their day. With Clemency, now she's older, it will often involve the politics of relationships and the crushes the girls and boys are starting to have at school. My cup of love is complete. I am reminded of the need to cherish these moments, to enjoy them fully while my children are still young.

Love Letters to Our Children

When our children fall asleep, they should close their eyes feeling all is well in the world. One way to help them do that is to think of all the little things you have noticed about them that day or across the week and tell them.

This idea came from an exercise I did when I finished my first counselling course with the children's mental health charity Place2Be. Our lecturers, Georgia and Beq, had each student write an 'appreciation' note to one another. We wrote little notes that listed what we most appreciated about each other: our values and what we had contributed to the course or personally. It proved to be a very moving exercise and we all valued the notes we received.

At times when I want to top up my children's cups, I will take time to say out loud what I think of as appreciation notes, or love letters, before bedtime. When they are drowsy and calm, I lay my hand gently on their chest and tell them things I have noticed about them.

'I'm so proud of you; you are such a wonderful person.'

'I loved the way you were so fearless when you went on the zip wire this week.'

'I love your laughter; it makes the whole world light up.'

'I loved how Daddy gave you the giggles with his impression of Wilbur's future girlfriends, and how it made you laugh.'

These truths are not only wonderful for our children to hear, but they remind us of the genuine appreciation we have for our children and how much we love them. I don't do it all the time as it might lose its authenticity and value, but I find it works beautifully, especially if we have had a difficult day. Appreciation notes can help our children to remember and think of all the good stuff that's happened and they help soften any ruptures and soothe worries away.

Valuing our children for who they are, not what they do, goes a long way to building their all-important sense of self.

As the child psychiatrist Dr Gordon Neufeld sums up so eloquently: 'Children must feel an invitation to exist in our presence, exactly the way they are.'

WISE OWL WISDOMS

- A child's behaviour is a reflection of how they feel.

- The child who feels safe is the child who behaves safely.

- Children need to feel connected to the adults they have around them.

- We are all on a spectrum of attachment and can learn how to become more 'secure'.

- Investing our energy, love and time in the relationship we enjoy with our children is critical to ensuring our crucial pillar of CONNECTION is in place.

Chapter Seven

CREATIVITY – The Importance of Attachment Play

When we delight in playing with our children, so our children will delight in us.

Play is another powerful tool for repairing fragile or lost connections with our children. If we want to deepen our connection with our children, we should always make time for play. As the playwright George Bernard Shaw said: 'We don't stop playing because we grow old. We grow old because we stop playing.'

One of my clients, Dan, a corporate lawyer, was concerned that his relationship with his son seemed to be suffering. He told me that when he had returned home from work and his eight-year-old son had said to him: 'Go away! I don't want to play with you. I hate you!' Dan felt dejected and deflated to be rebuffed by a son whom he loves dearly. 'I felt vulnerable. I'd asked my son if he wanted to play, knowing that I had been away for much of the week. I had missed him and wanted him to know, but being rejected felt like I had given my son power over me. I hated it. So, I turned around and said, "Fine. Suit yourself!" And I walked away.

I felt so childish, but I didn't know how to handle my son's rejection.'

When I asked Dan how old he felt at that moment, he responded instantly: 'Eight!'

'And what was that like for you?' I asked, gently.

Dan stopped, shook his head and swore with surprise. 'I can't believe it. It took me back to when my friends wouldn't play with me!'

It's quite common to find ourselves more at odds with our children when they are a similar age to when we experienced difficulties in childhood. We might find ourselves more sensitive and easily triggered by the things they do and say. The relief Dan felt at realising it was his own inner and long-held hurt that had triggered him, rather than his son, meant he could take a step back from his behaviour and be compassionate with himself as a parent. He could also get curious about his son's response, to see what had really driven his rejection.

'I wonder if he was just angry that I've been away. I haven't been home much and me suddenly asking him to play probably felt like I wanted everything on my terms. Perhaps I needed to build up to it, even apologise for my absence.'

Later that week, Dan messaged me to say he had written a card to his son, which said: 'I'm sorry I have been working so much. I have really missed you. I would love to play if you want.' He slid it under his son's bedroom door. Five minutes later, a reply was pushed back with a scrawled: 'OK.'

Dan wrote that the play session he had that night with his son was liberating. He felt accepted, and his son clearly delighted in having his dad say sorry for the time he had been away. Perhaps it had allowed Dan's son to change the story he had been telling himself, that 'my dad loves his work more than me'.

Being playful in our parenting not only liberates our children's joy, but it can also liberate our own.

MAN-OEUVRES WITH MIKE

Timekeeping is one of my biggest bugbears. In the military, we'd end up in a tank of icy cold water if we didn't turn up on time. I've realised how it impacted my parenting. I'd get cross if the kids weren't up and ready in the mornings. I'd go into their room, clap my hands and shout, 'Come on, time to get up!' Clemency especially would push back, growling at me. I realise now how much a child's baboon hates surprise. Me going in like a Sergeant Major would set us both up for a difficult morning. Inspired by watching how Kate so often makes the children laugh, I asked them how they would like to be woken up. Wilbur said, 'With music!' So now they choose the song and I have to wake them up by singing it (badly). It tickled me, because they don't choose your average kid songs. They pick the chorus to songs like 'Highway to Hell' and 'Teenage Dirtbag'. It's now become a thing in our house: the kids put in a 'request' at bedtime and I love waking them up knowing I'll get a laugh rather than a grumpy grouch. Win–win.

Your children may not love your routines, but when we cheerfully insist on them, everyday routines become habits. They can also provide opportunities for play. When the children were younger, I found I had a choice between either battling them into the bath at bedtime or I could put on a 'giant' voice and stomp round the room bellowing, 'FEE FI FO FUM! I smell Wilbur's stinky bum! Be he here or be he there, I'll put him in, in his underwear!' (I'm not sure about your children but for my son, anything poo, fart-or bottom-related is always a winner.) Being playful isn't about being funny all the time or making jokes if your child is sad. It's about helping them be more open to and experience the positive connection that will see your parenting get much, much easier. That much I can guarantee.

Play gives us a greater insight into our children's inner worlds. In the therapy room, I learn most from a child when I get down on the floor and play with them. The same goes for parenting, because children and young people instinctively play in order to sort out or understand their world. Play is their language, a vital part of child development. Play comes in many guises, but in general, I think of it as quality time where a child feels safe and able to express themselves with an adult who feels comfortable to follow their lead. It's about being together in a fun, light atmosphere, where our phones are set aside and our focus is solely on our children. Inviting your children to play – even if they're 12 – can see some surprising requests and choices. Especially as children head towards their teenage years, they can sometimes find comfort in your play routines of old.

Even Wilbur, with his penchant for more physical play, still loves nothing more than sitting with me and creating Lego houses and boats for us to play with in the bath. Or we'll just hang out in their bedrooms, talking, experimenting with hairstyles or doing art together. Even the most resistant of my teenage clients in therapy will soon join me on the floor and start finger-painting or engaging in sand play, once trust in the therapeutic relationship is established and the magic of us just 'being' is there.

The rough-and-tumble games of physical play, where our bodies connect, are incredibly valuable too. They enhance the development of our children's little owl, putting her to the task of regulating those big baboon impulses and bringing him back to calm after excitement, or keeping him focused during a task. Indeed, neuroscientist Jaak Panksepp even questioned whether many children diagnosed with ADHD might simply be 'play deprived'.

Our play must always be child-led; that is to say, we should always give our children the choice of what they do. A friend shared with me that at a recent corporate event, she and the other delegates were encouraged to participate in what was described as a play-based icebreaker. A box of Lego pieces appeared and they were each told to make a duck in under a minute. My friend said everyone worked diligently to create their duck while she felt an overwhelming sense of pressure. She felt stressed and resentful that a supposedly fun activity was being measured and directed. Once everyone had shared their ducks, she asked what the purpose of the exercise had been. The response was: 'This is how to play.'

Except it's not.

Play should not be time pressured. It should not feel competitive. It should not be prescriptive. It should not be for show. It should be unconditional: we should never threaten to withdraw our play sessions as a punishment.

Play should start with an invitation. If, like Dan, you get rejected, it might be a sign your child feels disconnected and you'll need to invest time in building up the connection again. It might be they're mad at you for being at work all day and they want to 'punish' you, or it might be the first time you've ever asked that question and they are so shocked, they're not sure what you mean! Accept their response with a smile and say, 'Oh, OK, maybe not now. But I would love to spend more time with you. I know I've been busy and I wanted to see what you might like to do. You can decide when it's the right time for you.'

For most children, though, the offer of time spent with you can soon see them accepting your invitation. Given time with us is what our children crave more than anything in the world.

> ## BRAIN BOX
>
> 'There is enormous value in our children having the opportunity to express themselves verbally and non-verbally in play. We all need to offer children a place to just be themselves. Children express their emotions and feelings through play – it enables them to understand and manage their experiences. To encourage this, as adults, we need to be playful ourselves.'
>
> — Catherine Roche, Chief Executive Officer, Place2Be

One of the first things I tell the children in my therapy room when we agree the rules around our time together is that they are 'in charge'. That means they get to decide what we'll do in the room. The joy (and often disbelief) on their faces brings joy to me too. It highlights how little autonomy our children often feel that they have, constricted as they are by school and timetables, by homework and clubs. There really is too little time in any given day where they can just 'be'.

If you do invite your child to 'play', you can decide together what you can do and what you can't. Ideally, the fewer rules the better. So perhaps you might say: 'The only things we can't do in our play are things that might not be safe for you or for me to do. For example, we can jump on the bed, but if I think we are getting too excited and the bed might break, we will have to stop. And we can't play in the living room as there are too many sharp edges.'

An anxious child might find invitations to play overwhelming. They might find there is too much choice – too many toys in the room, for example – in which case you can make some gentle suggestions while giving them the impression of autonomy. 'We could get the puzzles out, we could read a book or we could get the cookery books out and do some baking?' You might try: 'We could go outside and roll around on the grass. We might do some hand painting or play dress-up. You can do my hair or I can do yours…' Suggesting just a few things at a time can warm them up, and once they realise they really can take charge, the sky can be the limit!

Your children might enjoy being silly or they might prefer being silent. They might seek out your physical presence and even climb on your lap as my own children sometimes do. Wilbur will often sit between my legs, which I hold in a V-shape. He can lean on me while he does a puzzle and I, in turn, take comfort in the quiet time, feeling my own body regulate in response. Once your children are calm, however, they will often climb off you and move around more.

Try to mirror their body language if you can. If your child sits cross-legged, try to do the same. We don't have to worry about what to say. Just giving your children your time and presence is therapeutic enough. When we play in this way it allows our children's internal worlds to unfold. We might imagine that the lizard and baboon get to come down from the tree and gambol happily in the grass below.

Depending on how you feel about mess, you might want to throw in a boundary: 'We can make a complete mess, so long as we put things back!' It is worth noting, however, that some children might feel a real and urgent need to make a mess. It's often a way of the unconscious expressing itself. If your child delights in getting messy, find a way for them to be able to do that – for example by using a large waterproof tablecloth outside if they want to do hand painting or other messy play.

The key is for your children to have some sense of freedom. If we keep everything tidied away all the time, the less chance they will play with their toys and the more chance you have of a bored baboon on your hands.

MAN-OEUVRES WITH MIKE

As parents, we have to learn to live in chaos. The military trained me to keep my things neat and tidy and I've had to learn not to lose my rag when Wilbur decides to 'post' his pants through the gaps in the bannisters ready for me or Kate to collect, rather than put them in his laundry basket. I have come to accept, using Kate's concept, that his then six-year-old 'primitive' brain doesn't get why that's frustrating. 'Pant-posting' is simply much more fun. Letting this particular issue go meant I actually joined him, showing him how to make a parachute out of his pants, which we sent down to Kate to catch. A few goes of that and I found another 'game': who could aim their pants and socks into the laundry basket most accurately? I had to laugh when I saw how much easier it was to get him to put his dirty laundry in the basket that way than by me moaning at him!

The more we can introduce playfulness into our daily routine, the higher the chance of on board, bonded behaviour.

Playtime Inspiration

Draw My Day

This is a variation of Download My Day, which I describe in the Toolbox Tips in Chapter Six on page 119. It is another easy way to encourage a 'download' and reconnect after a day away from each other. Drawing images rather than speaking or writing words is an effective way of allowing our unconscious to 'speak'. It works especially well for children who might prefer to draw or show you images to give you an idea of their day.

I remember doing this with my own children. In one of our games, around Clemency's sixth birthday, I recall her drawing a cupcake then putting a big cross through it. She then drew some scribbles next to the cake in yellow. She had taken some homemade cupcakes into school that day to celebrate but clearly something was up.

'Ah,' I said. 'I see you've drawn a cupcake, but you've crossed it out?'

Asking the open question invites a reply, without asking why, which can shut a child down.

Clemency said, 'I didn't like my cupcakes. They weren't any good.'

I reflected Clemency's words back to her.

'Ah, so you didn't like the cupcakes. They weren't any good?'

Again, naming a difficult truth fires off a truth arrow that can lance any 'emotional boil'. It also invites her to tell me more.

'No, they weren't any good!' she confirmed and looks at me sadly.

Clemency then had a little cry. Wilbur watched as I soothed her tears and rocked her. His even littler owl was seeing empathy in play. In a short time, my six-year-old was smiling again as she told me how much fun it was when everyone sang happy birthday. A therapy trick whenever my children, or children in the therapy room, create any art is to ask: 'What title would you give this?' Or: 'If the scribble/drawing could talk what would it say?' These are good ways to get further insight. Clemency decided her drawing was called 'Wibbly Wobbly Cake Day', which summed up the mix of emotions rather well! Games like Draw My Day can work wonders for allowing our children to name and put their fears on the page in a very simple way that often diffuses their potency.

Needy

There might be some nights when you sense your children are a little 'wired' and need to offload some energy of the stress response before you can find that all-important calm. When he was seven, Wilbur created a game he called Needy. (He chose it, and we don't need to be Sigmund Freud to see his unconscious at play!) He would stand at the entrance to one bedroom with me standing behind. I had to give him a two-second start and he would run across the landing to his bedroom, where he'd jump into his bed and pull the duvet up over his head. I'd chase him and if any part of him was still exposed, he had told me I was allowed to tickle it.

I am mindful of tickling. Bodily autonomy for a child is vital, so tickling should always be at the child's behest and we must always stop if they ask us to. Wilbur was so good at the game, however, that I rarely got the chance, but the chase and merely the anticipation of a tickle had him squealing and me howling with laughter.

We'd boundary the game before we started and agreed on how long we would play, given that I didn't want him too excited just before bedtime. It needed to be just enough to discharge any excess energy from the day, but not to tip Wilbur's stress response the wrong way. Just as I do with children in the therapy room, when we boundary games in advance we can gently remind our children when we have five minutes to go. It helps to keep the energy contained and expectations in check. It also helps Wilbur's little owl to practise that all-important emotional regulation as I bring him back to calm with an: 'Oh wow, that was so much fun! Now we can go get ready for bed.'

Having me alongside while Wilbur released his energy kept his behaviour safe and connected us through the joy of play. However tired I was at that time of night, I never failed to enjoy the game. His roars of laughter were food for the soul. And while Mike is typically not an 'imaginary' game player with the kids, preferring to connect with them through sport or puzzles and learning, Wilbur explained the rules and asked him if he would play. To hear my husband's and son's roars of laughter, as well as the stomping of their feet on the landing above, was heaven.

Physical play can be just as creative and beneficial in terms of building your children's confidence and connectedness with you. Here's a quick checklist of physical games you might like to try:

- Pillow fights
- Throwing a blow-up ball back and forth across the bed
- Throwing soft toys at a target
- Hide and seek
- Rolling around on the floor
- Rolling your children up in a blanket and unrolling them again.

One of my colleagues, psychologist Dr Lawrence Cohen, writes wonderful books about play. He advocates regular 'roughhousing' games that he says are great for child development and family harmony. His top tips include:

- Make play safe, but don't worry too much. 'Children need to take risks, because in risky play they learn how their body works and how to manage risk.'
- Have a dedicated area free from sharp edges and away from glass doors.
- Don't be afraid to 'roughhouse'. 'Good rough and tumble play is more like dancing than fighting.'
- Roughhousing builds confidence in children as long as adults or older children don't dominate and overpower smaller children.
- Usually let the child win! 'Don't worry that your child will become "over-confident" or lose their respect for you. On the contrary, they will learn a vital moral lesson, that bigger people should hold back their superior strength during play so that it remains fun for everyone.'
- Pause if someone gets hurt, even if it's an imaginary injury! 'The purpose of roughhousing is not to toughen kids up, but to let them know that they can be physically and emotionally safe even while using all their strength and power. However, there is no need to stop the game abruptly just because of a minor injury or some tears. Provide comfort, listen empathically to the tears, then get back to playing.'
- No holding children down and tickling them. 'Unfortunately this kind of tickling overwhelms the nervous system. A quick little jab-tickle, or pretend tickle,

can bring a more enjoyable type of laughter and is less overstimulating.'

- Good signs are giggling! 'You know you are on the right track when you see a child working hard, in a joyful way, to tackle you or bop you with a pillow.'

- Let your child be the one who is 'stronger' or, as Dr Cohen puts it 'more competent'. 'I like to exaggerate my abilities – you will never knock me over, you will never escape!'

- 'If in doubt, fall over. Young children especially love to give you a little push and have you fall over dramatically. If that makes them laugh – do it again. And again...'

BRAIN BOX

'I like to start every roughhousing session with a good strong connection, such as a hug, shaking hands, high fives, or bowing to one another "to show respect before fighting to the death!" as one young boy put it to me. Then it's great to end roughhousing with another symbolic connection. During roughhousing play you can build connection by tuning in to your child, noticing their intensity level, their eye contact, and their mood.'

— Dr Lawrence Cohen, author of *Playful Parenting*

A final note on physical play. Roughhousing, as Dr Lawrence Cohen also observes, can trigger big feelings. If that's excitement: wonderful. But other intense feelings can arise, from sadness (if a child is reminded of a time when they didn't have this fun play) to anger (if play tips over into something more). If a child tips into a blind rage or does not give you eye contact, bring the energy down again, observing they seem to be having some 'big feelings' and you want to help. You might say 'Oh, WOW, I can see that you're upset/angry. I'm so sorry – how can Mummy/Daddy help?' Remind your child they are safe and your job is to keep them safe. Gently suggest you both sit with the big feelings. It can be another great way to release any emotional energy and, as always, there is repair to be had from any rupture. Trust that you being there and available will help strengthen your connection with your child.

All good things come to an end. When time is short, it's a good idea to negotiate an end to the play session, so your children know in advance what to expect. Even so, when I tell my children it's time to put things away, I can empathise that it's a difficult moment. 'Oh, I know; it's so hard to stop now when we have been having so much fun! I love it too. Can we do it again tomorrow night?'

You can negotiate an extra five minutes, to bank lots of goodwill. But then, when it comes to 'our time is up now, guys', you can remind your children that toys need to be cleared away before supper time, or that it's time for 'listening ears on' as we get ready for bed.

I tend to have firm boundaries on things that matter to me. For example, 'I gave you an extra five minutes but now we need to calm down for some quiet time,' rather than force my children to pick up every last Lego brick. If we impose our own need for neatness onto our children, it can undermine all the goodwill we have built up. Equally, play offers us the chance to help our children to work within boundaries, and again, it involves both a little owl as well as baboon.

Humour is a good tool if your children resist tidying up with you and you've asked them to. In that case, I might put one of their soft toys on their head and say, 'Oh, Tiger, I know you love Clemency so, so, so much, but she has to put you to bed now! Clemency will give you a kiss goodnight. Is that what you want?' Laughing, Clemency will kiss the tiger and put him in his box.

I joke that Clemency will become a brilliant lawyer when she's older as she can negotiate me into a corner any time when I am tired. And that's okay. Sometimes I 'give in' to my children's demands, but, equally, on nights when I want some down time, it's okay to be firm and remind them of what we have agreed. 'I know it's hard to stop now, darling. I know you want to play and we have had such a good time! Would you like to throw your cuddly toys in their bin to get that crossness out, or would you like to throw them to me and see how many I can catch?'

Children work with us much more easily when we work with them. We are still in charge, we are still in command of the ship and, as we've seen, we can still set limits if we are all to feel safe. But our children must feel heard and showing our understanding that it can be difficult to stop playing is a good way of doing this.

Finally, find ways to say no while still saying yes. In my child-counselling training we played the 'Yes, and...' game. You can try it with your children as you tidy things away or get ready for bed. Each of you says a sentence that is joined by 'and yes' or 'yes and'.

'It's time to go to bed and yes, I will help you!'

'And yes, I can leave my Lego house up?'

'You can leave your Lego house up and yes, we can play with it tomorrow!'

'And yes, we have time for a bedtime story too?'

'Oh yes, and I'm going to tell you how much I love you!'

When we tell our children that we want to spend time with them, what we're really telling them is: you matter to me and I enjoy being with you. Parenting today is often sadly so time-compromised that it can be difficult sometimes to find the enthusiasm. But I can guarantee you'll never regret saying yes to play. Even just ten minutes a day, spent in child-led play, can be food for the soul and a saviour for your connection. Six hundred seconds that play a fundamental part in restoring calm and connectedness, and in future-proofing your relationship, and your child's mental health.

WISE OWL WISDOMS

- Play remains hugely beneficial for children between five and 12 years old.

- Play with friends is important, but time spent playing with us is still crucial.

- Play helps our children to make sense of their world.

- Play informs their sense of self.

- Play restores our connection after a busy day.

- Play improves behaviour, because our children will want to please us when we say yes to play!

Chapter Eight

CURIOSITY – Why Curiosity is King – or Queen!

Rather than wondering, 'What's wrong with you?' instead we must wonder, 'What's going on for you?'

At bedtime, Clemency shared with me that she had seen Wilbur being 'naughty' in dance class at school. Wilbur looked ashamed. I don't encourage telling tales, but my son's face told me there was something to explore. I felt a stab of shame myself (what parent likes to think of their child misbehaving at school) but overrode my own baboon discomfort to stay in wise owl and gently ask, 'Sweetheart, can you tell me more?'

Wilbur looked at me defiantly and blurted crossly, 'I don't LIKE the dance teacher! He tells me off!'

In moments like these, when our children are on the defensive, it can put us on the defensive too. This is often a hangover from our own childhoods. If we were taught to defer to those in authority and to always say 'kind things' it can see us drop into those dastardly Ds (see Chapter Six) and immediately defend the person, especially a teacher, with an, 'Oh, Wilbur, he's really nice. If he's telling you off, you must have been doing something 'naughty'!'

Alternatively, we might succumb to the shame that can arise because we feel our children's behaviour reflects poorly on us as parents. We might offload or project that shame and guilt onto our children. 'Oh, Wilbur, what did you do? How could you?'

I will admit those thoughts fleetingly crossed my mind (old habits die hard). But instead, I paused and took a deep breath, giving my wise owl time to step in. I met Wilbur's gaze, and with genuine interest and a tone that suggested I was curious, I said, 'Oh, sweetheart! What happened?'

Using a 'what happened?' question is a great neutral way to show your child you want to understand things from their perspective. It immediately soothes a bounding baboon, who senses he'll get a 'fair hearing' and helps our children to engage their little owl, who must step in to help the baboon make his case. When your child's little owl can work alongside the baboon, some serious lessons can be learned. Using a curious question – one that is not loaded with judgement – is more likely to help our children to tell us the truth about things that have happened, trusting we are not going to jump to the instant conclusion that they must be in the wrong.

Asking 'what happened?' also keeps emotions alive, rather than shutting them down with a 'WHY did you do that?' question.

'I didn't want to dance!' Wilbur shouted, his anger a reactive defence. Knowing that beneath anger lies hurt, and also fear, allowed me to keep calm and curious. I responded with a head tilt and a curious expression. 'Oh, so you didn't want to dance?'

Wilbur's voice became 'whiny'; the voice of a child with something painful to share.

'He puts me by the window and everyone comes past and laughs at me when I try to dance!'

That feeling of being humiliated in front of our peers, of being laughed at if we make a mistake, is something we can all relate to. Being laughed at creates a deep sense of hurt and Wilbur's eyes filled with tears. Brain neuroimaging studies reveal why. They show how the brain areas activated during distress caused by social exclusion are also those activated during physical pain.

I think that's worth repeating. Our children experience psychological pain when they feel excluded from friendship groups or if they feel rejected by us.

It's why, when our children reveal something painful, they are at their most vulnerable. Suppose a child has experienced a rejection by their peers. In that case, there can also be a profoundly unconscious fear that you might reject them too.

This can feel unbearable.

These are the moments that give us such a rich opportunity to build trust and connection.

I reached out my arms and with genuine warmth and pain in my voice I said, 'Oh wow, Wilbur. So you had to stand by the window and dance, and everyone who came past could see you?'

As painful as it can feel to say the words, repeating and reflecting what our children tell us is enormously powerful. I showed Wilbur that I 'get' how embarrassing it must have felt. It shows him that I care more about understanding his experience than telling him off.

You will need to really feel your child's hurt in these moments. Our children know instantly if they are being patronised. Few of us enjoy being 'watched' when we feel self-conscious. I can recall my time when rehearsing with Aljaž Škorjanec for *Strictly Come Dancing*. He was a fabulously fit 28-year-old and I was a non-dancing 48-year-old mother of two. Aljaž would often invite groups of people to watch us practise our routine. I'd push on through with a faux grin on my face, my inner wise owl reassuring me it was only my pride that might die a little if I got something wrong. But if I was tired and feeling wobbly, I would tell Aljaž, 'No! I'm not ready!' and in protest I would sometimes act silly and mess around – just as Wilbur had done – by distracting the audience, making them laugh; in fact, anything rather than perform!

Back in the bedroom, Wilbur told me: 'They were laughing! Clemency was laughing!'

He was letting me know I had missed a crucial bit of the story: people were laughing at him. That's where the pain was: not only in being watched, but in being laughed at.

I repeated what he'd said, a tone of crossness in my voice to match his own. 'And they were laughing at you?' The tone of our voice needs to match the energy and intensity of our children's, so they know we don't just hear what they are telling us, but we feel it too.

'Yes!' he cried, and then his tears really flowed. When a truth arrow hits home, it often turns on the tear tap. We are not being 'mean' doing this. Remember, bearing witness to our child's pain and distress, and soothing away those tears and fears, BUILDS emotional resilience in the longer term. But first we need to 'exorcise' the hurt and painful experience so it doesn't get stuck as a negative memory or association. In repeating our child's words back to them, we endorse that we really do 'get' how painful that experience must have been.

Wilbur curled up on my lap and I rocked him back and forth, repeating, 'It's OK, it's OK; Mummy's got you.' Irrespective of age, tender words are very soothing for a distressed brain. Clemency looked across in concern. I didn't have to tell her in that moment how upset Wilbur was. She could see it. I could tell from her expression that she also realised her behaviour in laughing had been rather mean.

'I'm sorry, Wilbur,' she said, with genuine remorse.

Wilbur was really crying now; loud sobs and big fat tears.

BRAIN BOX

'When a child feels safe, when you are emotionally available, they move from explosive rage to sobbing, a release of often years of grief and fear and desperate aloneness.'

— Camila Batmanghelidjh, Psychotherapist, *Shattered Lives*

Don't be afraid or resist if your children are crying. It can be difficult if we have not been parented this way, but as the Jewish proverb goes: 'What soap is for the body, tears are for the soul.' I like to think of tears as flushing away all those stress and anxiety hormones, rather than leaving them in the body, stuck and stagnant.

Contrary to what we might fear (that once we encourage our children's tears they might never stop), over time, and with practice, these regular 'grieving' processes take less and less time. Wilbur's true distress lasted for all of a minute. When he stopped crying, he looked up and said brightly: 'I did a really good football slide though, Mummy!'

I smiled. 'Ah, OK! So, am I right in thinking that the teacher got cross because he thought you weren't listening and paying attention, and that you were doing football slides instead?'

Wilbur looked sheepish.

It's a good idea to repeat what we have understood about the whole picture, just to be sure we understand the facts fully and accurately.

'So, in dance class you get put by the window and everyone comes past and laughs, so you don't want to dance and instead you do slide tackles across the floor?'

Both children were smiling. We could all see 'the big picture'. Once Wilbur's lizard and baboon were calm, I could engage his little owl to see if she could come up with a solution, because there's still a boundary around his behaviour and it was an important lesson for her to learn.

'OK. So, sweetheart, what do you think would be a good solution here? Because you do have to take the dance class and you do need to pay attention to your teacher.'

Thinking hard, Wilbur suggested: 'I could go in the other corner? No one will see me there.'

What a great solution! I asked Wilbur if he felt able to ask his teacher to swap places, or if he would like me to email the dance teacher and explain. I am always happy to facilitate something that might feel a little big for him to handle alone. However, allowing your child to resolve something themselves can be very empowering. It allows them and their little owl to take ownership of situations in future. Wilbur decided he could ask the teacher himself, but also said he would like me to email too, so, ultimately, we did both!

Problem solving this way gives our children agency over both their behaviour and how to state their needs. Just a single ten-minute conversation led to Wilbur recently declaring dance as one of his favourite classes. He certainly developed a better relationship with his teacher, who, once he understood Wilbur's behaviour was more nervous than 'naughty', began giving him house points and a high five for being so brilliant and engaged in class. The boundary still stands on his behaviour – he still has to go to dance class and he still has to listen to his teacher. But now everyone's happy and the solution was such a simple one.

Knowing that our brain actively feels 'pain' when under threat of social exclusion or being laughed at is something we can all relate to. If adults find such situations difficult, we can indeed find more empathy for the child who 'acts out' rather than risks 'public humiliation'. It can be helpful at home and in school. I hope, using science, we can all use more curiosity to consider more playful, kinder and certainly more effective ways of bringing a child's behaviour 'on board'.

TOOLKIT TIP
Curious Questions Don't Start With Why?

Ask a child 'why?' and we will often be met with shrug or an 'I dunno!'

Remember, our children often genuinely *won't know* why they have behaved a certain way if their non-thinking lizard and baboon have been in the driving seat!

Curious questions that begin with an 'I wonder …' are a more helpful way to open up the conversation. They also help our children's little owl to reflect and better understand their behaviour too.

A curious question is an open-ended one loaded with warmth, conveying our willingness to understand. So rather than asking 'why did you do that?', we can ask simply 'what happened?', or 'what was that like for you?'

TOOLKIT TIPS
Be More Owl

When our children tell us they hate their teacher, their friend or even us, it can see us immediately drop into our Ds and move to defend, dismiss or diminish. But that's our stuff. You are your child's most powerful advocate and these are the moments when they need the help of your wise owl, not a defensive baboon. In these moments we can remember to OWL:

O – 'Oh, sweetheart. Can you tell me more?' Or, 'Oh, what happened?'

W – 'I wonder what that was like for you?' (When she/he said that / when they did this / when that happened.)

L – Lean in, Listen and show Love.

Showing your child unconditional love when they are vulnerable will strengthen your connection and sets your relationship up for life.

I include many more scripts and suggested questions and responses in Chapter 12, Conversations that Count (Page 229), and I hope they will be of help. Find one or two that sit comfortably with you and try them out. Short, simple sentences work best: the key is the warmth of your voice and your genuine curiosity.

Put Aside the Personal

Matt is a father to two girls: Zara seven, and Faith, four. He told me his eldest daughter had started using words he found incredibly disrespectful and even hurtful. Things like: 'I HATE you! You're a bumhole.'

He told me he found it really triggering. (And it is incredibly difficult for us to respond to our children with compassion and empathy when we're hit by an immediate feeling of hurt and disrespect.) But Matt said he didn't want to keep responding in baboon, shouting back and sending his daughter to her room.

I asked him to show me where he had felt it when his daughter had spoken to him that way. Matt immediately pointed to his chest. When I asked him what the feeling was, he told me 'hurt and rejected'. Without further prompting he said, 'It made me feel like I did as a child when I never felt heard and I did not feel my feelings were respected.'

Whenever we are triggered by our children's behaviour, it usually means it's activated an old wound from our childhood, and, precisely as Matt identified, it's generally related to not feeling heard or respected ourselves when we were young.

Child psychologist Dr Laura Markham says: 'Because that wound is a story we tell ourselves, like "No one ever listens to me," we're always looking for confirming evidence that that's the way the world is.'

It's why having counselling, joining parenting groups and asking for support can be so helpful for parents. We ALL carry wounds from our childhood. Realising that we are not alone, and that we are not terrible parents, helps us to reflect on our behaviour with compassion, realising we're often just parenting from a place of hurt.

Being curious takes courage, but when we address and heal those hurts it will deepen the connection we have with our children. Because, when we 'put aside our personal,' we can look beyond our child's behaviour and have compassion. We can immediately see that our children use hurtful words when they're hurting. And yes, it's most often when *they* don't feel heard, or that their feelings are being respected! Being curious allows us to LISTEN to what our children are telling us, often in the only way they know how. In doing that we can repair and can take great pride and comfort that we're breaking transgenerational cycles of hurt.

The next time Matt's daughter told him 'I HATE you! You SMELL! You're a bumhole!' he said he felt able to reflect the words back with a genuine and authentic curiosity: 'Oh darling, Zara. So you HATE me, I SMELL *and* I am a bumhole?!' (He said he even had to suppress a smile at that point, given how clearly childlike it sounded.) Rather than seeing his daughter as the enemy, and taking her words personally, Matt said he felt a jolt of compassion for his little girl who was so cross and he suddenly felt really curious to know why. He wanted to understand her, in a way he wished his parents had understood him.

Matt said Zara stopped in her tracks, shocked that her father hadn't responded in his typical baboon fashion. Matt continued with genuine concern. 'You must be SO MAD at me to speak that way. I want to understand. Can you tell me more?'

Zara immediately yelled: 'You NEVER play any more. You shouted yesterday. I don't like it when you shout.'

And THERE it was. Zara LOVES her daddy. She wants so much to spend time with him because he's fun and they get to sit in the garden, and she feels so seen and heard when her funny stories make him laugh. She feels confused when he's at his computer and he shushes her or waves her away. Inside, she tells herself the story 'he doesn't love me any more'. No wonder she's wearing a defensive armour of anger – it's so much easier to wear than fear.

These are the moments that offer us such rich opportunity for repair by using the simple tool of SAS that I introduced in my first book.

S – Say what you see or hear.

A – Acknowledge the upset, to allow us to quickly get to a place where we can

S – Soothe. To heal the pain that hides behind our children's hurtful words.

Matt told his daughter: 'I'm so sorry. I'm hearing that you have been missing me. I have been missing you too.'

He explained that he had a project at work that he'd had to finish. But he emphasised it wasn't because he didn't love Zara or that he preferred to be doing that. He acknowledged: 'I know that must feel horrid when it seems like I don't have time for you. My work is SOOO boring (!) and I much prefer my time with you! I love it when we play and I am so sorry that I shouted yesterday.'

Being conspiratorial, especially on matters of work and how we find it much less interesting than our children, helps to lighten what can often feel a heavy load for us both. It allows our children to really trust that we find more joy in being with them than we do anything else.

Young children don't yet have 'work' in context. They don't know where we go or what we're doing, or why it's so important. When we leave the house or sit in our home office all consumed and concentrating on our work, waving our rumbunctious children away, it can leave them feeling very rejected and confused. 'Why on earth would Mummy/Daddy prefer to spend time doing that, when they could be with me?' They can then internalise the story that we want to be away from them, which can drive an unconscious fear of not being 'enough'. Having conversations around work, or even taking your children into work for a day, can really help them to understand that work is something adults must do to 'pay for our food and for our toys'. But always remember to emphasise that it 'doesn't mean I don't love you'.

Matt said he put away his phone and made a great show of switching off his computer. He showed Zara he was really listening to what she had told him. He wanted her to know he much preferred time spent with her. His little girl took his hand and they had a wonderful half hour of play. Matt said he had never felt as connected to his daughter as they were then. With her feelings, and his own, now soothed, he felt able to tell her: 'Hey, Zaza, I've had SO much fun! Thank you for reminding me that we need to play together more. If I ever forget again, do you think you can remind me – or give me a sign to let me know you are mad so you don't have to use the mad words to be heard?'

MAN-OEUVRES WITH MIKE

I was the youngest of six children and the age gap between us was 17 years. My dad died when I was 11. so I spent a lot of my early childhood alone.

I realise today I never really felt seen or heard as a child, and so one of my biggest triggers now is if my children aren't listening to me. I can literally feel it in my gut. Talking about it with Kate made me realise how personally I was taking my children's behaviour. Once I could 'put aside the personal', I could respond from a place of wise owl rather than my baboon. For example, at supper time, when Wilbur is kicking a ball outside and I am calling him in for supper, I can get cross quickly because it feels like he's ignoring me on purpose. When I can accept that with his baboon in play mode it is genuinely much harder for his little owl to cut through, I can remain calm. Rather than shouting out to him, and becoming baboon when

I am inevitably ignored, I walk out, crouch down to his level, look him in the eyes, smile and say: 'Hey, Wilbur, dinner's ready.' It's amazing that it works so quickly and easily without me getting stressed and enraged.

I receive quite a few messages from parents, many fathers, actually, who echo Mike and Matt's comments. Callum is a psychotherapist who reached out one Easter when his five-year-old was on overwhelm. He'd read my first book and so was aware of the technique 'Stop SN-O-T', which again encourages us to put aside our personal:

First **STOP**: take a breath.

Remember, this is **S'Not** personal!

Observe your child's behaviour. Ask yourself: what might these words / behaviours really be about?

Turn it around. When we are able to think about a thing from our children's perspective, we can then wise owl and turn things around.

PARENT PONDER
Callum, father to Alfie, 5

Easter thanks for your book! I'm currently sitting upstairs in the loo, taking a deep breath, reminding myself to STOP SN-O-T. My son's just had a full-on meltdown and I got cross because it felt like all my efforts to create an Easter morning to remember had gone pear-shaped. My parents didn't do it for me, so I wanted to create special memories for Alfie. But a morning of fun activities and sugar have clearly caught up. I felt hurt because it felt like his tantrum ruined everything. I'm up here reminding myself it's not personal, it's just overwhelm! I'm off to give him some big hugs and chill out. We can do the egg hunt tomorrow!

Being able to reflect on our behaviour and why we respond to our children in the way we do can be a tricky thing to master and it is something I found having personal therapy incredibly helpful for. But having these honest conversations with friends and people we trust can be therapeutic too.

You might make a list – don't let your child see it! – of your triggers so you can consider them with curiosity.

I personally used to get triggered when:

- the children weren't listening and it meant we'd be late.
- they were fighting.
- or if they complained that I'd brought them 'the wrong snack' after school.

Being curious allowed me to consider the following:

- As a child, I was always criticised for being 'scatty' and late. Anyone formally diagnosed with ADHD, as I am, will know how shaming it can be to be called out for having a scattered mind. When I am late, I feel a sense of shame, that I am going to be judged, that my children's tardiness reflects directly on me.

- I get on brilliantly with my older sister now, but we had terrible fights when we were children. We shared a bedroom and a fair few punches and kicks. It triggers me if I see my own children physically fighting, not only because of the obvious, but I suspect because of the frightening feelings and negative associations it also invokes within me.
- The attachment style of my childhood was 'avoidant', which means I can feel rejected if I have tried to do something nice for the people I love and they 'reject' me.

You may feel exposed and vulnerable making such a list. You might even feel a bit silly. But we all carry old hurts and we do our own mental health a great service if we can be curious about them. If your 'hurts' feel childlike, it's because we experienced them as children and so we recall them as such. Paying attention to the little person inside you and being curious about how we felt as children allows our inner child to feel heard, which then serves to reduce the more reactive behaviours we usually like least about ourselves as a parent. At least, I know they do for me.

When I can soothe my own inner child, I can reassure myself, that it's ok if I am a little bit late this morning. When I am parenting solo, it's hard to chaperone two children and a puppy out of the door and be on time for school! Once I have dropped my old fears around judgement, we have a much happier journey to school than if I allowed my baboon and his old wounds to take over.

On the topic of tardiness, do cut yourself and your kids some slack in the mornings. I know it's typically a stressful time of day, given we have the deadline for school. But remember that children live very much in the present, because their baboon does not wear a watch – he has little concept of traffic to navigate and school gates that close. Considering the stress response, and that the baboon has little grasp of time, allows me to forgive my children, and me, and I either get up half an hour earlier to give ourselves more of a fighting chance, or shrug and think, it's ok if we are five minutes' late on occasion!

When my children were younger and they would niggle and fight, I would remind myself to take a deep breath and engage my wise owl, separating them and working on their emotional regulation rather than shout.

On the days I take my children a snack, I remind myself in advance that they might be starving and tired, so any complaints will not be about me or the snack; they need to be met with a soothing wise owl who understands.

The psychologist Oliver James observes that we either 'robotically reproduce, or react against, the care we received as children'. Being curious about our own childhood experience, what served us and what did not, helps us to gain a sense of 'self hood' as James calls it. We can serve our children and their mental health if we are first curious about and address our own.

TOOLKIT TIPS

I wonder ...

The more we can reflect on our own behaviour, the better we can help our children reflect on theirs. Using reflection followed up by 'I wonder' questions are great in that regard.

If our children tell us 'I HATE Ilyan! He said Liverpool are rubbish because they lost last night!', we can take a moment to reflect on what the meaning of HATE might be in that moment. Then we can help our children to reflect too, perhaps by asking: 'Oh, so I am hearing that you felt really angry when Ilyan said your football team was rubbish? I wonder if his words about your football team made part of you feel a bit rubbish too?'

In response to: 'I HATE Jennifer – she says she's not my friend any more!', we might say: 'I hear how much it hurt when Jennifer said she's not your friend any more. I wonder if it also felt a bit scary too because our baboon can worry if he thinks we'll be left alone?'

The list of 'I wonder' questions is endless. Using our curiosity to consider what our children are really feeling helps us to wonder aloud, firing a few truth arrows as we go:

'I'm wondering if a part of you is missing Grandma? It is really hard when we miss someone and want them back.'

'I wonder if a part of you was angry that Daddy has been away and that's what you wanted to let him know when you told him "go away"?'

'I wonder if a part of you was just trying to protect yourself?'

'I wonder if you were cross because it's your sister's birthday and all the attention is on her, and 'I'm wondering if you need a little attention too?'

'I wonder if you feel a bit wobbly about going back to school?'

'I wonder if it feels hard to be missing your friend?'

'I wonder what it's like for you when you get so angry you forget to use your words?'

'I wonder if part of you isn't sure that I won't get cross, so you don't tell me when things are hard at school?'

Remember to notice the positive emotions your child might be feeling, too: 'I wonder if you are feeling really proud that you got the lead part in the school play. I noticed how your eyes sparkled when I picked you up from school!'

In her excellent book, *Inside I'm Hurting*, the teacher and therapist Louise Bombèr quotes a teaching assistant who describes the powerful example of this process in action.

'I was quite amazed at how effective it can be to say, "I wonder if you are feeling anxious about the different teacher in class today and that's why you are refusing to sit on your chair." By guessing what the child's anxieties might be out loud, using my intuition, I was able to alleviate him of some of that anxiety. The child would feel someone understood and then we could look at ways to help him.'

If your family is experiencing separation or divorce, or if there has been a death or significant adversity, we can use our curiosity to reflect on how our children might be feeling. As hard as some emotions can be to name out loud, it might be the only way to be sure you are helping your children grieve, whatever big losses they are experiencing.

I am so, so sorry you have had to see us arguing. I'm wondering what it's like for you when we do?

I'm wondering what it's like not to have Daddy here?

I'm wondering what it's like when Mummy has to go away for a long time?

I'm wondering what it's like for you to see me crying?

I'm wondering what it's like for you when I shout like that?

I'm wondering if it feels lonely sometimes?

Finally, curiosity goes both ways. If you can open up about your own childhood – perhaps through sharing stories where your parents didn't get things quite right for you and didn't respond well to difficulties – it can really help your child to understand that your yelling is less about them and more about your own dysregulation, and that you weren't taught about emotions in the way that you are trying to teach them. In this way, we do something we call 'psychoeducate' our children. In essence, they get to understand that our behaviour sometimes is not because we don't like our children, but because we don't know any better, because that's what our parents did with us. This can be a very moving and powerful conversation to have, especially for older children. As Mika, who's ten, told her therapist of her mother: 'It's not because she's bad or that she doesn't love me; she's really trying to learn not to shout but her mum shouted at her.'

Being curious helps us to break unhealthy transgenerational cycles and unburden ourselves of some of our own childhood hurts and pain too.

WISE OWL WISDOMS

- Being curious about our children's experiences allows important conversations to open up.

- Keeping curious helps us to ditch our 'D's of dismiss, defend, diminish or deny!

- 'I wonder' questions can help our children to own their feelings and reflect on and better understand their own behaviour.

- Remembering 'OWL' reminds us to stop and observe, be curious, wonder, listen and most of all show our children unconditional love.

- Keeping curious allows us to break old and unhelpful cycles of parenting.

- When it comes to parenting, curiosity really is king (or queen!).

Chapter Nine

COMMUNICATION – It's a Two-way Street

Children don't talk nicely to parents who don't talk nicely to them.

Communication is a hallmark of our species. It's how our ancestors survived living and hunting in groups. Their survival depended on their ability to communicate and to process information well. It meant each individual could relax in the group, feeling safe and secure. The same goes for our children today.

How we communicate with our children has an enormous influence on their wellbeing because our children's brains are wired to attune not only to what we say but how we say it, and what our body language conveys to them too.

BRAIN BOX

'Negative looks and interactions are remembered and stored. A negative look can also trigger a biochemical response, just as the positive face does. The mother's disapproving face can trigger stress hormones such as cortisol, which stops the endorphins and dopamine neurons in their tracks and also stops the pleasurable feelings they generate. These looks have a powerful impact on the growing child.'

— Dr Sue Gerhardt, Psychotherapist, *Why Love Matters*

MRI scans show how children's brains respond when faced by negative, frightening or aggressive images. If we shout at our children, or shout in their presence, their stress response will be triggered and their lizard and baboon WILL react.

None of us can get it right all the time. There cannot be a parent alive who has not raised their voice or shot a disapproving look at their child! We are human, and for many parents today, we are also juggling plates for much of the time, which means our behaviour will at times be more 'stressed out' too. We have looked at ways to try to reduce our stress, or rather how we manage it, but we do want to be mindful when it comes to 'projecting' our stress onto our children, because how we talk to them is ultimately also how they will talk to us – and, importantly, how they'll talk to themselves.

Research shows we need to praise our children six times for every one criticism. So we might want to ask ourselves whether our children are being told off more than they are being praised, whether they are being given more negative than positive attention? We might then reflect on how much praise we received when we were children and determine to change the way we parent in turn.

We have seen how unhealthy cycles can be broken when we

feel able to take responsibility for our own behaviour, when we address our stress and apologise for the times we get things wrong. We can break this cycle when we learn to regulate our own big emotions and teach our children how to do the same.

If we have lost our rag, we can apologise and tell our children: 'I am so sorry to have raised my voice. I can see that I have frightened you.' Or: 'I am so sorry I used those words; I can see I have hurt your feelings.' Or: 'I am so sorry; I should have spoken to you more kindly.'

Again, in doing this we are supporting that all-important 'rupture and repair' process that psychoanalysts Donald Winnicott and Melanie Klein identified as such an essential part of parenting. When our children realise that we all make mistakes and that we, too, are fallible, it demonstrates that we can recover from our fallibility and forgive ourselves.

Donald Winnicott talked about being a 'good enough parent' and that's important to hold on to. We don't need to be perfect, but we *can* aim to be 'good enough'. I talk to my own children, and some clients, about how adults can make mistakes with their behaviour, very often because we were not taught how to behave more appropriately ourselves. This is not to excuse ourselves when we do or say things we regret, but we want to convey to our children that we want to be better, just as we want them to 'be better' too.

As the psychoanalytic psychotherapist Dr Sue Gerhardt explains, the communications we have with our children result in 'an inner library of images that can be referred to that will become increasingly complex and loaded with associations and thoughts as the child grows up'. Our children's sense of self, whether they feel 'likeable' and 'valued', is born of their exchanges with us, with their teachers and others around them. It's why 'labels' like 'stupid', 'careless', 'scatty', 'daydreamer' or 'difficult' are … well, they ARE 'naughty'!

BRAIN BOX

'One of the main reasons children behave badly is that the way a parent is relating to a child is activating the wrong part of a child's brain. You will have a horrible time with your child if you activate her lower-brain RAGE, FEAR, or DISTRESS systems. You can have a delightful time if you activate her lower-brain PLAY, SEEKING or CARE systems.'

— Dr Margot Sunderland, Child Psychotherapist,
The Science of Parenting

We might not even realise we are doing it, especially if our parents have done it to us, but comments like 'you're being silly', 'stop being a crybaby' or 'you're so difficult', or even 'why are you not like your sister?' stick, and they sting. We have seen that the amygdala, our baboon, 'tags' memories of negative events, making them easier to remember (a survival mechanism given we want to avoid negative things in life). We want to consider how many positive things we say to our children each day because our tendency towards 'negativity bias' leaves them focusing on the negative feedback they receive from us rather than the things we say with love.

Research shows that not only does shame impact our children's psychology but it can impact them physiologically too. A series of studies show how acute threats to the social self – that is, how our children feel they 'fit in' – increase proinflammatory cytokine activity and cortisol, and that these changes occur in concert with shame. As child psychotherapist Dr Margot Sunderland explains: 'The effect on our biology is essentially just the same as when we have suffered a physical wound.'

BRAIN BOX

'People don't realise that verbal putdowns constitute emotional abuse, which is particularly lethal in childhood when the brain is forming and the child is developing a sense of self. It's so easy to "introject", to take inside yourself, those early negative messages and believe them to be true. They then become part of an inner critic and we don't realise we keep replaying those discouraging voices for years, long after the actual critical person is no longer in our lives (e.g. a teacher) or we don't live with that person anymore (a parent).'
— Dr Margot Sunderland, Child Psychotherapist,
Draw on Your Emotions

Even though the science is clear on the potential long-term consequences and damage to a child's mental and physical well-being, the information has yet to filter into some primary schools, who still practice behaviour management policies that involve shaming children, to effect 'good behaviour'. I often hear from parents whose children attend primary schools that practice policies like sitting 'naughty' children on chairs to face the wall in a classroom of their peers. Or who put photos of a child on the 'wicked witch' chart vs the 'snow white' one, for misdemeanours like 'talking in class' or being 'late'. If we are to support our children's mental health, it is worth asking to see your primary school behaviour management policy to see if it aligns with the latest science and is supportive of your child's mental health.

Communication, as they say, is a two-way street. We cannot expect our children to want to collaborate and work with us if we're constantly calling them names or undermining their sense of self.

Lose Your Voice and Give Your Child Theirs

During a period of high stress at work, I lost my voice. Being unable to speak for two weeks meant I had to write things down or use sign language with my children. While they found it amusing, it had a dramatic impact on me. It made me realise how the stress I had been experiencing had often led to me raising my voice in order to be heard above the hubbub of family life. I reflected how the stress had impacted not only my own physical health, but also my parenting.

When my voice returned, I took them aside and said, 'Mummy really noticed how quiet the house was when I lost my voice. I think I've been too much shouty "fun-sponge" and not enough "fun" Mum. What do you think?'

This conversation led to us drawing up a 'scoresheet' and with the children giving feedback on Mike's and my performance as parents! This can be a lovely way to give your children more agency at home. Using humour, saying sorry when we get things wrong and being honest with our children are some of the most valuable things we can do as parents. Giving my children THEIR voice, asking them to score me and Mike, worked out to be such a blessing. The children loved giving us both feedback, telling me they needed more fun 'Mummy time' and that 'Daddy has to do more fun games'. You might try it with your children too. Think of it like an appraisal – only a fun one! – except this is for the most important job you'll ever have.

You could also try 'losing' your voice for a week – or, more specifically, to be aware of HOW you speak with your children; to turn the volume down from shouty. Be aware of any internal feelings of stress and consider how you can release them in a healthier way. Direct your stress energy away from shouting and into some of the healthy exercises we looked at in Chapter Three. You could suggest that everyone walks from where they are, whether upstairs or in another room, and rather than shouting out to each other what they need, they walk to the person, gain eye contact and speak their 'needs' instead. At home, it meant the children would come to me ahead of any sibling squabbles and calmly 'report' what had happened, knowing I would respond calmly, rather than me hearing the children shouting and then yelling up at them to 'stop SHOUTING!' in turn.

Cancel Critical Comments

I recently spent an hour on the touchline watching my son and daughter play football. A father sat in a deck chair next to me, recording a running commentary on his phone – a second-by-second narrative of his son's performance in the game. 'Look at you, just standing there – why aren't you moving? You need to move on the ball. Look at the others – they're all chasing the ball and you're daydreaming. Why did you miss that shot?! What's wrong with you?!' I felt heartbroken, imagining the child exuberant after a fun game only to have the entire match and his father's critical commentary replayed to him when he got home. I have compassion for the father, who would highly likely have had parents who did the same to him, even perhaps thinking it was constructive. But we must be very mindful of how we balance our critique. If we have something constructive to share, better to start with a positive comment, then reflect on what might be improved, then end with something positive to balance things out.

Measure your Tone

Psychiatrist and neuroscientist Dr Dan Siegel uses a simple but effective exercise to demonstrate the difference in the power dynamic between a parent and child, and the impact our tone and words can have on how our children feel.

In a seminar I attended, he prepared us briefly for an exercise he said he would try, before shouting loudly at the audience the words NO! NO! NO!

He asked us to close our eyes and reflect on the impact of his words on our body.

I felt tears prick my eyes and anxiety in my solar plexus – that area central to the breastbone where we can hold our anxious emotions. It brought me back to a time of hearing shouting as a child.

'Now place your hands, one on your breastbone and one on your stomach,' he told us. And then he followed up by saying 'yes' three times, kindly and gently.

The difference in how it felt was extraordinary. I felt immediately soothed and comforted.

Consider the times we might rage in baboon when we could have soothed, and then consider how you want your child to remember their exchanges with you.

PARENT PONDER

Sam, parent to Lucy, 5

'I was shocked to learn that children need six positives to every negative. I realised it's been the other way around for too long in our household. Changing this one simple thing, pointing out all the times my daughter has been getting things right rather than when she did something wrong, has changed our relationship entirely.'

Considering how you communicate with your children can fundamentally improve your relationship. Better to start now than during those hormonally charged, more rebellious teenage years that lie ahead. It's vital for mental health, too, given how we've seen that our children will internalise their thoughts if they don't feel able to communicate them. You might be surprised by the very 'small' worries your children hold on to that can feel massive to them, but which are very easy to unpick and resolve when they feel able to share them with us.

PARENT PONDER

Feiza, mother to Ali, 9

My son was showing signs of anxiety before school and when I spoke with his teacher she said just recently it seemed that he was finding it difficult to concentrate in class. I asked him directly: 'Ali, you seem anxious about school.

Can you tell me what's bothering you?' I expected him to shut down, but he immediately confessed he was scared that if he did not pass his exams he would have to go down a year and leave all his friends. This was absolutely not the case, but I was shocked he had been carrying that burden alone. I told him I would double-check with his teacher as he really was so sure. When I spoke to her, she said absolutely not! My son had clearly misunderstood what his class had been told about a test they had coming up, and no wonder he felt pressure! And no wonder he wasn't able to focus on anything else in class with that massive thought in his head as the exam approached.

The 'stories' children tell themselves can create unnecessary anxiety and angst. Anxiety can be more easily remedied when we have our strong pillars of our Cs in place. When our connection with our children is secure, it will see us having more open and honest conversations, and we can quickly alleviate heavy emotional loads.

All Behaviour is Communication

As it's often said, all behaviour is communication. Whether your child has had a big test at school, a trip or even a playdate; anything that sees a change in routine, tires them out, or tips them over with joy or excitement, you are more likely to see big behaviour driven by the stress response.

Wilbur recently had a playdate with a new friend from school and I anticipated there might be an outburst as soon as he waved his friend goodbye. His face had gone from sunny to stormy the second the door closed and he seemed cross when I said it was then time for a bath. He snarled and stormed upstairs saying, 'I want to watch TV!'

These are the times we must 'hold the line', overlook the niggling, cross behaviour and get curious about what might be beneath. I took a breath, engaged my wise owl over my baboon and said, 'Wilbur, you seem upset.' (Stating the bleedin' obvious – clearly) 'Mummy wants to help.'

'No!'

Another beat, another breath.

'Wilbur?'

A muffled voice shouted, 'Come up then.'

When I headed upstairs, Wilbur was in Clemency's bedroom, his eyes wet. He turned to me when I walked in. I sensed his baboon was on the verge of a blowout. So, I sat on the bed, just out of reach so I didn't trigger Wilbur's baboon with my over imposing presence. Tucking my legs up beneath me and with a face full of concern, I said, 'You seem really upset. Can you tell me what's going on?'

'I don't want to have a bath. You never let me watch TV. It's only half past six!' he shouted at me furiously.

I laid a boundary to contain what I felt could now escalate. 'Wilbur, can you use your words with Mummy kindly, please?'

'Well, I don't want to have a bath.'

I knew this was not about the bath. It wasn't typical behaviour. When our children behave this way, there's always something driving the behaviour. I guessed that something had happened during the playdate and I wanted to find out more!

Using compassion, 'holding the space' and laying a gentle boundary allowed Wilbur to trust that I was willing to help. Holding his defiant gaze, I said, 'Is it just about the bath or is there something more?' Quick as a flash, Wilbur responded, 'Ash never said anything about my bedroom!'

Wilbur had a new bunk bed. He has a small bedroom and I had bought it because I wanted to create more space beneath his bed for him to play. He was super proud of it, with his favourite football posters and books on a shelf beneath the bunk, with a grown-up light to read in bed.

But his friend had not noticed. (Interior design was clearly not high on his list of priorities, given the excitement of a playdate.)

It suddenly made sense why Wilbur had chosen his sister's bedroom to hide out in. He had been so proud of his newly decorated room and his bunk bed, but his friend had not noticed – which to Wilbur's baboon must have felt like a 'rejection'. Once again, we are reminded how social rejection is so painful that Wilbur was genuinely experiencing pain.

'Oh, sweetheart. That must be so tough. You have a new bed. You are so proud of your bedroom. You were so excited and you wanted your friend to notice.'

I do not drop into my Ds by denying it or dismissing what he has told me. I don't say, 'Oh come on, it doesn't matter, you love your bedroom and that's what counts.' Or, 'Is that all? Come on, stop being a baby, hurry up and get a bath.' Instead I acknowledge and validate what it is he is telling me. I reflect it back to let him know that I understand.

Taking just a few seconds to communicate that I wanted to understand my son's upset worked wonders in terms of him feeling seen and heard by me. My truth arrows hit their mark and his tear tank opened up. Wilbur cried a little harder, then looked at me. I put my hand out, sensing that he would take it now we were connected – my wise owl to his little one. He took my hand and pulled himself up.

'Mummy?' he said, as though nothing had just happened.

'Yes, darling.'

'Can we read together tonight?'

'After your bath, yes, absolutely.'

And that was it. No further discussion, no 'refusals', just a grin and a sense of relief that the painful feeling had been released.

After his bath, we went to his room and curled up together. No more mention of playdates or bunk beds, no more worries or woes.

Our children need to be able to release big feelings and, often, they can only do that safely with our help. When they share their vulnerabilities and worries we need to hold the space for them, not get caught up in how they are behaving. I can appreciate it can take a bit of practise, and faith, if we do feel triggered (as most of us do) when our children say NO and refuse to do something we ask! But if we can set aside that 'personal' and get beneath the NO, we will find that they are not being 'naughty'; they just have an underlying need, a fear, a worry that they need your help to resolve.

Our Communication Counts

Communication is important for our wellbeing too. If we weren't helped to communicate our own needs as children, we might find it difficult to express our needs as adults. It can leave us feeling overwhelmed, unheard, and often a little stuck. Asking for help, finding support, in community, in friends, in support networks, can go a long way towards helping us to break any negative parenting cycles and communicate more effectively with our children.

PARENT PONDER

Ian, father to Joe, 16, Josh, 14 and James, 8

When I lost my wife to breast cancer, our family was devastated. We have three boys: two teenagers and an eight-year-old. I was completely lost. One of the things I found most difficult for the boys was the loss of order at home. My wife had been amazing at homemaking and kept things really well. After she died, the house became cluttered and we were tripping over things, which left my sons too ashamed to have anyone over. This compounded the loneliness I think we all felt.

When I spoke to my son's counsellor at school, I admitted this was one of the things I was finding most difficult and also felt ashamed about. She was amazing. She made me laugh when she told me about her own house when her husband is away. We looked at ways I could get help to get back on track. It took time, but the biggest issue was the shame, which I realised I no longer needed to carry.

Solo parenting is hard enough, as you will know if you are divorced, widowed or single by choice. Ian's grief was compounded by his sense of not being 'enough' for his sons, for not keeping the house the way his wife had done. When he was able to communicate this to somebody, to share his worries, he found it so much easier to put down his own 'suitcase' of guilt and move forward. In doing so, he suddenly found he could get the house clear. He found it allowed him to grieve fully for the wife and mother his family had lost and found the 'space' to grieve more fully with his sons too.

Co-parenting can bring its own difficulties too. One mum recently shared with me how fractious things were becoming at home over the 'lack of order' when her husband arrived home. He had grown up in an extremely chaotic household and we explored that his lizard brain was likely more wired for hyper-vigilance, with a need to keep everything 'in its place' because it created a sense of safety.

Children who grow up in environments where they don't always feel secure can develop a biological adaptation called hyper-vigilance. Think of it as having a baboon and lizard, in fact the entire nervous system, much more 'on guard' and alert to any sensory changes in the environment that might spell danger. The need for security can sometimes manifest in obsessional compulsive behaviours where the brain's desire to find security and safety can be met by keeping or doing things a certain way.

While her husband's behaviour was understandable in light of his childhood circumstances, Mum was also struggling because with young children she said she could not keep the house totally 'in order' every day. She loved her husband, but his irritability when he got home made her feel judged as a mother and as a woman, and was undermining their relationship.

The solution lay in mutual communication.

The couple came together to discuss how they could find a way through.

They wrote out all the potential solutions, brainstorming as a team, rather than each feeling judged.

Once her husband had felt able to reflect that his baboon behaviour when he came home from work was due to the fear he had experienced as a child when he found the house in chaos, he was able to see beyond the fear and consider the 'data' in real time instead. He accepted that if he saw the boys' muddled boots in the hall, that it might be more appropriate to consider whether his wife had had a 'difficult' and busy day. He actually then felt empowered to offer to help, as her husband, rather than responding from old wounds from childhood. Mum told me she felt she had a 'new husband' and that she in turn felt more accommodating and gentle, recognising that her husband's need for order came from a place not of criticism but of fear.

Through communication, they worked together to become more of a partnership. And, as can so often happen, the children's behavioural issues that they had initially wanted to discuss suddenly 'went away'!

If we are baboon to baboon at home, then we can expect our children's behaviour to be more baboon too. Stress is contagious.

Working on our relationships, asking for help if we are parenting alone, getting support, and being open and curious to finding solutions for our own problems can often be a huge step towards seeing our children's behaviour resolving more happily and readily in turn.

WISE OWL WISDOMS

- How we talk to our children is how they will ultimately 'talk to themselves'.

- It's not just our words that count – it's our tone, volume and body language too.

- All behaviour is communication – keeping curious, and keeping calm, enables your child to be vulnerable and offload worries.

- Communicating *our* needs is important too. Asking for help and explaining how we feel can go a long way towards helping our children communicate *their* needs calmly and ask for help too.

Chapter Ten

COMPASSION – How to Keep an Open Heart, Even if it Feels Like Your Child Has Closed Theirs

We can only understand when we care,
and we can only care when we understand.

To future-proof the mental health of our children, we must ensure they feel valued, safe, loved and understood. For that to happen, they must experience our compassion. Compassion is defined as the sympathy and concern we feel for the sufferings or misfortunes of others. It literally means 'to suffer with'.

Neuroscience shows us that children DO suffer when they're in emotional turmoil. So, while their behaviour can often test us, we must stay alongside them when they are struggling – not send them away to suffer in silence. It is when children have to suffer *alone* that long-term worrying consequences can occur.

It requires us to be compassionate to our children, even when their behaviour is at its very worst. We must let go of those old-school notions of 'naughty' and disregard the belief that we should punish or discipline our children for 'bad behaviour' to disappear. The *Oxford Dictionary* definition of the word 'discipline' is the 'practice of training people to obey rules or a code of behaviour, using punishment to correct disobedience'.

Hmmm.

It all sounds rather Victorian to me. Absolutely, yes, we MUST teach our children good conduct, but why the need to punish? Children need boundaries because they create structure and security and keep us and our children safe. But it is absolutely possible to have boundaries that aren't based on punishment. If we wish to successfully discipline our children we need to, in the words of Dr Gabor Maté, 'make them our disciples'. It is our job to teach our children how to behave. We can only successfully do that when *we* MODEL the compassionate behaviour we want to see. When we practice punishment over compassion, we undermine our cause.

While physical or corporal punishment is thankfully no longer considered justifiable or acceptable in schools and was (finally) outlawed across the UK in 2003, as I talked about in Chapter Nine, many schools do still use *psychological* punishment to effect 'good' behaviour; the aforementioned children's names or photographs displayed on 'good' and 'bad' boards in the classroom being just one example. Writing lines or having break times withdrawn, or brandishing red cards for 'bad' behaviour all shame children or to instil fear to ensure they'll 'toe the line'.

In 2019, Susanne McCafferty, headteacher of Bainsford Primary School in Falkirk, ripped up her school's behaviour policy. She had written it herself some years earlier, but said she was horrified when she realised how shaming and stigmatising these policies were. Interviewed at an ACE-Aware Nation event, she explained what happened to children who were struggling to behave:

'They got a warning card, it was yellow, that said WARNING! right across it. If they did it again, they got a red card, which said CONSEQUENCE and then the child would lose what we called golden time. So, come Friday, when the children would get their hour's golden time, there would be some children who would be still working because they had lost time and we didn't think that was beneficial to anybody in the school.'

McCafferty said her views changed after watching a TED Talk by the pioneering paediatrician Dr Nadine Burke Harris. Dr Burke Harris explained how adverse childhood experiences often play a significant role in impacting a child's behaviour.

Adverse childhood experiences (ACES) are considered traumatic events that occur before the age of eighteen. They can include neglect, abuse, poverty, the death of a parent, parental separation, having a parent with mental health issues and/or substance addiction. ACES affect large numbers of the population. In fact, in England *almost half of all adults* will have experienced at least one adverse childhood experience, and nearly 10% of children will experience four ACES or more.

Susanne McCafferty said, 'I thought to myself, that is definitely what I am looking at. I am looking at children who are coming into school who are already in a state of anxiety and they do not need me or anyone else adding to their anxiety. What they need from us is for someone to listen to them, to help regulate themselves, and to look at what's happening in their lives. And we would tell the children we were there for them and that we want to help them as much as we can.'

She reached out to her teachers, parents and children and created a new, collaborative 'relationship agreement', which understood 'naughty' as a need and raised greater awareness around the science of behaviour. Priority was given to understanding a child's behaviour rather than seeking simply to punish them. She said it had led to incredible progress, both in the children's conduct and in staff reporting feeling more confident and capable to respond compassionately in return.

Not every child who 'acts out' is displaying trauma, but when we can consider behaviour as an expression of need, everything changes. When we seek to *ease* a child's distress rather than escalate it, we more likely create loyal 'disciples' who more readily and authentically want to follow our lead. Children become more committed students in every sense.

Back in Falkirk, 'recognition boards' replaced behaviour charts. Children had individual positive targets to aspire to, with their names going up on the wall to HIGHLIGHT their personal achievements. Rather than putting children in 'isolation booths' (I am still incredulous this is sanctioned in schools today), McCafferty says her school introduced a 'peace room', where children could elect to go, still with their work, but in a space that offered a quieter environment if they felt they were losing focus or not managing very well in class that day. She says it has made a massive difference for children experiencing difficulties at home; to have quiet time out, to feel safe and able to focus. When asked why she thought more schools had not adopted this more compassionate approach McCafferty replied: 'Because it's easier to punish children than to take the time to talk to them about what's happened.' As the interviewer Gary Robinson reflected, 'It's not about punishment, it's about kindness.'

It's about having healthy boundaries around behaviour, too. Boundaries in their simplest form help children understand what behaviour *is* acceptable, and what is not. They help to create a predictable routine, for example: 'we clean our teeth before bedtime and after breakfast'. They create a secure environment for our children, and for parents and carers too. When we are confident our children understand where the boundaries are at home and what is expected of them, it helps us to offer flexibility where we consider it appropriate and equally experience the generosity of feeling that is compassion. For instance, in the therapy room I invite children to share some pretty big emotions. I can only remain calm, and compassionate when those big emotions arrive, because I have boundaried with the child what might happen in advance. I do that using something we call contracting. I also ensure all my Cs are in place, just as I do with my own children at home.

I'll share more on this in the next chapter, Contracts and Crisis Management, and show you how to do the same.

Experiencing compassion, and that generosity of feeling towards our children, means we can offer them choices without feeling that our authority has been compromised. For example, if your child is finding it difficult to stop playing and get ready for their bath, we can have compassion that it IS really HARD to stop playing instantly, especially when they're having so much fun!

Without boundaries *we* don't feel safe either. It means our baboon interprets any 'refusals' as a direct threat to his authority. The story he tells himself is that if he doesn't take control now, he'll lose control later. This is where we see ourselves parenting in baboon, stepping in using force, fear, threats and control. It might see us raise our voice in anger: 'STOP PLAYING THIS INSTANT! I am going to count to three and you had better get in the bath or else!'

We've all been there – but compare *that* baboon response with that of our more compassionate wise owl. With the benefit of perspective, with her boundaries in place, she does *not* feel threatened. She can see how much fun our children's own baboon is having and how difficult it is to stop playing 'this instant'!

She can be compassionate with our children's plight and empathise with how hard it is to stop when a child is simply having too much fun. It means her response can be both playful and compassionate:

'You are having SO much fun! I'm hearing that you REALLY don't want to get ready for the bath! OK, sweetheart, I understand. Do you want to choose to have five more minutes of play and then jump into the bath?'

Being confident that we can hold boundaries around behaviour allows us to be more flexible and offer our children choices, knowing that in doing so we help them to develop a greater sense of agency, which is important for later in life. When children can exercise choice, they can also learn from the natural consequence of their choices.

We might say, 'OK, darling. Five more minutes of play time – but then it's definitely bath time, OK! Shall we shake on it? Great, because if we don't, there's less time for us to play with the boats in the bath.'

We are not threatening our children here, we are teaching them that actions have natural consequences. They can still choose to play but if the play goes on too long, they'll miss out on the other activities on offer.

We can patiently (don't think they'll get there overnight!) explain to our children that if we don't get our things ready for school the night before, we might forget our gym bag in the morning – and that's not ideal! If we don't get to bed on time, we might not get a good enough sleep, and it can leave us grumpy and tired the next day. If we don't take a coat, we might feel cold at the park later. And conversely (and I like to focus on the positive outcomes more than negative!), we can demonstrate that life feels a lot simpler, much easier and is a lot more fun when we are organised, when we have enough sleep and when we can practice good self-care.

Developmental psychologist Dr Suzanne Zeedyk reflects that 'Our culture teaches us to think of "consequences" as an inherently bad thing, something that adults dish out to children as punishment. "Natural consequences", though, are simply what occurs as a result of children's actions. It is true that some of those will be uncomfortable, but some will also be pleasurable. By letting children experience the natural consequences of their actions, they gain a better sense of themselves and their relation to the world. It is much healthier. What is fascinating is that this is such an unusual way for our culture to frame the idea of "consequences".'

Demonstrating unconditional compassion, rather than punishing our children when they do get things wrong, empowers them to make choices in life without fear of 'mistakes'. Offering our children choices and explaining the potential consequences of those choices gives them the opportunity to consider their actions. Then, if they do make a mistake, they can remember and make a different choice next time!

If we punish or shame, we teach our children their only option is to comply. They will have little way of knowing what they like and want in life, and what they don't. If they constantly feel afraid of making a mistake for fear of being punished or publicly shamed, we will have children reduced to compliant 'versions' of the person they're meant to be.

It's why the more compassion we show our children, the greater their sense of self. In our unconditional compassion we convey a crucial message: 'even when you make mistakes, you are loved, and accepted, as you are.'

In modelling compassion and kindness and showing our children we value them, even when they get things wrong, we show them how to model compassion for themselves and others, when they make mistakes too. If we are serious about raising free-thinking, resilient adults who are capable of solving problems, and are able to tolerate and learn from failure, we can raise a generation who will effect positive change in the world.

We need compassion and empathy to survive as a species. The future of our planet depends upon it. Our children can only care and have compassion for the people and environment around them when they have experienced compassion and care for themselves. If our children are to play their part in creating a truly 'better world' they will need empathy and compassion in huge supply. But they can only catch it by spending time in our presence or in the presence of other emotionally available adults who can mirror it for them.

Science has only relatively recently revealed why the human qualities and values of compassion, empathy and kindness are 'caught rather than taught'.

In the early 1990s, researchers discovered that we have a type of brain cell known as a mirror neuron. Mirror neurons light up when we perform an action, *as well as* when we see another person performing it. For example, mirror neurons fire in our brains when we smile, or someone smiles at us. In seeing the smile, we feel the smile. It's how babies learn: by imitating us.

If we want children to embody the crucial human qualities of compassion, empathy and kindness, we need to model it. If society and systems continue to punish children when they make mistakes, we cannot be surprised if our children go on to treat others in the same way too.

Compassion and Sense of Self

Self-determination theory suggests that all humans have three basic psychological needs:

- To feel connected to others.
- To feel competent at what we do.
- To feel authentic in our lives.

We offer our children the greatest opportunity to feel connected, competent and authentic when we treat them with what the humanistic psychologist Carl Rogers called unconditional positive regard. Showing unconditional positive regard means demonstrating empathy and support to someone, and accepting them for who they are, regardless of what they say or how they behave.

When we accept our children for who they are, and the values that they embody, we teach them to accept themselves. We help them develop a capacity for self-compassion. The ability to speak to themselves and others kindly, even when they get things wrong.

'Be Kind'

Kindness is the human quality of being friendly, generous and considerate. It's another beautiful quality that, as parents, we all hope to see in our children. Again, however, simply telling children to 'be kind' without modelling kindness ourselves won't work. We need to demonstrate spontaneous acts of kindness ourselves if our children are to demonstrate it too.

These qualities are crucial if future generations are to thrive. Yet, current events and the excessive exploitation of our planet's natural resources indicate these qualities are sadly very much in decline.

In her study, *Empathy and the Novel*, the literary scholar and poet Professor Suzanne Keen observes that 'the desire for dominance, division, and hierarchal relationships' has weakened empathy. She says that conventionally an empathic person is now more likely seen as a 'bleeding heart' who believes naively that understanding people will change them.

It hasn't always been this way. As I mentioned previously, not long ago in our history, societies functioned in small hunter-gatherer groups, with children raised by a multigenerational extended family that served as a strong and nurturing socialising force. Psychologists often pinpoint to England's Industrial Revolution in the late eighteenth century as bringing an end to that more collaborative, communal way of life. They say that while mechanised manufacturing transformed economies and led to significant global success, it created a new and very different way of life for families, one which had a profound and largely negative impact on their mental 'wealth'. Larger communities were brought together in more urban environments to work in factories, with people forced to live on top of one another in conditions that psychologists say led to an increased need for dominance to 'keep order' and retain control. It is here that, as a society, we saw qualities like compassion and empathy begin to decline, and where the economy began to dominate family life.

Compassion and Self-Care

The continued drive towards technological advancements come, in my view, at high cost to our children and our own quality of life. Despite previous promises to reduce the burden on our time, my bulging inbox begs to differ with the view that technology can make our lives more efficient, I'll admit that I often feel more enslaved. If *our* quality of life and work/life balance feels compromised, we should consider how much our children might feel compromised by it too.

Not all progress is progress. We must pay attention to and learn lessons from our past. The author and neurodevelopmental consultant Sally Goddard Blythe refers to recent generations when she says in her book, *Raising Happy Healthy Children*: 'Historically, society has never been very good at valuing motherhood. In the money centred culture of today, women and mothers are increasingly contributors to the gross national product and are not valued sufficiently (by themselves or by society more generally) for what they are contributing to family stability and society in the future, in their role as mothers.'

When we consider the critical importance of the earliest years of our children's lives and how much support is needed to ensure healthy brain development – and therefore future mental health – it seems obvious to say that a healthy society is one that gives significant consideration to the needs of parents as well as the needs of their children.

For many parents there are not enough hours in the day to work, to care for our children and ensure their needs are met, and still meet our own in the process. Self-compassion refers to a kind and nurturing attitude towards ourselves and in recognising that being imperfect is part of being human.

But I know many parents feel in crisis, overwhelmed by the demands made of them, of keeping house and on top of school admin and homework. With too little time to connect with others, there is often too little time to reach out for support.

We should not have to travel this journey alone. With compassion and in community, I think we can find a way. We can start by practising more self-compassion. Just as it's never too late to practise having more compassion for our children, it's never too late to practise it for ourselves.

One of the greatest gifts of therapy is in offering clients the experience of the compassion we likely did not have the privilege to experience when we were very young. In the presence of a skilled and emotionally available adult who holds us in the highest unconditional positive regard, we can slowly begin to learn to practice that compassion for ourselves.

But you don't need the help of a paid professional to experience this form of compassion. You can find it in community and among your friends. Find someone you feel you trust, someone who is 'emotionally available' and someone who might enjoy feeling a little compassion from you in return.

TOOLKIT TIPS
Compassionate Conversations

Here's an exercise that can prove extremely powerful for parents who find themselves on overwhelm and needing a safe space to offload. In psychotherapy training, we often practice what can be called dyads or focused listening. Essentially, two people sit and take turns to speak, while the other listens without interruption.

There can be great power in sitting with someone we trust, someone who can give us that confidential space, and time, to talk without feeling the need to jump in or problem-solve.

If you have a friend or someone you feel to be naturally compassionate, someone who is warm and kind and conveys understanding and whom you can trust, then you might try a form of focused listening exercise. It is a great way to both practice self-compassion, taking time to hear your thoughts and say them out loud, often finding solutions to problems as you do so.

You begin by doing the following:

Agree a specific amount of time you will each speak. It might vary from 30 seconds to five minutes or more, depending on how comfortable you each feel.

Agree on confidentiality. This means not sharing what each other has said with anyone else and not to mention to each other what was said at any other time.

Agree that you will not complain or criticise each other, or mutual acquaintances.

Discuss how you will make a note of the time and how you will bring each other's conversation to a close. The person who does the listening first might keep an eye on the clock, for example, or set a timer on the phone if it does not feel intrusive to do so. Then, when time is up, they can gently say 'that's time' or another expression that you mutually choose.

Then you speak, uninterrupted, without the listener saying a word.

You can speak about what's on your mind, anything that's happened during your day, or just how you're feeling in that moment. Whoever listens first simply listens. That's it. The role of the listener is not to speak, not to interpret or problem-solve, but to simply convey compassion for

whatever is being said by using body language. It might
be through eye contact (you can discuss both before and
after the first times you try this to see how much or little
eye contact you enjoy), it might be conveyed with a tilt of
the head, a soft 'uh huh', putting your palm to your chest if
something painful is shared. The role of listener is simply
to convey compassion in that moment for whatever it is
our friend, or partner, is sharing with us.

Honour the silence if the speaker finishes their sharing
before the time is up.

Then the roles are reversed.

This can be a very powerful and bonding exercise.
I know parents who began this exercise as a very informal
one-off and now make regular appointments with the other
parent, scheduling in their time, or just spontaneously
finding ten minutes together where they can. It is an
exercise that can work wonders for feeling heard and
to offload the niggles and worries we might have been
carrying during the day. It's also an incredibly powerful
way to practice modelling compassion, which you can then
go on to model yourself.

If you find this exercise difficult or find it hard to
find someone you feel you can speak to, there are other
exercises you can try where you speak with compassion
to yourself.

You might like to try sitting in front of a mirror and
staring at your reflection to really SEE yourself as you are.

Take your time. Smile. Look sad. Simply notice your
expression and the feelings you are sensing inside. You
might speak to yourself and say something kind about your
qualities, perhaps 'you are so lovely', 'you are such a kind

person', or 'I love how you smile'. Or 'I like the way you are'. You might even try 'I love you'.

It might feel difficult, or even silly, to say these things – if it does, notice that too. You might ask yourself but why is it so difficult or silly to say or hear nice things? And even perhaps you might reflect, so when did I last feel this way?

Notice your reaction when you speak, the words you use and how you say them. Notice how it feels inside when you speak kindly to yourself. And notice too if you find it difficult to find the words or even if the words are less than kind. It can be a very profound exercise to consider how it might feel to our children when we speak to them that way too.

Too often the difficulties we have practicing self-compassion in adulthood stem from the lack of compassion we experienced ourselves as a child. There is no judgement for our parents in this; again, how could they convey compassion if they had not also experienced it? But it does not mean we cannot now try to do this for ourselves. As we saw with the listening exercise, it can come in the presence of another caring adult. In this exercise, that caring adult is you.

TOOLKIT TIP

Connecting and Displaying Compassion for Yourself and your Inner Child

Take a photograph of yourself when you were younger and spend time looking at it, if it doesn't feel painful to do so. Sometimes seeing ourselves as children can bring up difficult feelings or memories and it will certainly help to reach out for professional support if this happens for you. Try though, if you can, to speak to that little girl or boy you see and tell them all the things you know they needed to hear back then. Notice how it feels to hear yourself speak so kindly. Resolve to keep practising, to keep these conversations going; in doing so, you connect with and strengthen your own inner sense of self.

The more you practice self-compassion, the more you can model it for your children. Consider that these are the Cs that break the cycle of generations: that set your children up for life.

As Susanne McCafferty showed, it's never too late to rip up the rulebook and do things differently. Just as it is never too late to change the way we interact with our children, so it's never too late to change the way we interact with ourselves.

Being kind and compassionate is a principle that should apply to everyone and it applies to our inner voice too.

WISE OWL WISDOMS

- Compassion is our ability to sit with the suffering of others.

- Practising compassion is crucial for our children's future sense of self.

- Children need to experience compassion to be able to model it.

- We need to be compassionate with ourselves too.

- The more compassion we have for ourselves, the more we help others to have it too.

Chapter Eleven

CONTRACTS AND CRISIS MANAGEMENT – Dealing with Distress

Children fear deeply the anger they have inside, that neither they, nor adults, seem able to control.

Emma contacted me because her daughter, Tara, who's nine, was 'completely blowing out' after school, with what Emma described as 'horrific temper tantrums'. She wanted to know if she was doing 'something wrong', because Tara's school described her daughter as 'an angel' and her grandparents said she was 'good as gold' for them.

Emma said she felt useless given 'everyone else seems better able to parent my seven-year-old than I can'.

The question 'why do I get all the bad behaviour?' is one parents often ask and it's essential to address.

When our children are forced to keep a lid on all the little stress responses, and the bursts of adrenaline and cortisol that accompany them, throughout any given day, they'll often explode when they get home. I asked Emma to consider where she thought her daughter felt most able to express her feelings and be her authentic self. At school, where she might get told off or punished? With relatives, where she must also be on her 'best behaviour'? Or when she got home to the person who loves her most, the person she trusts won't judge her or walk away?

Back-handed compliment it might seem, but if your children come home and explode with you, it's often because they feel safe enough in your presence to do so.

The trouble is, it doesn't always feel safe to us.

PARENT PONDER
Jenna, mother to Charlie, age 9

I'm a single parent and when my son gets physical, I feel really triggered. I am afraid because he's getting bigger and my fear is that if I can't control him, we'll all lose control. I'm frightened of what will happen next, and because I can see no other way of calming him down, I end up restraining him or pushing him. I feel like it all spirals out of control really quickly and I hate how I feel afterwards. It's like something has been broken.

It can be *very* frightening for parents when children spin out or melt down. It can see *our* stress response fired up and we find ourselves baboon versus baboon, feeling we have little option but to impose sanctions, remove favourite possessions, banish to bedrooms, or even use physical force to come out on top. These responses can often serve to escalate the situation, leaving us feeling we've lost control and, ultimately as Jenna identifies, that something has been broken.

What's often less acknowledged is that children can feel frightened by their behaviour too.

'There's a Monster Inside Me'

James is eight. He tells his therapist: 'It's scary to be so big when I am angry. Even the adults don't know what to do with me. It's like there's a monster inside me and I can't stop him.'

It can be very confusing for a child when they lose control and they can experience great shame about their behaviour afterwards. It is a common theme in my therapy room. When anger is so immense and potent that 'not even an adult can help' them, children often wonder what it says about them. Are they monsters? What a horrifying thought to have. Children fear deeply the anger they feel inside that neither they nor adults can seem to control.

Remember that when a child's stress response is triggered they are in a state of emotional pain and intense bodily arousal. The stress response triggers neurochemical and hormonal forces that, in the words of Dr Margot Sunderland, can 'overwhelm the mind and body like wildfire'.

Your child needs your help to put out the fire. Because, at this age, they still cannot do it alone.

This chapter looks at the type of challenging behaviour most of us will experience at some time. I offer guidance to help you feel confident to place firm boundaries around what is and is not acceptable when it comes to expressing big feelings – and to keep you and your child safe. I will share therapeutic interventions, with tools and scripts to help you stay calm during even the most energised of blowouts.

It is crucial, however, to make the distinction between behaviour that most of us will face from time to time as our children learn to regulate their emotions and the kind of behaviour that suggests it's time to ask for help.

This is critical. If your child is regularly displaying violent behaviour that is hurting you or themselves you MUST seek professional support. It is beyond the scope of this book to offer therapeutic interventions when there is child-on-parent violence. If you don't feel able to keep yourself and everyone in your house safe from immediate harm, there are many forms of professional help available. I have listed these in the resources section, including what happens if you do need to call the police or your local authority. You need to feel safe in your home and so do your children.

Child to Parent Violence (or CPV as it is sometimes called) is sadly becoming increasingly common and while it is mostly associated with teenagers, recorded incidents now include children as young as eight. Child to Parent violence is not 'normal' challenging behaviour; it causes parents to feel fearful, isolated and like they're treading on eggshells and it can have a profound impact on families.

BRAIN BOX

'It can be hard for parents to recognise whether the behaviour of their child or adolescent is violent or abusive. As a parent, always trust your instincts! You know when things are not okay. Violence from children and adolescents is NOT a normal part of growing up. Most children will act out at some stage however when the behaviour becomes controlling, threatening, intimidating or unsafe it stops being normal.'

www.whosincharge.uk

There are many courses offered to parents, especially foster parents or parents with adopted children or children who struggle due to developmental needs. One parent poignantly told me recently, 'I wish I had known this earlier.'

Having your C's in place is vital, because they build the connection and trust needed for the exercises I share in this chapter. If you do feel able to work with your child and you trust they will work with you, we can begin.

We start with prevention. Prevention is key, because when we can spot the tell-tale signs that our child's baboon brain is on the verge of tipping towards overwhelm, we can get ahead of many meltdowns by tackling them before they've reached 'crisis point'.

Generally, I have observed three stages or levels of upset and distress.

Level One

These are the low-lying, uncomfortable feelings we have when something is worrying or bothering us. They drive our children's more irritable behaviour. When our children bicker or niggle each other, or us, we should see it as a sign of niggling feelings within. This is why I typically look beyond my children's behaviour and focus instead on what might be driving it. Rather than tell my children off for 'being rude' if they grumble, grouch or even snap at me after school, I get curious:

'You seem a little cross. I'm wondering if everything's OK?'

'I'm noticing you're a bit irritable. Has something happened or are you just a little tired?'

'You seem a little fizzy... Can I help?'

'Have there been any Code Reds today?'

'I'm sensing you are getting bored. Shall we play a game?'

Clearly, you can play around with what you say, and how you say it, to suit you and your child, but generally we want to convey a sense of 'I am noticing that you don't seem your usual self and I want to know if I can help'.

Once your Cs are firmly in place, these conversations become much easier and free-flowing and you'll soon see your children opening up easily, with a 'YES! Mr Smith told me off for forgetting my gym shoes', or 'NO! I'm angry because Abe said he wasn't my best friend'.

It's then that we turn to our tool kit and use our skills of reflection, saying what we see and firing off any truth arrows to burst the emotional boils.

We can then soothe fears and tears with an empathetic and caring response.

'Oh, wow! I imagine that was HORRIBLE to be told off like that?'

You might add (as I often do), 'Actually, it's *my* fault that we forgot your shoes. I am so sorry you were told off, that's on me.'

You might throw in some humour and add, 'Mr Smith needs to come tell Mummy / Daddy off, not you!'

And reassure your child, 'It's my job to make sure that doesn't happen again and I am so sorry; let's write a note so we remember together next week.'

In response to friendship issues you might go in with an, 'Oh, darling, I imagine that really hurt your feelings?'

Recognising niggling behaviour as low-level distress – rather than 'naughty' – means we can very quickly work with our children and bring them back to calm.

If your child is still reluctant to engage, perhaps they shrug and remain cross, you can offer some one-to-one time with them later, typically bedtime, gently suggesting 'perhaps we can discuss it later, I really want to help'.

Holding a mirror up to our children's behaviour without shaming them allows them to reflect on how they are behaving. It allows them to join the dots on their own behaviour. This is how we teach them the important art of interoception, the ability to consider what's going on for them on the inside AND, significantly, how that might be influencing their behaviour on the outside. In time, your child's little owl will learn how to soothe the lizard and baboon herself BEFORE you even have to step in!

If we don't notice our children's niggles as a sign of discomfort within, they can 'stack up' on top of one another and escalate to Level Two.

Level Two

We might recognise Level Two distress in our children's bigger behaviour, when they start to act more erratically, for example when siblings raise their voices in play or when their behaviour becomes more aggressive. Scenarios in my own household where my children might display a heightened state of distress can include:

- If the children come back from the park having quarrelled
- After a long day at football camp and the 'wrong team won'
- If I haven't brought games for the children to play and they're bored on a long car journey. It can lead to niggles, then ultimately even physical fights in the back seat!

- After a busy party or if the children have had a 'high octane' playdate
- If one child feels excluded in a social setting, or feels they've been publicly shamed.

Remember, brain neuroimaging studies SHOW US that the parts of the brain activated during distress, particularly distress caused by social exclusion, are the same areas activated as when we experience physical pain.

We have seen how disappointment, embarrassment, shame, guilt, anger and excitement can all create intense and overwhelming emotional arousal. When we keep calm and curious about our child's experience we can still get in ahead of Level Two distress and support them to calm down. In fact, it's crucial that we do, because Level Two distress can escalate and intensify without our compassionate intervention.

I appreciate, however, that it can feel difficult to respond with empathy if our children's behaviour triggers *us* and activates our own stress response. To help us to put aside our personal, I imagine pulling on what I think of as a 'big empathy suit' BEFORE I head in to respond!

Big Empathy Suit

In my mind, the 'big empathy suit' is similar to the padded suit we see bomb disposal teams wear in the movies when they're called in to diffuse explosives. Our imaginary suit is padded full of love. Any harsh or painful words that might get hurled our way simply bounce off. Having the protection of the big empathy suit helps us to 'hold the space' in the room and catch the powerful waves of emotional energy that cascade out when our children project their sense of distress or hurt. Wearing extra, if imaginary, padding allows us to capture the energy of their emotional blast, without getting hurt ourselves.

The idea of wearing a big empathy suit does NOT mean we accept being physically hit or hurt by our children and we will talk about laying boundaries shortly.

Whenever I hear raised voices or howls of injustice or indignation between my children at home, I imagine pulling on my big empathy suit and head slowly and carefully towards the fray. My body language is crucial. Stride in too quickly, towering over my children, yelling, 'WHAT ARE YOU DOING?!' can inevitably only serve to escalate, rather than diffuse the situation.

Moving slowly, with my arms held out in a half crescent, palms open as though ready to offer up a large hug, helps me to hold the space in the room, but in a non-threatening way. Opening my arms this way allows me to 'capture' and contain the big waves of angry energy in the room, and it also invites my children towards me, my body language carrying with it the unspoken message: 'You can come to me if you're hurting.' This will all feel much easier and natural to do once all your Cs are firmly in place because the mutual foundations of trust and connection will be firmly established. When your child trusts you're able to hold their emotional pain when they are hurting, they will come to you readily. Who wants to free fall alone when they can have their trusted instructor alongside to steady them?

When you speak, your voice should be strong and in command. If you go in with a voice that is rather flat, it can sound meek and mild and it's likely your child won't 'hear' you. When our children are in distress their energy levels rise and we need to meet that energy if we are to engage. It's not so that you sound aggressive, but to convey an immediate sense that you are attuned to how they are feeling and that you 'get' how cross / angry / upset they are.

Our role is to help to contain our children's big feelings and then bring them back down from the brink. To do so, we need to be able to 'ride the wave' of their angry energy and bring it back to shore.

By way of example, my children recently stormed into the house, pushing past each other as they came through the door. They'd been to football camp and each declared the other to be the WORST brother / sister EVER!!

Clemency ran towards the bathroom, shouting behind her that it was HER TURN to have a shower first. It drove Wilbur wild with rage! He yelled: 'I HATE YOU SO MUCH RIGHT NOW, CLEMENCY!'

Clearly a moment ripe for intervention!

I walked towards Wilbur, my expression fully empathic. Rather than tell him off for shouting or using the word hate (which I hate) I:

Said what I saw, using a similar energy, tone and volume as his. 'Oh my darling, Wilbs, you are SO MAD right now!'
(Remember, terms of endearment like darling, sweetheart, my love, or other sweet nicknames that you have for your child can be very effective for immediately taking their baboon down a notch, so you can engage their little owl.)

Acknowledge the upset.

'You REALLY, REALLY wanted a shower, but Clemency's gone first?'

Soothe.

'Oh, sweetheart, that's tough. You REALLY wanted to have a shower first! Mummy understands. Come, let me help.'

We are not patronising, mollycoddling or mocking our children when we empathise with them in this way. I *get* that it's annoying for Wilbur if he wanted a shower and Clemency jumped in first. Our children's outrage can often seem trivial and even comedic – 'she got to the door before me and I wanted to be first!' – but we must keep a straight face and suppress our smiles, given we can trust there's usually more to our children's upsets than first meets the eye.

With my arms open wide, Wilbur comes towards me and I nod behind him for Clemency to head on into the shower. I will deal with the rights and wrongs of the argument later. For now, I want to focus on diffusing Wilbur's distress and I find the fastest way is to offer few words, a LOT of empathy and a warm, containing hug.

During Level Two distress, our children's baboons are usually too fired up to hear us clearly so we need to keep our sentences short and our tone soothing.

It was certainly *not* the right time for me to remind Wilbur that *he* went first in the shower yesterday – even though he did!

We should not try to force our children to come to us when they are hurting. For some children, hugs can feel triggering rather than soothing. We'll address what to do if your child does not like being held in the next section.

If your child does allow you to bring them in for a cuddle, it can help to gently sway back and forth as you hold them, offering a few soothing words. I tend to simply hush, 'it's OK, it's OK', which is often all it takes to see Wilbur or Clemency's parachute fully up, and calming them down.

It's at this point, when a child feels really seen, held and heard by you, that they'll often reveal the *true* underlying cause of their distress. On that day, as I held Wilbur in my arms, I sensed his body relax and he looked up at me and said, with his bottom lip quivering:

'AND CLEMENCY got the football trophy and I never got one, and someone scraped my foot with their studs!'

Ah! There it is! Now his tears can flow.

Wilbur sobbed for less than half a minute, enough to exorcise his grief in missing out to his sister on a trophy as well as the physical pain of the football stud scrape. Then he looked up at me with a grin to tell me about the 'brilliant' goal that he scored. We laughed as I helped him off with his football boots, wrinkling my nose in mock disgust at the smell of his socks. Then he was off happily for his shower, his howling and hurts done, and his projected anger at his sister healed.

If children feel forced to keep a lid on all their little Level One distresses without healthy release it can escalate to Level Two just as it did for Wilbur, and Tara at the start of the chapter. Level Two can also be caused by strong feelings such as:

- I felt really embarrassed.
- I am really disappointed.
- I am overexcited and don't know what to do with all this energy.
- I am bored, and my brain finds it 'painful'.

- I've kept a lid on all my Level One distress today and now all my niggles just need to explode!

In being that safe person for your child, the person they trust they can turn to, who won't turn away; with your big empathy suit on, and lots of hugs, ticking emotional bombs can be diffused in no time.

Catch your child *before* they're in free fall and your job as a parent/teacher/carer becomes much easier. What were once difficult exchanges can offer instead rich opportunity for building trust and firm foundations for future emotional regulation and resilience.

In an ideal world we'll always get ahead of our children's distress, readily donning our big empathy suit and offering support where it's needed. In an ideal world we can head off any melt-downs at the pass.

But who lives in an ideal world?

Level Three Distress: Otherwise Known as 'LOSING IT'

Without an emotionally available adult to help them, a child's distress can reach fever pitch quickly. It can see children lashing out with limbs or words, yelling, STOP! LEAVE ME ALONE! I HATE YOU! Or worse. They might throw things, hit others or hurt themselves. Level Three distress requires all our Cs in place if we are to bring our children (and us) down to earth safely.

Again, I will stress that if your child is *regularly* displaying distress at a level that feels beyond your control and if they are hurting you or any other member of the family, or if they are hurting themselves, then you MUST seek professional help.

It's important because, as well as providing your family with support, there might be additional underlying issues that your child will benefit from having specialist help to address.

Dr Peter Levine's work makes the important distinction between a child's reaction to grief and loss, and a child's reaction to trauma. I speak about this more in Chapter Fourteen. It's imperative that we furnish ourselves with all the information we need to help ourselves and our children in the most appropriate way.

Here, I offer a guide to enable you to accept and bear witness to a child's grief, loss and anger, while placing careful boundaries to ensure you and they remain safe while they discharge their emotions appropriately. You will need to use your instinct and intuition to guide you as to what you feel is manageable and appropriate for you in these circumstances. The guidance I share here I hope can therefore still be of use in giving you confidence to work with your children, as well as the courage and intuition to know when you might need support. My guidance cannot replace professional therapeutic support, but it is founded in the principles of somatic experiencing and trauma-informed care. The exercises I share are ones I use with my own children and some of my clients where appropriate too. You will need to decide what is manageable for you and what you feel will work best for your child.

Ultimately, our children need to trust we can hold the space for them when they are hurting and know what will happen if they blow out. Because, as James, the eight-year-old in therapy, articulated, it can be terrifying for a child when they don't feel emotionally held and contained. My former psychotherapist, Liza Elle, explained it this way: 'If we don't give our children boundaries, a child can feel like they might fall off the edge of the world.'

Thinking back to the skydiving analogy, imagine how you'd

feel if you were in a plane and about to jump, but you hadn't had any training. How terrifying not knowing what would happen next; how much we might panic if we found ourselves mid-air, with nothing and no one to help stop our fall.

As dramatic as it sounds, neuroscience shows us this IS how it can feel for children when their lizard and baboon go wild. If our children are to learn how to regulate their big emotions, they'll need to practise first. And they'll need us by their side when they do.

I'll show you how to be the calm instructor who jumps alongside your child when they're in emotional free fall, guiding them safely back to earth. It might feel a daunting task, especially if we have never been taught how to safely contain anger ourselves. It's why we need what I think of as a Crisis Management Plan. This is effectively an agreement, or contract, between us and our children so that we know what to do if we find ourselves in free fall. We need it because, as Mike often says in his line of work, fail to prepare, prepare to fail.

MAN-OEUVRES WITH MIKE

My company trains journalists who are heading off to conflict zones. It's how I met Kate when she was heading off to Iraq to cover the conflict there as a reporter. She took part in a hostile environment course and an element of the training involved experiential scenarios, including coming under fire and simulated hostage-taking. The exercise aims to prepare journalists mentally and physically for such emergencies. It allows everyone to know what their roles and responsibility will be in the event of a crisis. By practicing it in a safe environment first, the idea is that we create a form of 'muscle memory' so that, although still extremely frightening to come under fire in real life, the training and prior preparation helps our wise owl to remember what to do, even if the lizard and baboon initially freak out. I think Kate's concept of 'crisis management' in parenting is inspired, because I can totally relate to Jenna's experience (on page 196) of having her own baboon going from what I call 'flash-to-bang' when she's confronted by her son's blowout. When Wilbur gets enraged and stomps around the house shouting, I share Jenna's fear that if I don't exert my authority with him now, then I might lose control of him when he's older. I know lots of my friends who are dads also feel this way. Kate's approach – of preparing for parenting crises in advance – makes absolute sense. We need to help our children when they've been hijacked by their lizard and baboon and we can only do that by laying the groundwork first. I train journalists in how to keep calm 'under fire' and this is essentially what Kate's doing for parents too.

Crisis Management Plan

Drawing up a family contract or Crisis Management Plan in advance will really help. It helps to establish the 'ground rules' around behaviour and what you and your child can expect to happen the next time their emotions get the better of them.

Contracting is something I do in the very first therapy session I have with a child. Essentially it establishes who I am, what time we will meet, where, when and what we will do. It holds my behaviour to account and creates a sense of security in the room because the child then understands what is expected of them and what they can expect of me. Given it's my job to invite some pretty big emotions into the room it's also key for me to establish a clear boundary around behaviour. I explain that the only rule is: 'I don't hurt you, you don't hurt me, and we don't hurt the room.'

Creating a boundary or establishing a clear message around behaviour helps children to feel physically safe and psychologically 'held'. They 'know where they are'. In fact, most of us will feel psychologically safer when we have structure and certainty in our lives.

BRAIN BOX

'A society without structure is an extremely fertile ground for bad behaviour. Without the structure of rules and the law, we would have a breakdown in civilisation. It's just the same with children. They need the structure of clear house rules and clear routines.'

— Dr Margot Sunderland, Child Psychotherapist,
The Science of Parenting

The contract I create with a child in therapy is different to the agreement you're going to create at home. But in essence you want to create a Crisis Management Plan for how you can best support your child if they're experiencing distress that's hard to contain.

The Crisis Management Plan has three main aims:

1) It helps you and your child to consider and agree – just as Mike does with journalists – what everyone's role will be in the event of an (emotional) emergency.

2) It builds trust that you won't walk away when your child is at their most vulnerable.

3) It helps you to establish clear boundaries around what is and IS NOT acceptable behaviour – even when your child is in an emotional free fall.

It's important at this level that you feel confident your Cs are solid, so don't attempt this next step without investing your time putting those crucial pillars in place! Then, at a time when you and your child are calm and relaxed in each other's company, lightly introduce that you've been wondering how you might better support your child the next time 'our big feelings get the better of us'.

You can say that you have been thinking how you can best help them to bring their emotions into the room, but that you want to help them to keep themselves (and you) safe while they do.

'I want you to have somewhere safe where you can show me how you are feeling. Remember we said that all our emotions are welcome? Well, when some of them feel really big, I wanted to find somewhere we can go together, to let them out safely.'

Create a Safe Space

Invite your child to pick a room or space in your home where they feel safe and have room to express themselves. Explain: 'I want us to have somewhere we can go together when you have big feelings. Somewhere you will feel safe to invite them in and then let them out safely.' Using the word SAFE is key. It's a positive trigger for the baboon, because, to him, safety is EVERYTHING. It helps to keep him calm.

Ideally, the space you choose together will be carpeted, or

with soft rugs and furnishings, and without any sharp-edged furniture or breakables. Bedrooms are usually good places, but you and your child must each feel comfortable with the space. It can be a corner in a room, just so long as your child feels 'contained' in that space, and where no one, aside from you, will be able to watch them. It's the opposite to sending a child to their bedroom alone to calm down – this is something you are going to do as a team!

Once you've agreed on the space, you can even name it; put a poster on the door or wall to identify this is your child's special space, or 'safe spot' and be very clear this is where they can come if things start to spiral out of control.

Then you can gently remind your child of the boundary. 'OK, so now we have a space where we can do our offloading. If you feel angry or cross, can we agree that this is where you will show me?'

And again: 'The only rule is that we do not hurt each other, I do not hurt you and you do not hurt me, and we do not hurt the room.'

Look your child in the eyes as you say this. Your tone should convey confidence and authority. This is key. You are your child's flight instructor. You are teaching them how to handle themselves when they're in free fall. You can be fun, but you are firm when it comes to the limits and lines that are not to be crossed. If it feels necessary to say it, you might explain. 'If Mummy/Daddy does not feel safe, sadly I will not be able to stay with you. I want to help you to show me your big feelings but we will have to stop if you hurt me. I am going to try my hardest to help you to remember not to hit or hurt me but you understand we will sadly have to stop if we do?'

You can follow up brightly: 'OK, so we can't hit or hurt, BUT I'll tell you what we CAN do!'

Your tone here can even be playful. You want to engage your child's baboon and show him what he CAN do in the event of a crisis! There is no blaming or shaming in your tone. You are simply teaching your child the art of being angry.

Remind your child about their stress response and how the energy can feel really BIG (and even quite scary) inside. Reiterate that this is normal but that sometimes it can feel a bit too much to handle so it's a parent's job to stay and help.

You might find it useful to refer to any relevant books or films that you have watched that cover themes of emotional regulation, like *Inside Out* or perhaps the movie *Turning Red*, which lightly cover themes of emotional regulation and generational trauma, as well as some pre-teen themes.

Once your child has chosen where they want their safe space to be, you can then think about appropriate exercises that can help them to release those big feelings safely.

Here are just a few that I have used with my own children as well as the children in my clinical care. You can suggest one or two that you think your child might be comfortable to try. You can also invite your child to come up with their own!

Pillow Power

Pillow Power is a tool my children found particularly helpful when they were younger and that we still use on occasion today. They get to choose a pillow or a cushion that they can punch when they're angry. They might choose to pummel their bed mattress too. When my children were mad about something I would place the pillow on their bed and invite them to 'give it all you've got', encouraging them loudly to 'go for it!' while also naming out loud what it was that had got them so angry or enraged. It might be:

'I'm SO CROSS THAT MY BROTHER TOOK MY TOY!' Or: 'I HATE THAT I HAVE TO DO HOMEWORK!' I mentioned using a yoga bolster in Chapter Three, which can also be good for pummelling or giving a good squeeze! I'll sometimes encourage my children to holler or yell out what's making them so cross if they feel like doing that too.

Toy Throwing

Throwing soft toys against a wall is a great way to release negative energy! Invite your child to choose any appropriate soft toys or bean bags and explain that they can throw them at a designated wall in the safe space. You'll want to choose toys that are soft and have a little weight to them, but that will not break or break anything if they are thrown with force. It is essential that your child chooses which toys to throw, given some will have more sentimental or emotional value than others. In the therapy room, I have a big bucket of soft toys and puppets and, when a child is mid- release, I'll often crouch low by the bucket and pass the toys up to them one at a time. It offers up a wonderfully collaborative and even bonding experience, and sometimes I'll even see a knowing smile as even the most enraged child acknowledges the liberation in being given permission to release their anger by throwing the toys AS HARD AS THEY CAN! Exercises like these offer us an opportunity to experience a profound sense of connection. A priceless way for our children to show us their hurt and anger, but to do so together with you. The experience can form a very powerful glue, and of course the only 'person' getting hurt is the poor puppet or cuddly toy.

Shadow Boxing

The aim of these exercises is to encourage our children to graduate from using physical actions to using their words to tell us when they are angry. A good first step I find can be shadow boxing. I stand side by side with my clients or my children, punching the air in front of me, 'POW, POW' with my fists, *left right, left right*. As I do so, I loudly name the thing that I know is causing them hurt; whether that's a friendship issue or something else that has made them cross. It might even be something to do with me: 'Kate never brought the trampoline today and she let me down!' It's especially powerful when we name a hurt directly connected with us. Your child might be angry that you have not done/said something and in naming it out loud you are helping to diffuse and lance those emotional boils very effectively indeed. You can talk about yourself, speaking on behalf of your child: 'Daddy said I was a fussy eater and he hurt my feelings!'

You can continue to remind your child of the boundaries, especially with this exercise, reminding them gently but firmly that we can punch the air, *but not each other*. Our aim is to offer our children a safe outlet to practise venting and voicing their anger. In this way we help them to graduate to using their words to state how they feel, rather than have their fists do the talking for them. Exercises like these can help our children to go on to lay firm verbal boundaries with others. It can see remarkable results. One parent recently reported to me, having implemented these exercises, that she had overheard her youngest son, who at five she feared had been bearing the brunt of his older brothers' too-boisterous play, tell them loudly and firmly, 'NO! Stop it. That's not OK!'

Don't attempt anything that does not feel appropriate or that you instinctively know won't work for you or your child. But hopefully these exercises can serve as a prompt for you to identify alternative activities that might work for you instead. Some children like to tear up paper when they're angry. For some children, I will stick long rolls of paper up on the wall of the therapy room and they love ripping it off when they're cross. Others like to 'paint' their hands with water and smear their palms across the wall as a form of protest.

You could create a special box that is just for you and your child. Only toys they choose are put in the box and it only gets brought out when they need a release or to play with you. Getting the box out can be approached in a wonderfully conspiratorial way with your child (you could say with a wink, 'Shall we get the box out together?'). It allows you to intervene using play to diffuse what could otherwise become a big meltdown.

Rhythm Rocks

Remember, anything you can do with your children that is patterned, repetitive and rhythmic can work wonders for soothing an overstimulated nervous system. If your child is getting cross in the kitchen and you detect a potential for Level Three distress, you might suggest stomping to their safe space with you leading the way growling, howling, humming, singing out loud, as you go. Another exercise to possibly try is what I call the 'salsa shimmy', where you shake out the cross or nervous energy in the way we discussed in Chapter Three. If your children are younger, you might agree they can jump on the bed *but only while holding your hands* as that too can offer a lovely release. The key is to go to the safe space together and process those big feelings together.

Boundaries and Limits

Remember to identify which things in the room you cannot throw, hit, or jump on. Remind your child they'll need to hold your hands if they jump because your job is to keep them safe.

'My job is to keep you safe' is one of the most important sentences you can say to your child.

You are telling your child: it's my job to hold this space for you. I can do that even when you feel like you have a scary monster inside. Letting your child know that you are not scared of their behaviour means they don't have to be scared of their big feelings either.

It can take practice and time and, if a child does forget 'the rules' in the heat of the moment, you can firmly but calmly remind them, 'Remember, no hitting or hurting. I will do my hardest to help you but if you hit or hurt me we have to stop.' This can often be enough for the child to release their energy on the pillow instead. If they cannot work within the boundaries then you will have to stop and remove yourself from the situation. You can do this with confidence and say 'I am sorry because I want to stay, but I cannot allow you to hurt me.'

What happens when...

What happens if your child reaches Level Three distress and you go to their safe space, but then they tell you to LEAVE? For many of us, if we are experiencing painful feelings it can make us feel very vulnerable. Children often do not want to be seen by us, or indeed anyone when they are in such an emotional state. And we can hopefully understand that. It's important that our children have agency over what happens when they are in distress. If they ask us to leave, we will want to honour that; equally, we want to convey our love is unconditional, we will always love them and want to help them, even if they feel at their worst. You might say:

'I imagine it might feel uncomfortable to have me here. I could make myself small and sit in the corner if that feels better? My job is to keep you safe so I would like to stick around if it's OK, but if you *really* want me to leave, I will do as you ask. You are in charge.'

It's important to give your child the choice. Empowering them to decide what happens when they are upset means they must engage their little owl more than if it's you calling the shots. So long as the boundary around safe behaviour is adhered to, you can do as they ask and leave the safe space. You might offer to stay outside: 'Just in case you need me. You let me know'.

It's crucial to stress that: 'If you want me to come back, I always will.' Our children need to know that our love and support is unconditional. It's a powerful message to convey to your child: 'Even when you feel at your very worst, and most frightening, I am not frightened and I will not leave you if you are hurting'.

Sometimes, it might be that *your child* wants to leave the space. If a child moves to flight this can sometimes be the case. Again, discussing this in advance helps you and your child to consider ground rules around safety. You can explain that if they leave the room when they are really angry it might not be safe for them, or anyone around them – for example, if a child storms from the room they might lash out at a sibling without thinking. You can agree that they'll do a quick grounding exercise before they leave the safe space; anything from five deep breaths, or five star jumps and a shimmy. The exercise should be their choice. Doing a quick release exercise ensures your child will at least be slightly more grounded before they leave the room. Again, let them know that you will wait for them for a little while, in case they want to come back. This can prove a powerful incentive to return. If we're skydiving and in free fall, what might we prefer – to spin out, frightened and alone, or have a calm 'instructor' by our side, who can steady us as we fall?

Keeping your own baboon under control can be tricky if your child melts down in public or in front of relatives or friends. Our baboon doesn't like to feel embarrassed any more than our children's. Finding a place of 'safety', whether it's taking your child to another room if you are at someone else's house, to another, preferably quieter area if you are somewhere in public or at a party, can help take the pressure off you, and your child. It gives your wise owl the space to step in. It's much harder to successfully manage a meltdown with a baboon at the helm!

You can brainstorm this with your child, thinking about any places they have experienced difficulty before – perhaps noisy birthday parties, crowded events, shopping malls, on a noisy train or street, at a festival, playdate or at relatives' houses. You can wonder out loud: 'Where would we go if we were out shopping and you felt fizzy, do you think?' Or, 'What if we were at a party and all your friends were there?'

You can always make some suggestions and see if you both agree – you could suggest finding another room where no one was watching, or in the shopping mall you could find a bathroom stall, or a quiet corner. You won't have an immediate solution for each and every occasion, but often just thinking things through in advance in moments when you are both calm allows you to think more intuitively in those moments of emotional crisis. Brainstorming together this way builds trust and understanding between you. It builds a bond that will more likely have your child follow your lead. Again, far more appealing to stick close to my instructor if I am in free fall, rather than having to spin out all alone.

You can also game plan what should happen if the one rule of 'I don't hurt you and you don't hurt me' gets broken.

You can acknowledge big feelings while still reminding your child of the boundary.

'You're so MAD! Tell me with your words! Or can you stomp to show me how mad you are. But no hitting. Hitting hurts.'

You might tell your child, 'I will not allow you to hurt me, so if it's too difficult, I might have to step away and come closer again when you feel able to keep me safe and you safe.'

You might consider that you could pick up a pillow or yoga bolster to protect you but still allow your child to hit that if you feel comfortable holding it. I have done this before in the therapy room when a child has struggled to contain their behaviour, and I briefly held a large cushion up in front of me before gently lowering it to the floor, where the child carried on hitting the pillow from there.

Emphasise you will not touch your child if they are feeling overwhelmed, unless they reach out to you for help. While a hug or touch can feel containing and comforting during Level Two distress, at Level Three, when a child is in free fall it might serve only to infuriate and escalate the situation.

Your role during Level Three distress is to be a steadying presence and you don't need to touch or hold your child for that. Consider the job of the instructor on the skydive, keeping a safe distance, but not being too far away should the novice skydiver need a steadying hand. Being able to 'hold' the space in the room is often containing enough.

The first few times you and your child try this, it might feel difficult to remember the plan. In which case you will need to improvise and use your intuition. Do remember that in the middle of free fall you do not need to use many words – your child will not hear you above the noise.

You can simply say what you see: 'You are SO MAD right now! Mummy/Daddy can see it. Remember I can help.'

But remember too that when our children display high levels of distress we will often go into fight or flight ourselves.

So:

Remember to **BREATHE**. Taking those slow deep breaths that help us to keep calm.

Remind yourself, **'This Too Shall Pass.'** You might consider Level Three distress as a massive wave of energy. Much like an angry great wave out at sea, it will eventually lose its potency and power as it finally comes in to shore.

Feel confident to make yourself smaller, resisting the temptation to rise up and assert control! **Keep low and slow** when your child is in distress – it will serve you far more than if you try to assert yourself using your physical presence to gain control.

Hold the Line. Your child needs you to stay emotionally strong and hold the space for them in the moments when they are all at sea. Keep calm and trust that your comforting but confident presence sends a powerful message that 'we've got this'.

Don't panic! It takes time and practice so have faith: you are doing important work with your child.

Put aside your personal. Remember, when our children use 'hurtful' language, it's very often just a reflection of the 'hurt' they feel inside. Your child doesn't actually hate you, or want a new mum or dad, or whatever she's yelling. She's not 'behaving badly'. She feels hurt and scared and powerless, so she's pulling out the most upsetting thing she can think of, so you'll know how upset she is. When your child realises she doesn't have to raise her voice or go on the attack to be heard, she'll develop more capacity to express her feelings more appropriately next time.

Connect before Command. Do not get drawn into a battle of wills. If your child throws a pillow on the floor (rather than at the designated wall), or uses a rude word or tone, remember to look beyond the behaviour and focus on the connection you have with them. You can point to the wall and say with energy, 'You can throw it there!'

If we are going to teach our children the art of emotional regulation, they'll need to practise first. And they can only practise by experiencing what it's like to be in distress, and then to be helped by you to calm down.

And just as we can all feel great exhaustion after a big adrenaline rush, so too your child might seem worn out after a big release. You will see their energy reach a crescendo, and then dissipate, often leaving the child exhausted. This is sometimes referred to as 'the big adrenaline dump', leading to a child curling up somewhere, tired and still. It is then that we can move a little closer if it feels right to do so. There is no need to speak, your child is still 'riding their wave' – it's now just closer to shore. Stay with them in these moments and often you will find your child reaching out to you for comfort. Some children feel a huge sense of relief and even joy when they have been helped to safely navigate Level Three distress. They might start laughing or even dance around – it is a very poignant and even magical moment. You might even want to join in!

Contrary to what we might have thought, our children's biggest outbursts offer us the greatest opportunity for repair. When we remember that inside they are hurting, we can have faith that by being consistent, remaining calm, relying on our co-created contract, we can be confident we will know what to do. The calmer we are, the more our instincts will kick in.

PARENT PONDER
Mark, father to Rex, 8

Rex is our only son and the pressure on me to play can sometimes feel intense. I love it, but I notice the difference when his 12-year-old cousin, Joe, comes over and see the joy on his face when he has someone closer to his age to play with; someone he can also look up to and connect with. Recently, Joe came to stay and he and Rex had a brilliant few days. As soon as he left, however, Rex's mood shifted. He turned to my wife and pointed to a scrape on his chest, telling her it hurt. She empathised, but when she said it seemed OK, Rex became enraged and shouted at both of us, telling us: 'I hate you! You're so boring – you never play!' I was stunned, and actually felt really hurt given I'd played football with him and his cousin just that morning! I wanted to shout back and defend myself. It was a look from my wife that stopped me and I realised it was more than just the scrape. He was missing his cousin and, in his loss and pain, he was lashing out – at the only people he had left.

He stormed up to his room, really sobbing, poor kid. I was still quite angry, but something made me want to comfort him. I think I recognised a strong sense of loss that I had experienced at his age. Just something about his behaviour that said he was really grieving. When I went into his room, Rex threw a cuddly toy in my direction and told me to LEAVE! I stood outside his room, but something made me return. I climbed up onto his bunk and just lay there beside him. I didn't speak and didn't touch him. It felt important for him to work through his pain, but knowing I was there alongside him. Something seemed to shift. Rex kept sobbing with his head in the pillow, but he reached out his little arm in my direction, holding out his hand. Without any words being spoken, I took his hand and gave it a gentle squeeze. I felt quite emotional. Slowly, my boy came back to me and we cuddled. He had grieved his loss and now he was calm.

In this rather beautiful story, we can see how Rex was indeed grieving the loss of his cousin. We might also notice the symbolism of how he pointed to his chest, telling his mum that 'it hurt'. His heart likely did hurt. When we experience the joy of life, the company of those we care for, the crash of the low that follows can feel truly painful, triggering the brain chemical acetylcholine. It can make children (and adults) very angry and hostile. When our children are comforted, the acetylcholine comes back to its base rate and the child will feel calmed. Sometimes our children will feel safe and contained just by us sitting down next to them and talking gently and calmly. Sometimes, our presence can enrage them further. Don't be afraid to try different things in the moment, moving away or edging towards. The calmer you are, the more you can trust your instincts, just as Mark did, ultimately lying down and using his calming, loving presence to help to co-regulate his son.

The more confident you are, keeping your tone warm but firm, the more your child is likely to follow your lead. When a child trusts we can hold the space for them, they'll bring forth their most vulnerable selves.

BRAIN BOX

'As long as we feel safely held in the hearts and minds of the people who love us, we will climb mountains and cross deserts and stay up all night to finish projects. Children and adults will do anything for people they trust and whose opinion they value.'

— Dr Bessel van der Kolk, Psychiatrist, *The Body Keeps the Score*

It might take a few months, it might even take years (how many of us are still, as adults, learning how to regulate our own temper and big feelings?), but being able to relieve your child of their painful feelings, sitting alongside, not sending them to their rooms to deal with it alone, is not only going to help them to heal, it will help your relationship too. We can – and must – help our children to manage their anger responsibly. In doing so we also help ourselves.

Something magical happens when our children feel able to be vulnerable in our presence, able to show us all the ugliness they might feel inside, to 'project it out' rather than keep it all held in. If they try to push us away but still see us hold firm, holding the space for them, staying calm, keeping control, we see fear and trust form a powerful glue. When you stay true to your commitment that ALL emotions are welcome, and that you will not abandon your child when they're 'spinning out', I guarantee the gratitude they will show you is worth everything in the world.

MAN-OEUVRES WITH MIKE

I might not have believed it until I saw it for myself. We had an incident where Wilbur might ordinarily have blown up – when I had thrown his last piece of pizza away by accident. Trivial, I know, and something that would typically have me 'blow out' baboon-style back, telling him off for sounding so spoiled. Before I did, however, Wilbur literally stopped himself mid-shout and took a deep breath. He said, 'I'm sorry to shout, Daddy. It's just that I was really looking forward to it.'

Just as we are encouraging Wilbur to practise using his words to tell us how he feels rather than shouting them, we have to practise too.

Do not punish or criticise your child if they don't follow or remember all the rules when the time comes. Just as adults let their baboon get the better of them, so our children most certainly will too. This takes practice and it takes time. But the more you feel able to do it, the stronger your child's little owl will become and the fewer blowouts you will see.

Gaining true emotional regulation takes time, it takes our emotional investment, and it takes our faith and our patience. You will need to look after yourself in this process too, especially if previously you have not felt in control. All the exercises in

Chapter Three will help in this regard. Always take a moment to ground yourself before you try to ground your children. Because, as Peter Levine, who developed Somatic Experiencing in his excellent book, *Trauma-Proofing Your Kids*, says: 'Experiences with our adult clients in therapy confirm that often the most frightening part of an incident experienced as a child was their parents' horror reaction! Children "read" the facial expression of their caregiver as a barometer of how serious the danger or injury is.'

WISE OWL WISDOMS

- Prevention is key when it comes to dealing with distress.

- Be aware of the signs that tell us our children are in fight or flight and work quickly.

- Empathise, don't escalate.

- Imagining ourselves in a big padded empathy suit can help us to remain calm and offer comfort.

- Implementing a Crisis Management Plan will help you and your child work together as a team.

- Strategising in advance still won't guarantee that all will go according to plan and you must always prioritise your safety. But the more you both practise, the more confident you will be.

- You have every right to feel safe in your home and so do your children – always seek professional support should you feel you need it.

Chapter Twelve

CONVERSATIONS THAT COUNT –
What to Say When...

*Look beyond the behaviour and you
will see the pain.*

Sometimes it's just really helpful to know what to say when, and how to say it! We don't always have time to 'think' when our children are upset or 'acting out', so here are a few suggestions, scripts and sentences you might find helpful to have up your sleeve.

While this is by no means an exhaustive list, I hope the suggestions below will be useful for having conversations that count. Perhaps consider how you might respond to something specific that your child has said to you. Writing sentences down in advance can be very helpful for you to have an immediate 'wise owl reference' in the heat of the moment.

Reflection

Reflect, or repeat, your child's words back to them, using a similar tone and energy in your voice.

For example: 'The party was TERRIBLE!' We can respond: 'Oh, WOW! The party was Terrible?'

Leave the sentence hanging, with a pause to invite your child to tell you more. Or, if necessary, you can add:

'Can you tell me more?'

Reflection helps to open up the conversation, to get to the hurt that so often lies beneath 'hurt words'.

Put aside the Personal

If our children use hurtful language or say 'I hate you' we might respond:

'I get that! You are SO cross that I won't allow you to do x/y and I guess you are really disappointed. I get it. You really wanted it and now I am saying no. I am sorry it's so hard. I love you and sometimes I have to say no.'

Another good response might be: 'Ouch! You must be so upset to say that to me. I wonder if you're saying the worst thing in the world, so I will know how upset you are. Tell me why you're upset. I'm here, and I am listening.'

Ask Open-ended Questions

A closed question is one where we can only answer 'yes' or 'no'. Open questions invite a more elaborate answer. For example, rather than ask, 'Do you like bananas?', we can instead ask, 'What fruit do you like?'

'Do you like school?' becomes, 'How do you feel about school?'

'Is Nathan your best friend?' becomes, 'Tell me about your friends at school.'

And rather than, 'Did you have a difficult day?', we might ask, 'How did you feel about your day today?' Or, 'What did you enjoy most about today?'

We can all feel somewhat rejected if, having picked our children up and we ask, 'Did you have a good day?' and we get a yes/no reply but nothing more. Reframing the question will really help to open up the conversation.

I might ask, 'What was the best thing about your day today?' And if I suspect something tough has happened because of the scowl I see (!), I might try, 'What was the worst? Or what didn't you like about today?'

Avoid Assumptions

Rather than asking, 'Do you feel sad about Daddy not being here?', you might ask instead, 'What do you feel about Daddy not being here?' Or, 'How does it feel without Daddy here?'

And rather than asking, 'Were you angry with her for doing that?', you can ask, 'How did it make you feel when she did that?'

If there is loss or bereavement, you can try firing a few truth arrows to see how they land, but do do it gently.

'It can make us feel SO sad when Daddy is not here.' Or, 'I bet you felt really MAD when she did that?'

'Yes, you are sad. Mummy is sad that Grandma has gone. Mummy cries sometimes too.'

Or, 'I am sad too. It's OK to feel that way. You can tell me and Daddy/Mummy when you feel sad and we can sit here together and let the sadness out.'

'I understand, sweetheart. It's very normal to miss him. I miss him too.'

'We are sad because he has died and we won't get to see him again. It hurts.'

'Where is your sad? Mine is sitting here. Can you show me where yours is?'

'Let's sit with your sad for a bit. If your sad could speak, what would it say?'

'It can feel like a big feeling to have to sit with but I am here. It's OK, I am here. We can sit with the sad together.'

'Let's see if we can let the sad out. We can do that safely just by sitting quietly and feeling it, sensing where it sits in our body. We can do that together.'

Avoid Asking Why

Always avoid leaping to that question of 'WHY did you DO THAT?!' Instead, you can respond with an 'Oh my love, there were some big feelings there. Can you show how it feels using your stomping feet, or maybe a colour to show me how you're feeling?'

Try Not to Problem-solve

Always be mindful of immediately 'suggesting' solutions when our children share a problem. The key is first to EMPATHISE. Consider the response you'd appreciate if you shared your vulnerability with a friend or partner and they immediately tried to problem-solve (clearly trying to be helpful!) rather than listening and really hearing how you feel. Think how much more helpful it can be if we open up about something and our friend / partner responds:

'Oh, that sounds really difficult. I'm sorry it's been so hard.'

Or: 'Oh gosh, that must have been tricky. How are you feeling about it now …?'

And then instead of,

'Shouldn't you do x or y…?' Or, 'If it were me I would…'

We can say,

'What did you feel you wanted to do?' Or, 'What do you think would help?'

Only then might we open up with some possible solutions. You are not giving your child THE solution – you are inviting them to choose a solution themselves.

You can gently wonder,

'What do you think might happen if you tried to …?'

Or:

'What would you like to have happen?'

Or:

'What do you think might happen if you talked to them about that?'

If the problem is something that could prove difficult for the child to solve alone, you can pose potential solutions – but the emphasis again is the choice lies with the child.
I might wonder out loud, saying something like,

'Gosh, this sounds difficult. I can understand why you are worrying about it. I wonder what might help?'

And then,

'I guess there are a few options. You could talk to them yourself, you could ask me to help you or perhaps a teacher at school? Do any of those feel right to you?'

'I wonder'

Using 'I wonder if/what/how ...' allows us to fire off a few truth arrows and see if they land. They also give us a chance to pause for thought if your child has said something and you are not quite sure how to respond.

For example, if they say, 'I don't like school.' You might reply, 'Hmmm, I'm wondering what it is about school that you don't like?'

Stick to the child's words where you can. Stay curious with your child, use pauses and they will usually fill in their own 'gap' when they feel comfortable to do so.

You can use your 'I wonder' phrases as we looked at in Chapter Eight.

Talk about 'Parts'

Rather than talk about the child as a whole, you can speak about 'parts' of them being angry or sad. It helps children to realise that not all of them feels that way, enabling them to keep their emotions in perspective.

'I wonder if part of you is feeling sad [or mad or worried]?'

This also serves to help a child to visualise or isolate that part and even, with your help, to begin a dialogue with it. It allows them to get curious about why that 'part' might be sad, mad or feeling bad.

So you might invite:

'I wonder if the mad part of you can write down what it's so MAD about?'

'I wonder if the sad part can show me where it hurts?'

'I wonder if the worry can tell the teddy what it's worried about?'

If your child has done something that they have been told off for at school you can name it as a part, again rather than having the child feel that ALL of them feels that way:

'I wonder if a part of you felt ashamed / embarrassed / bad / guilty when that happened?'

By naming negative feelings you are letting your child know it's OK to feel the feeling, but that they can let it go. You are not judging them in this moment, just empathising that a part of them felt that way and they can talk to you about it.

Don't impose your feelings onto your child

Very often we can unconsciously impose our own feelings onto our children. For example, if our child tells us they don't like school and we didn't like school ourselves when we were young, we might say, 'Does school make you feel sad?'. Actually, it might be a child likes school most of the time, he just doesn't like the thought of having to do a spelling test tomorrow!

Acknowledge the emotion and show you accept it

Showing your child that you want to understand how things feel for them is the fastest, most sure-fire way to calm them down.

'Wilbs, I can see you are really cross. You wanted me to play with you?'

Leave a pause so your child can really open up both barrels: 'YES! I wanted you to come and play but you didn't!'

Remember, we don't have to agree with what our child wanted us to do, but we can honour how they feel as a result.

Then we can soothe. 'I am so sorry you are so upset. Daddy was too busy making supper to play. I am so sorry. It's hard when I am too busy to play. I really love my time with you, I have to make supper but shall we have some special play time before bed?!'

Don't impose your interpretation onto your children's drawings

When your child brings drawings or artwork back from school, or when they make them with you, resist the urge to interpret!

Rather than, 'Oh that man looks sad!' or 'Is that me?' or 'You have used a lot of black, are you sad?' Instead we can say, 'You are showing me your drawing! Can you tell me about it.'

Do make general observations. 'So you have painted blue here, and orange there...'

It shows your child you are really noticing what they have done.

You can also ask, if there are characters in the drawing, 'Tell me about this person [or dog or monster].'

You might even wonder – 'What are they feeling?'

Asking your child to give their drawing a title can be a very useful exercise. It helps them to add a 'full stop' to what they have created and can also provide interesting insight – although again, no need to interpret!

Keep sentences short

If your child's lizard is 'fizzy' and their baboon bounding, remember that their 'thinking brain' is not getting a look-in. It's like trying to type on a computer when the hard drive is whirring.

So:

Keep what you are saying really simple.

Keep your sentences short.

Keep your voice soothing. We can only connect with our

children's limbic brain if we have warmth in our voice to convey compassion and curiosity.

Avoid the baboon-state bear-traps

Max, who is seven, is refusing to engage in his homework. He scribbles across his worksheet and gets up from the table and runs into the garden. He tells his mother, 'I don't care! I don't want to do this anymore.'

His mother, whose own baboon is in charge after a long day at work and now with the pressure of overseeing her son's homework, yells after him.

'Stop that now!'

'You need to do it NOW!'

Finally resorting to:

'I'll just have to phone your teacher to tell them you won't do your work!'

Feeling completely deskilled and disrespected, Max's mother asks me, 'What are the alternatives?'

Firstly, I remind parents that at this age, battling baboon to baboon over homework can often see us setting up a negative cycle with associations around school and education that are terribly unhelpful. Homework that requires parental oversight can, at this age, put unnecessary pressure on hard-working parents and can see them pitted against their children that proves much less helpful than if ten minutes of play was prescribed each evening.

Whenever we find ourselves in potential bear trap territory, we can remind ourselves to be playful – to be creative and use our curiosity.

Max's mum might take a pause – then take the paper that her son has scribbled on and ponder, 'Hmmm, it looks like Max has drawn a wibbly octopus here and he seems SUPER angry!' She might reply in a pretend octopus voice: 'I am so cross! I hate doing homework!'

Now Max's mum can have a conversation with the 'octopus'.

'Oh goodness, Mr Octopus, I am so sorry. It seems like you are bit stuck. Hold on, let me get Max, he might be able to help.'

Turning to Max, his mother might now say: 'Max, can you please help, Mr Octopus is really unhappy. How can we help him?'

Max might look at his mother still cross. Max's mother can then say with genuine empathy and concern, 'Are you OK, sweetheart? You look a little cross too. Would you like to sit with me for a little bit?'

You can remind your child your job is to keep them safe and to always listen and if they like, they can sit in the calming corner with you and just sit for a while. Sitting side by side with your child, allowing them to feel the security of your presence, of sensing that you want to help, will get you both much further down the line than punishment or threats ever can.

When you are both sat in your 'safe space' you can consider whether rather than simply being 'oppositional', your child is actually struggling with their homework or perhaps something at school is upsetting them. It might suggest the scribble is a way of expressing that inner hurt or frustration.

Mum might then say: 'Max, I'm wondering if this scribble is how you are feeling about doing the work?'

Pointing to her chest she might say, 'I am feeling a sense of frustration? Is that how it feels for you?'

'I know when I am frustrated I want to rip things up because they feel rubbish, and I sometimes want to scream and shout and get the "rubbish feeling" out.'

She might use an 'I wonder' question:

'I wonder if something else has upset you?'

'I wonder if you can help me to understand?'

These conversations take practice. They take time and patience, and we won't get it right every time. I appreciate it can feel counterintuitive to use empathy when a child is telling you NO! But thinking ahead to avoid the bear traps will help you to keep the all-important Cs in mind and respond from a place of compassion and curiosity, rather than letting your own baboon take charge.

Apologise

When we get it wrong, and all of us do, it is a great opportunity for learning. We can model to our children how we would like them to behave when they get things wrong too.

'I'm so sorry, I think I have said something that has made you even more upset. Can we look at what might have helped you so I can know for next time?'

That's a much more powerful response to a moment of anger than: 'OK, FINE, have it your way!' Or, 'Go to your room until you've calmed down!'

Showing that we are human, apologising where we get things wrong, allows our children to get things wrong and be human too.

If we experience a sense of fear, that we might lose our 'command' by apologising: it suggests our sense of command is fragile in the first instance. I want parents to feel 'in control', but not 'controlling' – there's an important difference. We can gain control and command when we first connect, ensuring your ten parenting pillars will give you a much firmer foundation from which to 'captain the ship'. You'll have little control over that 'flapping sail' until you do.

Children do generally want to co-operate with us. They know they need us – life is pretty scary without someone to take care of us! So if your child is behaving in an 'oppositional way', the first question is not to stamp down with more control – but to be curious about the disconnect they might be feeling. Connect before command and model the behaviour you want to see. Being able to admit to our children and ourselves that just as they will make mistakes, so we get things wrong too.

Working with you will always going to feel better than going it alone.

Tune in, don't turn away

Sometimes your child might say such things as 'I hate myself', 'I don't like myself', 'I felt really bad when I shouted' or 'I felt really bad when you told me off'.

This can be distressing. Our first response as parents can often be to resort to the Ds: defend, dismiss, deny and diminish. It's not because we're terrible parents, but because we likely want to do anything we can to avoid seeing our children in pain.

But if we want to help our children to exorcise their big feelings we must learn how to 'press into the pain'. We must learn how to 'tune in, and not turn away'.

We can only relieve our children of their painful feelings by helping them to release them. We can only do that when we help them to grieve, to let them go. If it doesn't feel triggering to you, try saying the following statements out loud:

I am not worthy.

I am horrible.

I don't like myself.

I am bad.

No one likes me.

I hate myself.

These are really painful statements.

Yet many children will have similar thoughts every single day. In fact, I would go so far as to say most of our children will experience one or more of these negative thoughts at some point in their lives.

Would you rather they hold onto them, or share them with you and learn how to let them go?

Using the Ds does nothing to release our children from that pain.

When your child tells you something that feels painful, they are sharing their pain with you. It's a sign they feel connected enough to you, that they trust you enough to be vulnerable, that they need your help.

Dismissing, diminishing or defending against this pain won't help.

But your empathy can.

It can be difficult to do, especially if we were not helped to experience and exorcise our own painful feelings when we were growing up. In the early stages of my own therapy, I learned how to connect with those long-held feelings by visualising myself as a little girl on the inside, the little girl who had taken on the role of holding on to all the painful stuff. This is in essence what we do psychologically – the psychoanalyst Melanie Klein referred to it as 'splitting'. Today we talk about internal family systems, both of which you might find helpful to research and I include references at the back of the book in that regard.

So what do we say when our child tells us, 'I feel like I'm a bad person'?

Repeating what your child has told you tells them you have heard them and that you are ready to hear more.

'You feel like a bad person...?'

If they just look at you, remember that their brain is now scanning your face and body to gauge your response. What are you communicating to them at that moment? Are you judging them? Do you think they are silly? Do YOU think they are a bad person?

So keep your face soft with genuine concern, your voice warm and mindful of your body language, so as not to trigger the baboon. He might not have been in this territory before, where he feels able to be vulnerable. It might make him more ready to close down again, if he thinks you will dismiss or deny him.

If your child seems unable to say anything further, you can follow up with: 'What a big thing to be carrying. How brave you are to share that with me. Has something happened to make you feel bad?'

Being able to stay with the feeling of 'bad' and naming it out loud tells your child you are not afraid of it, that you can talk about feeling bad without any sense of judgement. This can feel hugely liberating to a child who has been sitting with shame. You might say, 'I'm sorry if this is feeling really hard. Perhaps you could tell me why a part of you feels bad, or could you show me on paper?'

You can draw your child as a stick person with a speech bubble and write the words they have used inside: 'I feel like a bad person.'

Seeing the words on the paper and tuning in to the pain of the statement can help to guide you.

Now, you can direct your conversation and talk to the image on the paper. It helps to take the pressure off your child, it sees us talking more symbolically, but you can still talk as though to your child.

'Oh, Aidan, I am so sorry. How painful that must be to be carrying that. Can you tell me if there is something that is making you feel that way? Can you help me understand where this thought might come from, or what's happened to have you feel that way?'

Your child might blurt something out, or mutter under their breath. For example: 'Because yesterday I was mean to my sister and you told me off.'

'Ah, so yesterday when I told you off you were not only sad, you felt like a bad person. Perhaps you thought I think you are a bad person because I was telling you off?'

Note your child's response. They will nod if you have got it right. You might even see tears. Tears tell us our truth arrows have hit home.

'Oh sweetheart, what a big, big thing to have been carrying. I am so sorry. I was talking about your behaviour, not you. There is a big difference. Of course, we want to look after your sister. And I was concerned about her. But I am also concerned about you and if what I said upset you then you are right to tell me. I never want you to feel bad about yourself because of one behaviour yesterday. We can always change our behaviour. It is not who we are. It's just how we act sometimes, and we can always change that.'

We always want to distinguish between the child and their behaviour.

We can then use sentences like:

'I am so sorry, that must have felt so hard yesterday.'

'I am sorry that was the story you told yourself.'

'I love you so much. I love my children more than anything in the whole wide world [be careful not to say one child over the other here!]. I never want you to have to hold on to big feelings that are painful. I am so glad you felt able to share them with me. Thank you. Mummy might get things wrong sometimes. And now you have told me about yesterday, I can really see that you probably just wanted to play with your friends and not have your sister hanging around.'

Watch as the light of recognition goes on for your child as they hear that you really 'get' how they felt! That they were not being bad: they just wanted to play without their sister for once!

In these moments you can really build that connection between you. Your child might have more 'stories' they have been telling themselves that suddenly start spilling out.

'And you told me off for breaking the vase with my ball!'

'And you told Auntie Pamela that I had been 'naughty'!'

'And the teacher told me I was lazy!'

And, and, and... Press into the pain and you can help your child to find a release.

Choices and consequences

We can offer our children more agency by giving them choices: 'Do you want to tidy your room now or later?' Or 'Do you want to have a bath now or after you eat supper?'

If my children are not listening when I am asking them to help me tidy the kitchen I might stop and remind them: 'Guys, I want to have a readathon with you tonight but if we don't work as a team, I won't have time to sit with you if I am left to tidy up the kitchen alone.' They can then reflect, do some 'little owl' thinking and make a choice.

If a child breaks something in anger, we can encourage them to consider how they can repair the consequence of their actions, perhaps saving the money to buy a replacement, or helping you to fix the item.

Don't fall into power struggles in choices and consequences – you want to work wise owl to little owl, pondering the choices and options you have together, then working through the potential consequences of those actions. This is how we help our children to regulate and problem-solve for themselves in the future.

Finally, use your words wisely and remember to praise more than you criticise!

Relate to educate

After big feelings have been released, you might tell a story to help your children to put their behaviour into context, talking them through what happened in a 'wondering way'.

'You wanted a biscuit. I said no. You were sad and disappointed. You got so angry. Those were some big feelings. I saw and heard how angry you were. But you did so well. You used your words and you remembered not to hit. Well done. Everyone needs to cry sometimes. Now you feel better. Thank you for showing me safely how you felt.'

Very often young children want to hear the story of how they got mad and cried, and how they resolved. As long as it's an empathic story, not a judgemental lecture! It helps them understand themselves and ensures they feel seen and heard.

PART THREE

Testing Times in the Real World

In Part Three, we look at some of the big arenas our children will now step into, often without us by their side. We will explore how best we can help them, and how to help themselves, building something crucial for mental well-being: a healthy sense of self.

While it's beyond the scope of this book to do justice to every situation our children will encounter in their primary years, I have tried to focus on a few areas where difficulties might typically arise.

Chapter Thirteen

School, Shaming and Separation Anxiety

*'Shame is the deepest of the "negative emotions",
a feeling we will do almost anything to avoid.'*
Dr Gabor Maté, *When the Body Says No*

Kirsten, mum to Joe, five, reached out to me on Instagram because Joe had been refusing to go to school. 'He keeps saying he has a stomach ache. It's so frustrating to have to try to persuade him and my husband and I are worried it will become a permanent thing if we can't persuade him to go.' Kirsten said she was resorting to bribes and even threats ('The headteacher will come and tell us off!'), even though she hated doing so. She admitted it had only upset her son more, leading to furious outbursts when she and her husband attempted to coax him out of the door.

Kirsten said her doctor said there was nothing medically wrong with Joe, so I asked her to consider her son's behaviour from the perspective of his five-year-old brain. What if Joe wasn't being 'difficult on purpose'? What if he just had a baboon who was fearful and, if so, why? Kirsten had been using the 'naughty' step with Joe and I suggested she try my soothing stair approach instead. Just before bedtime when Joe was snuggled up on her lap, she sat on the top stair and rocked him back and forth, before asking: 'Darling Joe, I am so sorry you are getting so upset about school. Can you help me to understand what it is you're finding difficult?'

Kirsten explained to me what happened next.

'I gently rocked him back and forth in my arms. I asked Joe again if he could tell me what it was that he hated about school. He immediately blurted out that he keeps getting hit by another child! He started sobbing and sobbing as though he'd never stop. He must have been holding in all that fear and hurt for so long and I was heartbroken to think he'd been carrying it alone. My husband and I had been dealing with him as though he was being 'naughty', yet all the time he was just petrified about going back into a classroom where he was afraid he'd be hit.'

Kirsten deployed SAS. First, she said what she saw: 'Oh no, Joe. How upsetting for you and how scary too. It's not OK for someone to hit you!' Then, she acknowledged the upset: 'No wonder you have not wanted to go to school!' Kirsten told me she also added an all-important apology of her own, for not understanding Joe sooner. Then, she soothed: 'It's OK. You are really brave to tell us. Remember, it's our job to keep you safe. We can help make this better. No one should be hurting anyone at school and now we can help.'

Kirsten told me Joe sank into her arms, and that it felt as if a great burden had been lifted. There is certainly a lightness to our children's energy when we help them offload an emotional burden. Kirsten said Joe stopped crying and turned to her and said, 'It's OK though, Mummy. It's just like having a bull in a field. I know I have to ignore him.'

Kirsten was amazed that her son had made the analogy. At just five! Our children are indeed more perceptive than we might give them credit for and they will often find quite sophisticated ways to contextualise what they are going through. I also reflected how stressful it must be for a little boy if he feels he has to face a 'raging bull' every day. No wonder he was finding it so difficult to leave the house!

Kirsten organised a meeting with the school and, with support for both boys, the matter was happily resolved.

There's always a cause for our children's behaviour; our job gets much easier when we can translate their Morse code.

School

Whether your child is starting out, moving up to senior school or is somewhere in between, plenty of situations will arise in any given day where your child's stress response will be triggered. It might be a teacher shouting or telling them off in class, difficulties with other children, as poor Joe experienced, or any manner of other issues that can feel incredibly triggering for children at this age. When our children feel understood, it results in increased brain activity associated with reward, positive feelings and social connection – all things that will support your relationship and ultimately your child's behaviour.

Separation Anxiety

If your child is struggling to separate from you, your first question should be why. What is it that your child's baboon doesn't find safe? Working with them, you might consider the first time your child found a transition tricky. Perhaps at nursery school. Remember, the baboon banks negative memories and they get tagged and remembered more quickly than positive ones. Any previous upsets can get triggered and projected when a child starts primary school. Staying curious and compassionate allows us to sit with our children and ask gently, 'I wonder if there is a part of you that remembers another time when being away from me felt difficult?'

Exploring difficult feelings carefully and tenderly is the most sure-fire way to exorcising them. Remember all the tools you now have at your disposal. You might ask your child to show you how it feels in their body when they have to leave you at the gate and what that feeling might say if it could speak? Separation anxiety is not a sign of weakness. It's simply the sign of a child who has a brain signalling that it doesn't feel safe.

Resolving separation anxiety can take time. There are no quick fixes, but ensuring your connection is strong, that you are keeping the lines of communication open, is much more likely to help your child build resilience and confidence slowly, rather than seeing them forced to cope with that anxiety alone. As always, never be afraid to seek help, either at school or support groups or contact a child therapist or counsellor – the more support you and your child have, the more quickly the issue is likely to be resolved.

Try to resist any well-intentioned, but sadly ill-informed advice you might receive to 'just drop and go, they'll be fine!' We have seen that when a child is afraid, their brain and body are awash with stress hormones. We also know that one of the best ways to lower stress levels is to spend time with an emotionally available adult. If a support teacher is available whom your child trusts and who has the time and understanding and can use calming techniques to ensure your child has a gentle transition, then great. Otherwise, it is worth working with the school for a period to go in with your child, to a place where you can help them to regulate, ultimately giving them the confidence to go in alone.

I know there is often an anxiety that 'if I do it now, he'll want me to do this every day'. But given everything you have learned, you know this is not how the brain works! Your child will be 'fine' when they feel fine. And that means being reassured they are safe. Once they feel safe, the anxiety – and often the behaviour – will typically dissipate.

Research has shown that children transitioning from nursery to primary school experience an increase in the stress hormone cortisol and suggests it can take as many as three to six months before cortisol concentration returns to baseline levels. It's why I would like to see 'bonding benches' outside every nursery, Reception and Year 1 entrances, where parents can sit with their children for a short period before school; away from pressure, or prying eyes in the queue. Somewhere that parents and children can co-regulate, using any of the somatic exercises I shared in Chapters Three, Four and Five. Not every child will need it, but it can be enormously helpful for a child who is experiencing some anxiety to have a safe place where they can sing a song or do some star jumps with their parents, finding creative and playful ways to release the energy of their fizzy lizard or bounding baboon. Yes, it can take an initial extra investment of our time, but better to invest it now to help our children return to calm, rather than having a child for whom separations are always associated with a sense of anxiety – and leaving them sitting with their adrenaline and cortisol coursing for the rest of the day.

This is important to note for children who struggle with regulating big emotions, or children who have experienced trauma. One teacher shared with me that a young girl who created 'chaos' at the school gate when leaving her foster carer could become calm and focused after just five minutes doing an obstacle course using the climbing frames in the playground.

Five minutes can be all that is needed to allow a child who is struggling with the transition to face the school day more confidently and calmly.

Parent Self-care for Tricky Separations

As parents, we can wonder why, after a tricky drop-off, we get the feedback from school staff that they are 'fine once they get to class'. If the teachers are warm and caring and understand the psychological significance of attachment, then that's wonderful because you can feel reassured your child is fine because they do indeed 'feel fine' given the new relational connections they are building at school. But do check in with your children because we also know they might rather be 'sitting' on their still fizzy stress response and 'fawning' or masking their 'not fine feelings' and, if so, that will need addressing.

Some schools install a camera in the Reception classrooms for a short period to reassure new parents waiting in the Reception hall that their children are well and happy, and that's a lovely idea if parents can sit and feel comfortable to watch while their children settle in. Separations are a big deal and it helps everyone involved when everyone feels contained and all our feelings are seen and heard!

In that regard, we know that our children pay great attention to our body language, facial expression and our tone of voice. Your nervous system communicates directly with your child's nervous system so it's good to be mindful that if we found separations difficult when we were younger, our own stress can be contagious. It can be helpful to arrange to speak with or spend an extra five minutes at the gate with your child's new teacher or a teaching assistant who will be your child's key person in class. If your child watches you having a relaxed chat with that person, their brain and nervous system registers: 'Mummy/Daddy thinks this person is safe, so I am safe to be with them too.'

Work with your child, acknowledge any wobbles and reassure them it's normal to find change and transitions difficult. Remember to use your creativity, coming up with playful solutions that can help your child feel connected to you, enduring the absence of your separation.

Holding in Mind Guessing Game

Child psychotherapist Emma Connor from Your Space Therapies shares this lovely game for children experiencing separation distress:

She calls it the 'Holding in Mind Guessing Game' and, as she explains, this is how it works.

Ask the child to choose a time of day for you to focus on them and guess what they are doing (you may want to playfully demonstrate what your super focused face looks like!).

At that time, you draw a picture of what you think the child is doing, fold it up and have it ready for school pick-up.

At school pick-up be excited to have the 'big reveal'; give your child the picture and see if you guessed right. This provides a lovely connection at pick-up (which can obviously be a time of big emotions) – this provides playfulness to support a successful reunion.

You probably didn't guess right! But, demonstrating to

your child you have held them in mind is the most important thing, not getting it right! You can say you will focus even harder next time.

The child could keep a scrapbook of the pictures, showing all the times the parent/carer guessed right and when they didn't. This creates a creative record of all the times they have been held in mind.

Creative Connections

For Wilbur's first week in Reception, I made up a song for us to sing before school: 'I love you and you love me, I'll be back for you at three!' Very often young children just need to know we are coming back! Remember, their baboon does not wear a watch and five minutes could be the same as five hours (or five days!) without having an accurate context of time.

Connection Bracelets

I am aware of schools who offer families 'connection bracelets' that children can wear to school. Parents 'load up' the bracelet with kisses each morning and the children can hold the bracelet to their cheek if they need a reassuring top-up of Mummy or Daddy's love during the day. Getting the transition right in the first few weeks – whether that's to primary school or for an older child heading to senior school – can pay dividends in the long run. Taking time off work or negotiating an earlier finish time during the first week or two so you can pick your child up personally (only if your 11-year-old wants it, that is!) can help to establish firmer foundations for the long term.

School Refusals

We are seeing an increasing number of children refusing outright to attend school. The effect of Covid and the extended lockdowns have had a massive impact. The organisation Not Fine in School was created as a resource for families with children who were experiencing barriers to attending school. The organisation launched in 2018 with 100 members. Post lockdown, they have nearly 40,000.

On their website they say 'Barriers often relate to unmet Special Educational Needs and Disabilities (diagnosed or suspected), physical or mental illness, bullying and assault, trauma, excessive academic pressure, overly strict behaviour policies, a missing sense of belonging, and an irrelevant curriculum.'

Psychotherapist and author Philippa Perry writes: 'What seems to be happening in the UK educational system is that the individual pupil is seen as the whole problem rather than acknowledging that the school environment and unhelpful government policies around targets are a part of this, too.' She continues: 'One size does not fit all. Many of our schools are not fit environments for our children – they are too noisy, scary and overwhelming, while resources are too stretched to do much about it.'

It is beyond the scope of this book to write in-depth about this issue, much as I would like to. What I will say is that if your child is finding the school environment difficult, please do not feel you and they must struggle alone. Every school and local authority should have what is known as EBSA (Emotionally Based School Avoidance) guidance. EBSA is a term that covers children and young people who experience challenges in attending school due to negative feelings (such as anxiety).

I have included recommended reading at the back of the book

and listed support groups too. If your child is refusing to go to school, there is a reason for it. When we take our children's feelings seriously and honour them, we help them to feel safer and in turn more understood. Working with schools to recognise the need for children to feel safe, with an adult they trust is vital.

Bullying

Ultimately, all our children need to feel safe at school. Every school should have effective measures to protect children from being bullied or becoming bullies. You can and should enlist the help of your school in that regard, but having your Cs in place will support your children's sense of self, and their ability to navigate other children, and enlist your help if they are having difficulty.

The NSPCC defines bullying as 'behaviour that hurts someone else. It includes name calling, hitting, pushing, spreading rumours, threatening or undermining someone. It can happen anywhere – at school, at home or online. It's usually repeated over a long period of time and can hurt a child both physically and emotionally.'

Bullying is not something any child should have to tolerate. We know some children who have been bullied can suffer post-traumatic stress disorder. As we saw with Joe, if a child does not feel safe at school, they can have problems sleeping, eating and suffer from stomach aches, headaches and other symptoms. It can affect a child's ability to learn and can ultimately be enormously damaging to a child's health.

Playtimes are the most common times when bullying occurs, yet they are typically the most understaffed periods in school. Wilbur once told me about a child who kept hitting him in the playground. Wilbur said he had 'told the teacher', but that the teacher had simply told the boys to 'play nicely' and 'be kind'. I arranged to meet with the teacher and asked her with genuine curiosity: how would you feel if a parent came into school and hit you and when you reported it to your headteacher, she told you to just 'be kind'?!

To understand our children, we must put ourselves in their shoes. Not only are they smaller, but they have a still-immature brain. Playtimes are some of the most stressful times in terms of triggering their threat system – the amygdala – the baboon.

It's not enough to tell children to just 'be kind' if bullying or overly rough behaviour is taking place. If schools, and society are really serious about tackling bullying, it would be best to resource playtimes with staff in sufficient numbers who have clear oversight and have been trained in both conflict resolution and understand the damaging impact bullying has on a child's still-developing brain.

BRAIN BOX

'The brain experiences social pain with the very same neural networks that recognise physical pain. The old adage that sticks and stones may break our bones but names can never hurt us is simply not true! The experience of social defeat and rejection can bring on feelings of shame – I am not good enough, I am not accepted, I am not lovable, I don't matter. These feelings can really affect our ability to think well of ourselves – the roots of self-esteem. It is vital that we take seriously any indication by a child that they have been bullied and respond with validation and empathy to their perceived experience, even if we have a very different view of the events. Physical pain and emotional

> pain are ameliorated through social support – our
> sensitivity to pain is reduced when someone connects
> with us in this way.'
> — Julie Harmieson, Director of Education and National Strategy
> Trauma Informed Schools UK (TISUK)

Left alone with feelings of rejection, a child's emotional pain will intensify. It can lead to that child projecting their feelings of shame and pain on to another child in turn, victimising them in the way they have been hurt. In psychotherapy we understand that we often attack in others what we cannot bear in ourselves. It explains why children will tend to pick on a child who displays vulnerability. Julie Harmieson says it is why 'it is so very important in incidences of bullying to work with both the victim and the offender, to be compassionate to the emotional pain that drives the need to make another hurt in the way you were.'

Organisations like Trauma Informed Schools and the NSPCC offer some excellent resources, as do many other organisations and children's mental health charities, and I reference them at the back of the book. If your child has experienced bullying, or you suspect might even be the bully, it is always best to ask for support and therapy and counselling can help enormously in this regard. The NSPCC advises that 'if you find out your child has done something to hurt someone else, you're likely to feel angry, disappointed or any number of other strong emotions. Explain that what they're doing is unacceptable. Children and young people don't always realise what they're doing is bullying, or understand how much their actions have hurt someone.'

Helping our children early on prevents unwelcome and harmful behavioural traits from developing further down the line. It is worth noting that students who perceive their school to be supportive are more likely to report bullying. It should also be considered that if we want to prevent a child's aggressive or controlling behaviour from being repeated, we must actively first seek to understand what's driving it. Children who bully might well be witnessing violence within the home or elsewhere, or are being bullied themselves. While punishing a child for their behaviour might be thought to 'work' in the short term, it is unlikely to resolve happily for the child, or those around them, in the future.

BRAIN BOX

'What punishment does, at best, is immediately suppress the behaviour. The trouble is, the research is unequivocal: what happens is the behaviour returns at the same rate.'

— Dr Alan Kazdin, Sterling Professor of Psychology and Child Psychiatry at Yale University and Director of the Yale Parenting Center

Bullying can take place between siblings too and is much underreported. We must recognise that 'hurt children, hurt children' and it is increasingly clear from research that sibling bullying is contributing to the bullying epidemic. Being bullied as a child can have a devastating effect which lasts a lifetime. It's important to address and tackle the underlying issues rather than dismiss or minimise bullying behaviour by telling one of your children, 'oh, they're only teasing'. If your child is being bullied by their sibling and does not yet have sufficient 'wise owl' capacity to share with you the depth of their emotional suffering, it can see them in a threatened baboon state and potentially also see him/her bullying other children in turn.

I will share more practical tips to support healthy sibling relationships in Chapter Fourteen.

Shame and a Child's Sense of Self

Shaming policies are sadly still adopted by many primary schools in order to maintain discipline. Keeping a child in during playtime, threatening them in front of peers with 'off breaks' or putting their photo on a behaviour chart in the classroom are all measures that are perceived to 'work'; but without appropriate guidance and support to contextualise the consequence, they can target a child's sense of self, simply leaving them thinking, 'If I do this, I am bad.'

> ### BRAIN BOX
>
> 'Shame is closely related to guilt, but there is a key qualitative difference. No audience is needed for feelings of guilt, no one else knows, for the guilty person is his own judge. Not so for shame. The humiliation of shame requires disapproval or ridicule by others.'
>
> — Dr Paul Ekman, Psychologist

Neuroscience reveals that a child's body responds to the psychological wounding of shame in the same way as a physical wound. If we are committed to supporting our children's mental health and wellbeing it would seem appropriate to replace these policies with evidence-based neurodevelopmental approaches that support parents, staff and children and ensure behaviour in the classroom is calm and receptive to learning.

Endings

Teachers are an incredibly vital presence in our children's lives and it's important to acknowledge the enormous value and influence they can have on our children's development and wellbeing. If your child has enjoyed a particularly strong bond with their teacher, it's important to recognise that they might experience a sense of loss around the end of the school year, or even at the end of term.

We need to allow space for these emotions and help our children to grieve the loss of that person. Some parents tell me they find it difficult to hear how much a teacher means to their child, but I hope we can be comforted that our children have experienced the warmth of another emotionally available adult when we have naturally not been around. Endings are very important to acknowledge given they can influence how our children approach future relationship endings later in life.

If your child is leaving their school, here are some suggestions that can help to make the separation a little easier.

Firstly, never spring change on your child or leave it until the last minute to tell them if they are changing schools or you are moving home! Change is difficult for most of us; the more time your child has to process the ending, the gentler and easier the transition will typically be. In therapy, I approach the ending of the therapeutic relationship from the very first day I am with a child! Hard though it can be for a child to experience an ending, this is an important process. It helps to ultimately build resilience and confidence that enables the child to move forward. If I left it until the last week to let the child know we were ending the therapeutic relationship, the shock of the ending would likely be very detrimental.

In the same way, you can begin talking to your child about their ending – whether you know a teacher is leaving, if it's coming up to the end of the school year, or the end of primary school itself.

Whatever emotions your child might (or might not) express, you can hold the space, tune into their tears or even just their silence, knowing that you can use your Cs to let them know you will be there as a consistent and steady presence, and together you will come through.

Your child might be invited to make a final drawing or piece of writing to say goodbye to the class. The drawing can either be brought home or kept in the class for their friends to remember them by. You can make something similar at home too.

Your child might make a portfolio of work they've achieved during their time in the class, to symbolise that what they experienced there is worthy of care and protection.

Other children in the class might prepare special cards to present to your child. At the presentation of the cards, other members of the group can be asked to say what it is about your child that they have appreciated and will remember.

Just as adults can find change difficult, so can our children. With the help of our Cs – and keeping curious – we can guide our children through these big life situations and transitions.

Chapter Fourteen

Screentime, Social Media and Self-Image

'Your cellphone has already replaced your camera, your calendar, your alarm clock. Don't let it replace your family.'

Smartphones and Screens

When he introduced the first iPhone in 2007, the then Apple CEO, Steve Jobs, said, 'Every once in a while, a revolutionary product comes along and changes everything.' He was right. Smartphones have radically changed how we think, work, play and communicate. It is interesting, however, that Steve Jobs was among tech moguls like Google CEO Sundar Pichai, former Facebook executive Chamath Palihapitiya and Snapchat CEO Evan Spiegel who all restrict the access their children have to devices.

According to Walter Isaacson, author of *Steve Jobs*, dinner in the Jobs household was held 'at the big long table in their kitchen, discussing books and history and a variety of things. No one ever pulled out an iPad or computer. The kids did not seem addicted at all to devices.'

The reference to 'addiction' is interesting because smartphones and screens are designed to make addicts of us – and our children. The content we can access via smartphones, and the way we consume it, taps into the brain's dopamine-driven feedback loop that keeps us hooked. Social media sites are designed to activate similar mechanisms in the brain as slot machines, and even cocaine.

Successful sales of books like Catherine Price's *How to Break up with Your Phone* suggest we are slowly waking up to the negative impact on our time, our sleep, our sense of self, our attention and our mental health. Yet the amount of time our children are spending on screens is increasing. The lockdown policy during the Covid pandemic served to increase children's screen usage significantly; a Harris Poll survey in 2020 found nearly seven in ten parents of five- to 17-year-olds said their children's screentime had increased, and 60% felt they 'have no choice but to allow it.'

One global analysis found primary school children's screentime had increased by an extra hour and 20 minutes a day on average.

Many schools continue to adopt a more tech and screen-based educational model for study, done both in and outside of school. But what is all this screentime doing to our children's brains – and ultimately their behaviour?

Early data from a landmark National Institutes of Health (NIH) study that began in 2018 indicates that children who spent more than two hours a day on screentime activities scored lower on language and thinking tests. And some children with more than seven hours a day of screentime experienced thinning of the brain's cortex, the area of the brain related to critical thinking and reasoning.

Certainly, there is now enough research emerging for us to question the wisdom of sitting our children passively in front of a screen for long periods. Carlota Nelson is the director of *Brain Matters*, a feature documentary about early brain development. Writing for UNICEF, she concludes: 'Unlike reading books which gives time for children to process words, images and voices, the constant absorption of on-screen images and messages affects a child's attention span and focus.' She adds that 'screens curtail the ability to control impulses given children need their dose of boredom. It teaches them how to cope with frustration and control their impulses. If young children are constantly being stimulated by screens, they forget how to rely on themselves or others for entertainment.'

We know that the more we repeat an activity, the more our brain changes in accordance. In 1949, the neuropsychologist Donald Hebb explained how pathways in the brain are formed and reinforced through repetition. He coined the phrase 'neurons that fire together, wire together'.

My father was a London licensed taxi driver. To gain his licence, he had to pass something called 'the Knowledge'. It involved years of dedication, driving around the labyrinth of London's 25,000 streets, committing them all to memory. In 2000, a team of neuroscientists at University College London published a study, having followed 79 aspiring taxi drivers for four years. Their research revealed that the successful candidates' hippocampus (part of the baboon memory bank) was larger than those candidates who had dropped out. Neurobiologist Howard Eichenbaum of Boston University observed of the study, 'It shows you can produce profound changes in the brain with training. That's a big deal.'

It is indeed a big deal, and something to consider as our

children – with their still-immature brains – spend increasingly significant portions of their day passively staring or scrolling on a screen. For just as neurons that fire together, wire together, so the opposite is also true.

Former Google design ethicist Tristan Harris went on to co-found the Centre for Humane Technology to raise awareness about how manipulative devices are, going so far as to say the addiction to smartphones is causing 'human downgrading'.

As I said in Chapter One, we parents are in the brain development business, so we – and schools – really want to ensure we are serving our children well.

Certainly, there are increasing moves to raise awareness of the addictive nature and the distraction of screens and smartphones. Parent-led groups like www.safescreens.org campaign want to see cigarette-style health warnings about screentime and all smartphone-related advertisements.

One of the most common arguments against regulation is that it should be for parents to monitor and restrict use. But, as you will know, screentime can be hard to police, and especially if you have a child nearing primary school leaving age when peer pressure to have a phone is a powerful thing. Children for whom social settings might be overwhelming can find comfort and solace in peer relationships they make online and certainly there are games and apps that I know many children enjoy from both an academic and recreational point of view.

More longitudinal studies and research is needed to clarify what might constitute 'healthy' or otherwise amounts of time on a screen for older children.

Without more specific and formal guidance for our primary-aged children, it leaves parents to decide what is right for us and our children. I know from personal experience how hard it can be to establish boundaries around screentime now they are used increasingly for homework as well as in play.

This is not to ignore benefits of screens; they can help us out when we're busy, and half an hour of our children watching something age-appropriate and fun can give us all a much-needed moment of quiet from time to time. Our smartphones and screens can be social life savers too when our loved ones live far away and for children who might seek more connections outside of school. Who hasn't enjoyed Face-Timing family around the world during birthday or festive celebrations, or holding up our phones so Grandma can watch our children race on sports day?

So, what can we do to ensure the time our children spend on their screens is as reasonable as can be?

For older children it can be helpful to talk about the research, explaining that screens are not simply passive and 'benign' in that they are programmed with algorithms designed to get them hooked. In an age-appropriate manner, we can also speak to our children about their brain and the stimulus it needs to grow healthily for the future. You could speak to your child about how their brain changes with the activities they do. Just as they will get good playing the piano, or learning to read when they do a 'little and often', so their brain can get 'lazy' if they are sat passively staring at a screen. If your children push back, you can explain that just as it is also your job to keep them physically safe, it is your job to ensure that their brain develops safely and healthily too. You can show them the research that reveals how our phone messes with our memory, our focus and can reduce our enjoyment and engagement with the world if we are constantly 'online'.

Many parents tell me of the struggle they have to remove their children's screens and the fights that can ensue. One mother even sent me a video of the 'tantrum' her five-year-old son had when she threatened to take his screen away. The distress our children display when we remove these 'objects of desire' is real. They are not being 'naughty' when they scream and shout. Recognising that screen use releases dopamine in the brain and negatively impacts impulse control helps us to be compassionate and realistic. If our children are now addicted, they need our help to be 'weaned off'. Physician Dr Kathryn Lorenz observes: 'If there's a struggle over stopping screen use, that's usually a warning sign that they're fairly addicted to it and their brains are really craving it.'

Be compassionate with your children if you have previously allowed them screentime but are now considering how best to reduce it. You might start by introducing a time limit (or removing them if you can) during the week, and a time limit at weekends – explaining why. We don't want to set ourselves up against our children. Neither of us is the enemy. But we do need to recognise that we have given them access to a device that is designed to be addictive. Our children are not responsible for creating the addiction, we are.

We can also, if we are honest (!), recognise that addiction in ourselves.

Part of successfully limiting our children's screentime is about setting a good example. Turning off the TV and putting our own phones away in front of our children is much more effective for modelling the behaviour we want to see.

Social Media

Our children should not be using social media yet. The minimum age to open an account on nearly every social media platform is currently 13. I know, however, that if you have teenagers, or your children are at the older end of the age range, social media will be on your radar and it is worth covering aspects of it here. Social media can be an incredibly effective force for good. I find it useful for connecting with other professionals working in the field of child mental health and I use my own social media channels to share and demonstrate tools that I hope can be helpful for families. But, as is also now abundantly clear, when it comes to our children's mental health it can also be a force for grave ill.

'We make body image issues worse for one in three teen girls,' said one slide from a 2019 presentation that was posted to Facebook's internal message board. Chamath Palihapitiya, who joined Facebook in 2007 and became its vice president for user growth, said in 2017 that he feels 'tremendous guilt' about the company he helped make: 'I think we have created tools that are ripping apart the social fabric of how society works.'

Being concerned about social media's impact on our children's self-image means we must also be mindful of the information we share about them. The data we share about our children today could be revealed by search algorithms for years to come.

Children's charities remind parents that the 'innocent' information we post today could be used by other children to make fun of them later, even bully them at senior school. They point out that potential employers might take issue with certain posts, and that digital kidnapping can see our children's images and identity repurposed – even turning up on disturbing websites and forums, some of them dedicated to child pornography.

Finally, when we share information about our children, we do well to recognise that we are giving away their data. Something they might not thank us for when they are adults and might want more specific ownership of their digital imprint.

When or if it does come to addressing the idea of your child having social media apps, it will be worth doing your research together. Look at the studies that show the evidence that demonstrates that some apps have an even stronger link to mental health problems than even 'screentime' more generally.

Share the research that shows that time spent passively scrolling does not generally make us feel more connected or happy. And discuss how social media apps are designed to keep people using them as long as possible.

If your child expresses a strong desire to go online and spend time on a social media app, you might ask them about their goals and what matters to them. You can use your curiosity if it feels appropriate to do so with a 'wondering question', exploring out loud what it is that's really driving the desire. 'I am wondering if there is a part of you that wants to feel affirmed as "pretty" or "popular" or "cool"?'

Many times in the therapy room, children might talk about their desire to 'be famous' and I respond with curiosity: 'Ah, so I wonder what it is about being famous that you think might feel so nice?'

The answers children give tend to be very revealing. There is an innocence and an inner need that we might want to then explore and use what we call 'psychoeducation' to reflect the true 'story' rather than the one they likely are telling themselves.

'So, if I am famous, everyone will know me? Or everyone will like me?'

'Well, you know, quite a lot of people who are famous thought the same thing. But if they are not happy in themselves, then it doesn't really work like that.'

You might even fire off a truth arrow with an: 'Ah, OK, so am I perhaps hearing that you are not feeling "pretty/cool/popular" enough right now? Can we chat more about that?'

These conversations can help you and your child have important conversations around self-esteem and body image, or any area of vulnerability where they might need some support.

Ensuring all your Cs are in place will help you to navigate this clearly tricky social and online landscape once your children come of age. Do research the issues and don't be afraid to seek advice.

Chapter Fifteen

Siblings

'It's very, very hard for children to have to share us. In fact, when a younger sibling is born, virtually all children worry that they aren't good enough – why else would their parents have gotten a newer, younger, model?'

– Clinical Psychologist, Dr Laura Markham

However much we prepare our children, the introduction of new additions to the household will always change the family dynamic, regardless of best intentions!

In my first book, I compared the arrival of a new sibling to a husband coming home with another woman, and I did not say that in jest!

Sibling rivalry has its roots in evolution. We see it across all aspects of the animal kingdom, where (mostly older) siblings will even go so far as to kill in the competition to survive. It is natural for our children to sometimes feel threatened and fight over resources, whether that's food, possessions, or the attention and love of Mum and Dad.

Growing up with siblings can offer our children great gifts of learning; how to express their needs without shouting or hitting, to delay gratification and learn how to live peacefully alongside others. But your children will experience deep and conflicting emotions too. Older children might have a deep sense of love and affection for younger siblings, while also experiencing sadness and even anger at the loss of the exclusive relationship they previously enjoyed with you/your partner. Younger children, who have never known life without having to share resources, might learn to work harder to attract your time and attention. Unconscious sibling rivalries can emerge that, if unchecked (or even unwittingly encouraged), can remain for the rest of their lives.

I was reminded of this while watching a Netflix documentary about Arnold Schwarzenegger. He spoke candidly about his upbringing and how his father facilitated constant and intense competition between him and his brother. Poignantly, he said their relationship was never close, and was ultimately estranged.

Many siblings will experience a natural sense of competition but if we want our children to become firm friends for life, we must be mindful to direct the energy of their innate competitiveness in healthy ways. At home, we adopt the approach (paraphrasing the Japanese author Haruki Murakami): 'The only opponent you have to beat is yourself, the way you were yesterday.'

Rather than jump straight to punish our children if they fight, say, or do mean things to each other, we can remember to use our curiosity and wonder what's really driving any hurtful behaviour. Strong statements like 'I HATE HER!' or 'I WISH SHE WOULD DIE' should make us curious about what our children might be feeling on the inside. As we have seen, hurtful words and expressions of hate typically have their roots in fear. 'I hate you', translated, might mean: 'I hate that you comforted my brother after I hit him, but you didn't comfort me' or 'I hate that my baby sister gets to spend more time with you because she doesn't have to go to school'. Ultimately our children's anger is a defence against the deep vulnerable feeling of 'I'm scared you might love them more.' As the neuroscientist Jaak Panksepp said, 'The language of loss is the language of pain.'

If you are observing excessive rivalry and jealousy among your children, it's very often a red flag that you'll need to strengthen your C of connection. When a child feels strongly connected and secure in our love, there is less need to feel 'threatened' if we praise their sibling or express delight in their achievements. Jealousy and possessiveness are displays of insecurity and dysregulation.

TOOLKIT TIP
The Power of 'One-to-One'

Siblings have to share A LOT; whether it's bedrooms, toys, mealtimes, the journey to school – and of course, US. Spending quality time one-to-one with each of your children can really help to minimise sibling rivalry. Ten minutes spent with each child every day can be enough to top up their emotional cup and ensure their sense of connection with you remains consistent and strong. It also conveys to each child that we value them as an individual. It helps to build a strong sense of self and I find it's often the best time for facilitating those conversations that count.

Personally, I find bath time and bedtime the easiest times to implement 'one-to-one time'. As well as catching up on the day, I'll often use the time to read a therapeutic story, some of which are my own, and some I will reference at the back. These offer a great opportunity to help each child connect with any unresolved feelings that might be affecting their behaviour.

Ideally, we would also spend a full hour of play with each child over the weekend too. An hour where they get to have exclusive time with you! One hour where they get to choose what to do; without having to consider an older or younger brother or sister. This is time where they get to be reminded of what it is to feel your wholly attentive love. They might want to go for a walk, climb a tree, do some colouring, reading, play a board game or head out bowling. The only boundaries are the obvious ones: that it doesn't cost you the earth, and it's safe and age-appropriate!

I find a certain magic happens in one-to-one time. It's when my children will most often open up to me about how they feel and with only one child to pay attention to, I can really shift and surrender to the world of my child.

I know some parents who, every year, will also try to take each of their children away by themselves for an entire weekend. They might go camping or stay home and ask grandparents to babysit siblings.

I appreciate that in busy households, especially if you are parenting solo, there are only so many hours in the day. But building in as much one-to-one time with each of your children can bring enormous benefits, not only to minimising sibling rivalry, but for us as parents too.

Sibling Rivalry and Conflict Resolution

Siblings who are close in age, same-sex and different temperaments might clash more than others, but ultimately, we will all see flashes of sibling rivalry in our children sometimes. Teaching our children the art of healthy conflict resolution is crucial if you want them to live happily and peacefully and learn how to work alongside others in the workplace and broader community later in life. But how?

If your children are a little older and attempting to resolve an argument themselves, it can be wise to first hold back and observe; seeing if they can succeed without you stepping in.

However, if they're struggling, don't leave your children to resolve conflict alone. It's a hard skill to master and without guidance it can see older, or more powerful children 'winning', which could instil an unhealthy power dynamic that can continue to play out throughout life.

If tempers are running high, take a pause before you act, imagine you are putting on that big empathy suit and notice your own feelings and the potential for fight or flight when you do. Taking a breath before you enter the fray means you get to model self-regulation and resolve conflict calmly, helping us much more than if we allow our baboon to enter the fray.

Empathise with and listen to each child – regardless of 'who has done what'. When each baboon feels heard, it's easier for little owls to swoop in. When you give each child a 'fair hearing', it builds up trust that it's better to ask for support if they are struggling, rather than trying to fight on alone. Firmly but calmly remind your children of your contract (see Chapter Eleven), which applies to behaviour with siblings too: 'no hitting, or hurting each other, or the room'.

Help your children to self-regulate, either doing a 'palm pause' or taking a deep breath before they tell you what has happened will take work and practice, but again, these are vital skills to master.

TOOLKIT TIP
Giant Stomping and Heave Ho-ing

This is a somatic exercise I might intuitively deploy in the therapy room if a client is having real difficulty with self-regulation. If they are stomping around the room, shouting and pounding their fists with rage and injustice, I might join them, stamping my feet too and repeating their words with the same energy before slowing myself down to stomp on the spot. Taking a deep breath, I then 'moan' the energy out, in what I can only describe as a deep 'hurgghhhhhhh', letting all my air and big energy out. Then, I reach up to 'capture' the angry energy and contain it, bringing it down before 'pushing' it down into the earth. It's a wonderfully grounding exercise for the nervous system and my clients will often stop and copy me, typically delighting in the sense of calm they feel after such an expressive yet safe release.

It can be a beautiful (and at appropriate times, fun) way of showing siblings how to release their anger, stomping around while they rant and rage, but sending all that energy down into the earth, rather than detonating and spraying their anger out onto those around them.

My children are now much better at resolving issues and arguments (having had a LOT of practice!) but there are still times when tiredness and irritability will creep in and they need my help to resolve the niggles.

Recently, Clemency hit Wilbur, leaving a mark on his arm, which is very unlike her. When he came to me wailing, I first used SAS to say what I saw.

'Oh, Wilbur! I can see you are hurt. Come, sweetheart – show Mummy.'

Using tender words, I offer up a cuddle, which serves to regulate him and ensure his baboon calms down, rather than escalating the fight he's clearly been having with his sister.

Now I can call Clemency into the room. Wilbur feels contained in my arms, which allows me to remain calm and keep curious. I want Clemency to see that I am concerned that Wilbur is hurt, but equally to trust that I will hear her side of the story. I start by saying what I SEE.

'Clemency – there is a red mark on Wilbur's arm. He's hurt and you look CROSS. What happened?' (I am not endorsing what she has done – this is the opening salvo to having a curious conversation!)

Clemency growls. 'Wilbur's always coming into my room and messing up my things!'

Ahh ... Now I do know that when Wilbur is bored, his little baboon brain can seek to 'create havoc' and torment Clemency just to prompt a reaction.

'Oh, Clemency, I'm sorry. I can understand why you might be annoyed and I am sorry that I wasn't there to help.'

I am still soothing and regulating Wilbur with a cuddle.

He knows I will listen to his side of the story too. I turn to him and say, 'OK, Wilbur, can *you* tell me what happened?'

Wilbur, in my arms, gives me a look that tells me all I need to know!

'Hmm. Wilbur, you do know that is Clemency's space. If you are bored, you must come to Mummy.'

I then turn back to Clemency, 'OK, sweetheart, I know that's frustrating, but you know we don't hit. If Wilbur won't leave when you've asked him to, do you think you can come to me rather than lashing out and hurting him?'

Understanding what has happened allows us to use our calm wise owl to address the big picture. Clemency's wise owl had tried to do the right thing and ask Wilbur to stop coming into her room. Clearly, after too many times, her baboon had eventually snapped.

In situations like these, I don't feel the need to punish. I want my children to be able to reflect and learn from the experience, understanding that Wilbur has been hurt and I am not happy about the behaviour. I want Clemency to reflect that she should have come to me to ask for help before tipping over into fight or flight. Working with both children helps them to understand where things went wrong and how they can repair and move forward.

'Wilbur, do you think you can use your words now and tell Clemency you wanted her attention, rather than teasing her to get it?'

Wilbur: 'I just wanted her to play with me!'

Clemency: 'But I didn't want to play right then!!'

Me: 'OK, so can you have that conversation together now and see if you can find a solution that works, rather than shouting and hitting?'

Wilbur: 'I'm sorry, Clemency. I was bored; I just wanted to play with you.'

Clemency: 'I'm sorry that I lost my temper. If you sit quietly, you can play in my room. I don't want to play right now, though, so you just need to wait until I have finished reading, OK?'

Me: 'OK, that's really kind of Clemency, Wilbur; she's saying if you respect her room, and do as she asks, you can stay and perhaps she will play with you when she's ready. But do you think you can sit alone for that long or do you need my help?'

Wilbur: 'I can read a book. It's OK, thank you, Clemency.'

Conscious conflict resolution takes time and practice. It's tough enough for adults to master! But listening to both children, using SAS – once again, say what you see, acknowledge the upset, then soothe – we can help each of our children to feel heard and seen. I am also modelling the calm behaviour I want to see in future rather than yelling at Clemency for hitting her brother or telling Wilbur off for annoying her. Ultimately, it sees both children apologise to the other authentically, respecting each other's perspective and learning to come to me more quickly in future before things escalate.

I am also reminded that for Wilbur, his busy brain needs stimulation and that's my job, not Clemency's. Helping Wilbur reflect on his behaviour helps him to understand that his baboon often acts out when he is bored. We can look at this together and find ways to support his baboon, giving him more SEEKING activities to do, such as playing, problem solving and fun stuff that keeps him active. This will help him elsewhere too – at school, for example. It means he can be more self-aware and come to me in future when he's feeling bored, or needs attention, rather than falling into a destructive cycle of 'creating carnage' in order to feel 'alive'.

Clemency learns she can trust that she can come to me for support before she tips over into baboon mode herself; using words to maintain her boundaries without resorting to using her fists.

Our children come as discrete packages with their own characteristics and personalities and will have different ways of behaving and being. No child has ever had the same 'parenting' in that our first-borns will have had our time and care exclusively before their siblings arrived on the scene! Younger children have only ever known life with other children around and will often have learned they need to work harder to get your attention.

Parents can sometimes identify one child as the 'difficult one' or 'problem child'. It can happen often in families with three children. Not only can negative labels stick, but it sees us missing important cues about what it is that their behaviour is really telling us. Perhaps the third child simply feels left out and is doing whatever it takes to be seen?

Embrace your children as individuals, with their own individual way of expressing themselves. One child might scream and shout when they're angry, another might retreat into angry sulking or silence. Using your Cs will encourage them both to communicate their feelings more healthily and ensure they each get to feel heard.

Boundaries and How to Place Them

It's important to teach our children how to place firm boundaries around their space and their bodies. Not only will it help to ensure siblings learn to respect each other, but it will serve our children in later life too.

TOOLKIT TIP

Palm Power

This is something I suggested to Clemency after the bedroom 'boredom' battle.

If a sibling, or another child, is invading our space, we can throw our arms out in front of us, holding our hands upright, palms facing our 'opponent', saying a very firm and loud STOP! or NO! as we do. This practice not only helps a child to discharge the 'fight' energy of the stress response but is also a very strong and clear signal of 'NO!'.

Palm power helps our children to place a virtual boundary around themselves and their body, and, if we are within earshot, it gives us a clear signal that it might be time to step in.

Encourage your children to practise saying STOP! or NO! using different volumes or tones of voice. If a child or adult breaches their boundary in the future, it can help them to more readily find that same strong voice to defend themselves without feeling the need for their fists to do the talking for them.

We want our children to become adults for whom it feels normal and natural to place firm verbal boundaries around other people's behaviour. The more they practise, the more familiar and comfortable it will become to tell someone, 'No, that is NOT acceptable behaviour,' or, 'Stop what you are doing. I don't appreciate it.'

TOOLKIT TIP

Conflict Resolution: 'Speak From the I'

Part of my training to become a therapist involved participating in 'group therapy'. This is where students and one or more facilitators meet to interact and discuss a variety of different topics. Some of the subjects are designed to be contentious. The aim of the exercise is to allow everyone to feel heard, as well as find ways to resolve conflict if something is said that someone finds offensive or triggering. The only 'rule' was to always speak from the 'I'. So, rather than saying 'you hurt my feelings when you said that', or 'what you said was really offensive', we learned to say, 'when you said x, I felt like that'. Speaking from the 'I' allows us to take ownership of our feelings, rather than blaming someone for how they 'made us feel'. It allows us to state our needs if something is said that we find offensive or disagree with. In this way, the other person can consider and reflect whether they might have expressed themselves differently or given more consideration to the impact their words might have had. It also allows the person who feels offended to interrogate their reaction and reflect whether it was directly related to what was said, or perhaps came from a place of previous hurt.

For siblings, we can encourage them to speak from the 'I' when they are trying resolve an argument or when they have upset each other. Clemency might tell Wilbur, 'When you took the biggest bowl of porridge it felt like you didn't care about me.' Or Wilbur might tell Mike in the park after a meltdown, 'I'm sorry, I got cross. It's just when you took Clemency out to buy a new bike yesterday, I felt jealous

because I have to have her old one.' (Genuine story –
Wilbur is nine now and his little owl is gaining her wings!)

We can use this tool effectively in our adult relationships
too. As we saw in Chapter Nine on communication, being
able to speak from the 'I' helps us to resolve matters that
feel incredibly important to us, because they feel very
personal. So, rather than get cross and irritable with our
partners when they are clearly distracted and we are trying
to download our day, we might say, 'When I try to talk to
you but you pick up your phone and I can see you're only
half listening, I feel rejected.'

This gives them the space to respond – calmly, and less
defensively, because when we share something that shows
our vulnerability (rather than use our baboon defence), we
can engage wise owl to wise owl, given we can all instantly
appreciate how that sense of rejection can feel.

Working towards mutual understanding in this way can take
practice, but it's great for our children to see if we want them to
model that behaviour too. It means we are helping them achieve
the crucial life skill of what Professor Peter Fonagy, CEO of the
Anna Freud Centre, calls 'mentalisation' (see page 26).

Quick-fire Solutions to Universal Sibling Squabbles

Back-of-the-Car Bickering

Boredom can create havoc with backseat behaviour! Prevention
is always better than cure, so mindful of not just sticking our

children in front of a screen, we must plan ahead of situations like long journeys and bring games, audio books, activities and actively consider what our children can do that will keep busy minds busy.

Stick a note on the dashboard that says CALM! It's hugely stressful on long journeys when the kids are fighting in the back. I confess this is one area of parenting where my baboon is often on a hair trigger and if there's carnage in the car, I advise you to pull over somewhere safe and regulate. Remember, our baboons get stressed out by anything that feels unsafe and being in charge of a fast-moving vehicle when soft toys and lord knows what else are being launched from the back seat is a sure-fire way to see our baboons literally in the driving seat!

Create a car contract that outlines who gets to sit where, how often they swap seats, whether someone will go in the front if the children are arguing, and if so, who? It should also cover using kind words, that there is no hitting (or kicking!), and what happens if there is? Will we pull over somewhere safe and everyone gets out for a kick stretch and 20 star jumps? Prior preparation, as they say in the military, prevents poor performance!

Setting off while your children are sleepy, whether early in the morning or later at night, is a reliable way to have them fall asleep so you can journey in peace.

And if you don't have that option, and all else fails, for long journeys you might do what we have learned to do (the hard way!) and create a mid-seat separation using pillows or luggage to reduce the opportunities for niggling.

Sharing

When our children refuse to share, it can feel quite triggering – given how we might feel we are failing in our duty to raise decent, civilised and generous-spirited little people. The truth is, it can still be quite hard for children to share at this age, especially with toys that might have an emotional attachment. And, while we want our children to notice and acknowledge the needs of others, we don't want them to think they have to give up cherished possessions just because someone else asks for them. In essence, we don't want children who become adults who have been conditioned to put other people's needs before their own.

But we do want to teach empathy, impulse control, working well in a team and negotiation skills. So, how?

Empower your children to feel able to ask for what they want, but also help them to accept that if their sibling is playing with that particular toy, they will need to wait until the sibling is happy to hand it over. Some psychologists call this 'long turn taking'. We might need to help our children with this initially, given turn taking in this way is something of a skill to master. In our house, it has sometimes meant I have sat and played with the child who was waiting – but, in time, this does become easier. It's a good investment of our time because we are helping our children to understand that:

- I might cry for things, but I won't always get my way.
- I can sit and wait for things, trusting 'all will be well' (self-regulation).
- It's OK if I find that difficult; Mummy and/or Daddy are there to help.
- It feels really good when my sibling hands over the thing I

want. It means they understand my desire and have been kind. I can learn how to do that for them, too, and get to experience how it feels to be generous. I can think about my sibling's feelings when they're having to wait too.

- I can use my own things for as long as I want, which makes me feel good and empowered.

We need to help our children with sharing, understanding that it can be hard to do, but when we teach them this way of taking 'long turns' we are fostering empathy, warmth between siblings and a mutual sense of what it means to be kind.

Playdates

I always like my children to include the other on playdates where they can, but I won't enforce this because it can feel really special to have friends over. I also recognise that Wilbur's idea of fun might not be Clemency's, so I ask him to honour the fact she doesn't want him crashing into her room when she's trying to spend quiet time with a friend. It can be hard for one child to have to watch their sibling having fun, however, so I might suggest doing an activity together instead, giving us much-needed one-to-one time too.

Who Do You Love the Best?

We never want our children to think we love one child more than another. If your child is worrying that you do then it tells you those Cs need firming up. Many of us will say to our children 'I love you all the same', which is all good, but as our children get older we might want to be more specific.

I might say, 'Well now, that's a very interesting question because the answer is of course I love you both very, very much. You are both so, so special to me, I would be lost without each of you. There isn't another like you in the whole wide world so I can't compare!' I might go further still and emphasise: 'Do you know my love is so, so BIG! It's bigger than all the stars in all the sky. There's so much love I have enough for both of you just the same!'

If your child still seems unconvinced, we might want to delve a little deeper into the 'why' behind the question.

'But I am hearing that perhaps a part of you wonders if that is really true?'

'Perhaps there is a part of you that wonders if I might love Clemency more. Am I right?'

Again, don't be afraid to fire a little truth arrow here. If there are tears, it means that a hurt bubble has burst and now you can turn to soothe.

'Oh, sweetheart, what a big thing to have been holding. It's very normal for children to wonder sometimes if perhaps Mummy might love their brother or sister more. But what a big thing to have to carry. I wonder if there is anything that might have made you worry about that?'

And THEN you are likely to have those all-important conversations that count.

Using our C of curiosity helps us to understand not only the question, but the worry or fear behind it. Then you can trust your soothing, tender words will heal any hurts much more powerfully than you know.

Chapter Sixteen

Difference, Difficulties and 'Disorder'

'This might sound simple, but I cannot overstate this: the single most important thing is recognizing what the problem is in the first place.'
Paediatrician, Dr Nadine Burke Harris

My friend's father tragically died when she was just a baby. She recently shared with me that when she was at primary school, she told her friends her dad was a famous pop star to explain why he was never around. She perpetuated the fantasy even into adolescence and the lie became a source of great shame until a friend gently unburdened her of it.

Children have a universal and innate need to belong. The threat of social exclusion can feel unbearable to the ancient baboon brain. It means children are often very sensitive to and aware of 'differences', either in themselves or in others. They might have parents who are divorced, in prison, separated, same-sex, much older than those of their peers, or parents who might be less financially able. What might not be an issue for us can be a big deal for our children. It is vital that we consider every child's experience of school and how they view their place in the world. Laura Henry-Allain MBE, author of *My Skin, Your Skin*, does excellent work in this field. She says: 'We sometimes forget how important it is that every child needs to feel confident about their background, identity and who they are. On my travels, when I discuss the topic of identity, I invite children to draw, write or make marks about their families. I am blown away when children can show an understanding of who is in their family and where they come from in the world. Many parents comment that this was the first time their child had thought about their background. This is important for children's self-esteem and self-image; they know where they come from, even if their heritage is from a number of countries. Children should feel empowered to talk about food, language and celebrations that form a part of their cultural heritage and this does not come from a place of shame but a place of pride. It is important that teachers have an understanding of every child's background – their race, religion and culture, for example. We know, for instance, that not every child lives with a mum and dad and that children live in many different types of households: same-sex, kinship or lone parents, to name just a few.'

Professional curiosity and being comfortable asking sensitive questions about a child's experience is essential. Susanne McCafferty, the headteacher of Bainsford Primary School in Falkirk, says, 'When I started as a teacher, I moved into an area of significant deprivation; no one told me what home life might be like for the children in my care. I gave one boy a hard time because he hadn't brought his homework jotter in, thinking that his house was like my house. The headteacher took me aside, then took me to the wee boy's house, and I couldn't find a bed, never mind a homework jotter. That was hard-hitting, but I realised then that we have to start teaching children differently.'

Being considerate of a child's experience – whether they are looked-after children, they're bereaved, have parents going through a difficult divorce, or are having a tough time generally – and being mindful of the potential for feelings of difference, allows us to consider how that child might in turn then behave differently. Child psychiatrist Dr Bruce Perry suggests school staff record the number of positive interactions they have with children who are struggling, especially those who are relationally deprived, to ensure no child who needs support, and to feel secure, is overlooked.

Ensuring we create the strongest foundations by investing in all your Cs will ensure our children not only feel safer, and more connected, but also better understood.

Difficulty

The majority of us will sadly face difficulty at some stage in our lives; and that includes our children. Whether it's due to difference, having a disability, big life changes like divorce, separation, the loss of a loved one, moving house, changing school, illness, accidents or any other adversity, life is not without challenges and few of us are immune.

Research shows us that when we are supported by emotionally available adults who can support us to come through adversity, we can come through these difficult times.

Loss and Grief

We must recognise, however, that children can experience deep psychological pain when they experience loss. Losses can include bereavement, divorce, the loss of a teacher who changes jobs, a best friend who moves away, or the 'loss' of a parent who is now also preoccupied with caring for another child. Certainly, the pain of loss can see the release of high levels of the chemical called acetylcholine, which can make us feel very angry or hostile.

Having compassion for our children if they have difficulty adapting to changes to the family dynamic – or indeed other big life changes – is therefore vital. Showing our children our love, comfort and understanding (rather than punishment or judgement) when they experience losses in life will help not only to calm your child but also releases brain chemicals that are soothing.

BRAIN BOX

'The physical comforting of a grieving child will release natural calming opioids in the brain, coupled with the lovely emotion chemical, oxytocin. These will block the toxic chemistry of too high levels of acetylcholine (which can all too easily move a grieving child into anger). This is why it is vital for children who are suffering from loss to receive comfort.'

— Dr Margot Sunderland, Child Psychotherapist,
Helping Children with Loss

Dr Peter Levine and child therapist Maggie Kline cover issues of divorce and bereavement in their excellent book, *Trauma-Proofing Your Kids*. It's such a huge topic and so multifaceted that I cannot hope to do justice to the pain and grief both you and your children will likely experience if you are dealing with loss, but the main guidance I would give is:

If someone close to you dies, you might create pictures with your children to remember that person (or pet) by. Together, you might write a letter describing all the things you will miss about them and draw pictures of the things you will remember most. You might want to keep them in a keepsake box. Let your child come up with ways to remember people they are missing, whether that's a best friend who has moved away, a teacher who has left the school, or a loved one who has died. Finding ways to be together with your child, being there alongside them for the sad moments in life is very often all they will need to overcome.

You can do the same if you are moving house, changing school or changing your family circumstances. Talking through things in advance – what the new house will look like, what colour your child might want to paint their new room, what sports they might try at their new school, and what they will miss and look forward to – are all parts of meaningful conversations that help a child put the change into context and for their lizard and baboon to feel reassured. So long as your child has you as a steady presence, you can weather many storms. And if you too are feeling wobbly, you can share that with them! Showing your child you can be vulnerable and remain strong teaches a precious lesson.

Child bereavement charities and child counselling organisations are also excellent places to start looking for support if your child is having a very difficult time processing a bereavement or change in family circumstances. I find Dr Margot Sunderland's therapeutic stories for children enormously helpful too, especially *The Day the Sea Went Out* and *The Frog Who Longed for the Moon to Smile*.

Don't forget the enormous value of community during times of adversity, too; whether through faith, friendship, family, or therapy, finding someone to walk alongside *you* during tough times means we are much more likely to be able to come through ourselves, and in turn we can better support our children.

If your child is going through big changes and is displaying obsessive behaviours, expressing a desire to hurt themselves (or others); if you are finding them hard to reach, or at a loss how best to help, then do be proactive – reach out to your GP, or other health professionals, and to the support systems you have around you, whether in your community, online or at school. Seeking support and guidance should never be seen as a source of shame or weakness. My former psychotherapist Liza Elle often told me: 'It is the most courageous souls who ask for help.'

It's important that we do, because going through very stressful, frightening or distressing events can sometimes lead to trauma. Trauma refers to experiences or events that we find physically or psychologically overwhelming. The word trauma has Greek origins and means 'wound'.

As the clinician and trauma specialist Dr Gabor Maté summarises, trauma 'leaves an imprint in your nervous system, in your body, in your psyche, and then shows up in multiple ways that are not helpful to you later on'.

Trauma is one of the biggest, if not *the* biggest, cause of mental health issues in children – and ultimately in the adult they become.

As much as it can feel difficult, we do have to talk about trauma. Not least because research shows that you will likely either know someone or will yourself have personally experienced a traumatic event. The causes of trauma can vary, including both obvious capital T trauma, like war and natural disasters, and things that happen to vulnerable people that should not happen: for example, sexual abuse, emotional or physical neglect or violence in the family; as well as what is often referred to as small t trauma, which can also have long-term effects. Small t trauma can include feeling unloved, being bullied, family separations, verbal abuse, harsh criticism (even from a well-meaning parent) or rejection. Insidious social background factors such as living in poverty, racial discrimination and not feeling safe at home or in our neighbourhood are other factors we now consider in the context of trauma too.

Clinicians now understand that it's not the actual event that causes the trauma, but what happens inside us in response. Clinical Psychologist Dr Lucy Johnstone says this includes the meanings we attribute to situations. 'A child who isn't able to confide in an adult about abuse, and be comforted, is much more likely to develop a destructive meaning like "I am bad and it was my fault".'

What happens inside us depends on the care and support we receive from those people we have around us. This explains why some individuals respond differently to the same event. Dr Maté says trauma impacts our health and behaviour because 'children, especially highly sensitive children, can be wounded in various ways, including not having their emotional needs met, or not feeling seen and accepted, even by loving parents.'

Unresolved childhood trauma can significantly impact our future health. The CDC-Kaiser Permanente adverse childhood experiences (ACE) study is one of the largest investigations of childhood abuse and neglect and household challenges and has been replicated multiple times. It has revealed the long-term effects of unresolved trauma on long-term health and wellbeing.

Children are especially sensitive to stress and trauma because their brains and bodies are still developing. High doses of adversity in childhood can not only affect brain structure and function, they can affect a child's developing immune system, developing hormonal systems, and even the way our DNA is read and transcribed.

Adversity and trauma can be overcome, but not if our

children, or we, are left to cope alone. Throughout this book the information and exercises I have referenced can all be considered 'trauma-informed'. I collaborate with several trauma-informed organisations that support schools and I have referenced them and others if you are keen to find further resources. I also highly recommend watching a thought-provoking Ted Talk by the brilliant paediatrician and former surgeon general of California, Dr Nadine Burke Harris, who has made remarkable contributions in this field.

Dr Burke Harris describes her work as one filled with hope, and I would agree. Because, while the causes of trauma may appear complex and overwhelming, the solutions are often simpler than we might think. Based on her extensive scientific research, which examined over 16,000 journal articles, she found that sleep, exercise, nutrition, mindfulness, mental health and healthy relationships are the most significant factors in healing from trauma.

The trauma specialist Dr Peter Levine says, 'Trauma is perhaps the most avoided, ignored, belittled, denied, misunderstood and untreated cause of human suffering.'

I think it's because we might find it frightening, or fear it is too difficult to tackle. But that is not the case. During my research and training I have had the privilege of meeting exceptional people who have successfully overcome significant childhood trauma. They serve as proof – as do I – that while our childhood experiences can certainly shape us, they do not have to define who we become.

By ensuring a balance in these six elements of our lives, we can make a positive impact and regain our sense of direction, no matter how blown off course we might sometimes feel.

TOOLKIT TIPS
DOSE UP

We can start by dosing up on our happiness hormones: dopamine, oxytocin, serotonin and endorphin, or DOSE for short!

They are released during activities like dancing, exercising, listening to music, having a massage or even just a cuddle. Doing things that help us DOSE up are not just 'nice to haves', they are proven to counter the impact of toxic stress.

Oxytocin release, for example, has been shown to block the hormones responsible for triggering the fight or flight response. It means we have the biological capacity to counteract toxic stress through healthy relationships. In fact, Dr Nadine Burke Harris's studies have shown that high-quality nurturing relationships can actually alter a child's brain structure, which can be measured using MRI technology.

THIS is why I get excited – and why I write books! THIS is why I am clear that with your Cs in place – especially the Cs of compassion, connection and communication – you can not only revolutionise the relationship you have with your child, but you can be confident your LOVE can heal. THIS is why I believe, regardless of any adversity or difficulty, we must always hold on to hope.

TOOLKIT TIP

Repetition Rocks

Another way to change neural networks in the brain is through patterned, repetitive activities. Just as demonstrated by the London taxi driver study (see page 267), any neural network that is consistently activated will undergo transformation. To help a child who has experienced trauma regulate their emotions and achieve a more organised brain, we can introduce patterned, repetitive stimuli to engage the dysregulated neural networks involved in the stress response.

Techniques like the butterfly hug, which I described in Chapter Three, and powerful methods like EMDR (Eye Movement Desensitisation and Reprocessing) can be incredibly effective for self-regulation. EMDR in addition to psychotherapy can help people process negative images, emotions, beliefs and body sensations associated with traumatic memories that may feel stuck.

Other activities that involve repetition and rhythm can also help us and our children overcome difficulty and find emotional balance. These include walking, listening to music, practising rhythmic breathing, engaging in yoga or dance, playing the drums, stroking a pet, jumping on a trampoline, enjoying swings, receiving massages and many other everyday activities that can be structured to provide support. I introduced a rebounder trampoline in my therapy room, for example, for this very reason. It has proved transformative, offering five minutes of regulation for those children who need it at the start of each session, while also helping them to access challenging memories and emotions.

BRAIN BOX

'The rhythm of these experiences matter. The brain stem and diencephalon contain several powerful associations to rhythmic somatosensory activity created in utero and reinforced early in life. The brain makes associations between patterns of neural activity that co-occur. All cultures have some form of patterned, repetitive rhythmic activity as part of their healing and mourning rituals – dancing, drumming, and davening (swaying slightly while reciting liturgical prayers). EMDR and bilateral tapping are essentially variations of this patterned repetitive rhythmic somatosensory activity. By tapping into these strong "regulatory" memories while you are re-creating the cognitive image and affective memory of the traumatic event, you are able to short-circuit the "trauma" memory.'

— Dr Bruce Perry, Child Psychiatrist and

Trauma specialist

Dr Perry's research in the United States suggests that 30–40% of children there will be exposed to domestic violence, sexual abuse, physical abuse, serious natural disasters or car accidents among other small t and capital T traumas by the time they turn 18.

Trauma exists and, as much as it may be uncomfortable for us to confront, it is possible to overcome it when we face it together. It's important that we do because, as the psychiatrist and author of the *New York Times* bestseller *The Body Keeps the Score*, Dr Bessel van der Kolk warns that 'trauma occurs when we do not feel seen and understood'.

A warning we do well to heed when it comes to the diagnosis of behavioural 'disorders'.

'Disorder'

There has been a surge in the diagnosis of children who are said to have neurodevelopmental and behavioural disorders in recent years: you might already be aware of conditions such as attention deficit hyperactivity disorder (ADHD) and/or ADD, oppositional defiance disorder (ODD), obsessive compulsive disorder (OCD), sensory processing disorder (SPD), autism spectrum disorder (ASD) among many others. It would not be surprising to wonder whether one of these labels might provide an explanation if your child is struggling – or your child might have already received a diagnosis.

Neurodevelopmental disorders are defined as types of disorder that influence how the brain functions and alters neurological development, causing difficulties in social, cognitive and emotional functioning.

Clinical psychologist Dr Lucy Johnstone is passionate that parents feel sufficiently informed when it comes to the diagnosis of their children. She says, 'It may be helpful to be aware that the whole area of psychiatric diagnosis is very controversial. No one doubts that children really do struggle, for example, to concentrate, or manage their feelings, or make friends and relate to others, and so on. The key question is whether it makes sense to call this a mental health or neurodevelopmental "disorder", or whether their problems can be seen as reactions that are understandable in context.' She adds, 'Some professionals would take this further and argue that we do not have any scientific evidence that these children's brains are "wired differently" or that they have inherited genetic conditions. They would therefore be reluctant to give a diagnosis or prescribe medication such as Ritalin, except perhaps in extreme cases. All of these issues need to be considered very carefully, because every child is unique, and each of them will need a way forward that suits their particular strengths and difficulties.'

It is beyond the scope of this book to devote sufficient depth to such a complex topic, but as someone who has experienced both complex trauma, and who is formally diagnosed as having ADHD, I would like to share some personal reflections and research in the hope it may prove helpful, as well as reassuring.

I would start by reiterating that our children are still children, regardless of diagnosis. They might have different ways of being, but all children still need the same things – to feel safe, seen, loved and understood. Every child will occasionally have difficulty with emotional regulation and children with additional needs often even more so. We can still help and support them when we have all of our Cs in place.

I appreciate parenting children who have higher needs is often challenging. I also know that it can create confusion and possibly even fear if our children are diagnosed with a label that includes the word 'disorder'. I hope it helps to remember that none of us have the monopoly on 'normal'. There really is no such thing. We are all on the 'human spectrum'; some children just view the world through a different lens and will do things a different way. Some of the greatest brains in history would now be considered 'on the spectrum' and there is an enormous amount of material in that regard if you ever want to share stories with your children that focus on their brain's brilliance and 'superpowers'.

We can help our children to build resilience and reach a profound understanding and sense of self-acceptance. We can help them to celebrate their gifts and their brilliant brains, rather than feeling a need to change who they are.

Having a formal diagnosis can bring us relief, offering a name for the problematic behaviours we might be witnessing and sometimes find so difficult to address: whether it's when our children find it hard to sit still, get easily distracted or dysregulated, whether they fidget, fight, are oppositional, obsessive, hypersensitive to noise, smell, taste or materials that they touch. A diagnosis can help us put these behaviours in more context, affording us more patience hopefully too.

We can appreciate that our child's behaviour is often not deliberate, which helps us to recognise when they are struggling and advocate for their needs. A formal diagnosis can help us secure more empathy and support, whether within the wider family, or with teaching staff at school.

Diagnosis can certainly bring us more clarity – BUT, there's also a danger that labels can create stereotypes, influencing the way others see our children, and how our children see themselves. Labels can create unrealistic expectations, or low expectations, when our children are capable of so much more. Some children can get 'lost in their label', believing it will always define the way they are. Labels can also lead to medication – which is a serious problem – if the label is wrong. Labels can also hide the context of a child's life – we might attribute their attention problems to 'ADHD' when in reality they might be witnessing domestic violence or being bullied.

Misdiagnosis is an issue of grave concern. By way of example, treating a child who does not have ADHD with medication is a serious breach of health and safety. ADHD, for instance, is primarily diagnosed based on answers given in questionnaires and interviews, making it a highly subjective process. According to Dr Nadine Burke Harris, the rate of misdiagnosis for ADHD is alarmingly high. In one example she says only three out of 100 children referred to her with ADHD actually had the disorder. Some professionals would argue that such a diagnosis does not provide much of an explanation, nor does it offer a medical cure. It is simply a way of saying 'This child's difficulties are severe'.

There is little question that many children are struggling with their behaviour, however, so what else might be going on? Clinicians point to what they call the 'muddle' between trauma and psychiatric diagnosis.

BRAIN BOX

'Many children and young people who've suffered traumatic life experiences are given the label of ADHD and/or ASD and sometimes medication without anyone ever asking what has happened to them in their life or hearing their story. The trouble is, there are many overlapping presenting symptoms between these two diagnoses and living with traumatic stress and a mind in torment. Being wrongly diagnosed then often results in yet more suffering for the traumatised child/young person as they are left with the fallout from their trauma, without appropriate intervention to help them heal.'

— Dr Margot Sunderland,
Child Psychotherapist

It's why Dr Sunderland says before considering any child for diagnosis, clinicians must first ask two questions: Why is the child behaving like this? What has happened to the child?

We would hope that misdiagnosis is rare, but the adverse childhood experience (ACE) study found that the more adversity and trauma a person experiences, the higher the chance of being diagnosed with ADHD, conduct disorder or being on the autism spectrum.

A very young child who is involved in a car crash, for example, might withdraw and stop speaking. If unaware of the incident, a clinician might be inclined to diagnose ASD, when the child's selective mutism is a result of their unresolved trauma. A child who is constantly angry, refusing to 'do as they're told', might be labelled as 'oppositional defiant' when the reality might be that they're struggling to cope with the abuse they're experiencing but are too ashamed to tell.

The evidence suggests that many children will be labelled as having a disorder when they are dealing with other underlying issues or may not have a disorder at all. So, if we are too quick to label, we might miss what it is our children's behaviour is telling us.

Take the example of Ella, who is seven. She was diagnosed with ASD due to poor eye contact, hypersensitivity to noise and social situations, and because she had eating problems. She shook her hands and was hyper-anxious about any change to routine. When Ella visited her aunt, all her symptoms disappeared.

Child psychiatrist Dr Sami Timimi is a critic of the concept of ASD and ADHD, because he says, 'the so-called tests' do not require behaviours to be present in all contexts. Regarding assessments for ASD, he explains that if a child's symptoms come and go, for example if they can hold conversations at home but not at school (or vice versa), if they can engage with some people but not others, if they can relax in certain settings but not others, then we might need to consider something other than ASD. As he says: 'If you have a neurological compromise, you have a neurological compromise. You can't turn it on and off.'

As technology progresses it will hopefully help to shed more light on neurological conditions and help improve the accuracy of diagnosis. It will also crucially prevent children being medicated for disorders they do not have.

For some children, medication is often reported to help, at least initially, but this is a topic that remains highly complex and controversial and it seems parents would be wise to first explore all available non-drug options for their children. I include resources at the back of the book for non-drug treatments for children diagnosed with ADHD, as well as teaching them the all-important and lifelong skill of self-regulation. It can be argued that this is more beneficial in the long run as medication does not 'solve' ADHD, and once medication is stopped, the behaviour often returns.

BRAIN BOX

'The use of psychostimulants in children with attention problems has been studied in more research projects than any other medication in child psychiatry. The results are mixed. With more than 5,000 studies reported, clearly there are immediate positive effects on attention for many children. However, in the best-controlled longitudinal studies psychostimulants show no superiority to nonpharmacological interventions and show significant negative effects on growth.'

— Dr Bruce Perry, Child Psychiatrist, Child Trauma Academy

Ultimately, irrespective of cause – whether it's neurological, trauma based, or both – we can help our children most when we focus on supporting them with their behaviour. We know that when children are helped to grieve, process and make sense of what has happened in their lives their previous symptoms and distressing behaviour are often alleviated.

I know how confusing, complex and overwhelming mental health issues can be and I can appreciate how concerned, even afraid, we can be when our children display behaviours we don't understand. But I do know there is hope and we can find answers when we come together in solidarity and support.

It can happen when we understand what drives behaviour, allowing us to focus less on a label and more on learning what our children really need. Our children are more than a diagnosis. Having a 'label' or challenging life experience does not define who we are.

Multiple clinicians and experts I have interviewed and whose work I have researched in the course of writing this book suggest that the rise in dysregulated behaviour in children should be considered in the context of recent changes in Western culture. The changes include how we now live in more isolated nuclear groups without the benefit and buffer of being part of an extended community. Parents are experiencing significant levels of stress, with a decrease in their own personal time and a decrease in quality, focused time spent engaging in play with their children. The intensified emphasis on academic performance in schools due to competition in national league tables, and the increase in social media and screen use, sees our children living a more static lifestyle, with academic subjects prioritised and physical activity often taking a back seat. Childrens' diets now see them consuming more sugar and fat and fewer essential vitamins, minerals and fatty acids. How can we not consider all these factors when trying to understand what's influencing our children's brain development and behaviour?

Perhaps it is time to consider that it is not our children who are dysfunctional or disordered, but rather the environment in which they are now being raised.

Nearly 20 years ago neuroscientist Jaak Panksepp warned that children moving less, and sitting still more in classrooms, could be contributing to the increase in the rate of diagnosis of ADHD. Influential educationalists like the late Sir Ken Robinson led calls for the school system to change, to accommodate more of the evidence-based practices that support healthy child development rather than the fixation on league tables and academic performance. Referencing the rise of psychological disorders in a popular post on YouTube, he said, 'Children for the most part are not suffering from a psychological condition. They're suffering from childhood.'

Clinicians also point to stressors in a child's environment that influence the development of their brains. There is now an overwhelming body of research that reveals how crucial the mother's physical environment, as well as her psychological health and emotional balance are for a child's healthy brain development. We now know, for instance, that a foetus in the womb feels a mother's stress directly.

As far back as 2004, researchers reported that infants born to women who were stressed or depressed had a significantly increased risk of developing learning and behavioural problems and 'may themselves be more vulnerable to depression or anxiety as they age'.

In his book *The Myth of Normal*, Dr Gabor Maté quotes nursing professor Dr Nicole Letourneau, at the University of Calgary, who tells him, 'We know prenatal depression and stress and anxiety can predict behaviour problems in the child. We can try to fix those behaviours in the kid years later, or we can medicate the child, or we can give pregnant women the support they need in the first place.'

In 2018, a group of psychologists and people who have used services published a framework for understanding why all of us, children and adults, sometimes struggle with a range of over-whelming emotions such as confusion, anger, fear, hopelessness, mood swings, hearing voices, self-harming, eating difficulties and so on. Instead of using diagnostic labels, The Power Threat Meaning Framework argues that these very real experiences can be understood in the context of our relationships and the social circumstances and standards of the society and culture we live in. When we fill in the gaps, we can clearly see why children (and adults) react as they do, and we can also see the most helpful way forward.

The Power Threat Meaning Framework, or PTMF, suggests four core questions which, instead of giving a diagnosis, can help us to better understand our distress. These questions are:

- What has happened to you?
- How did it affect you?
- What sense did you make of it?
- What are you having to do to survive?

We can take the notional example of Sam, a boy of seven, who is very disruptive at school. He has been referred for an assessment for possible ADHD. When we sensitively explore the questions (using our C's of curiosity and compassion):

What has happened to you? It becomes apparent that Sam is being bullied at school. At the same time, he shares that his parents are going through a divorce and are very preoccupied with their own problems.

How is this affecting you? Sam does not feel safe either at home or school and is very worried about losing contact with his father and younger sister.

What sense did you make of it? Sam is worried that the divorce must be his fault and perhaps his parents do not love him any more. He is scared of the children who are bullying him, and upset by the unkind things they say.

What are you having to do to survive? Sam has not felt able to tell anyone about his fears and so his only way of showing his distress is through his angry behaviour. He also hopes that this will help to keep the bullies away.

As a child therapist I work with many 'Sams'. When we remain curious about a child like Sam's experience and what might be driving their behaviour, we can consider whether Sam is being disruptive because he has ADHD, or whether his behaviour is a symptom of something else. We can wonder whether his lashing out angrily is a 'baboon' response to threat, given what is happening in his life.

When a parent or teacher is able to gain Sam's trust, they will be able to listen to his fears, to address the bullying and help him through the changes in his family life, using some of the ideas in this book, and building on his strengths and resources. On the other hand, a diagnosis of ADHD might miss the real problems, while giving him the same message as the children who are bullying him – that there is something wrong with him.

When we consider the complexities we currently face with our children's behaviour, never has the African proverb that it 'takes a village to raise a child' felt more poignant and prescient. If we really want to address the rise in 'disordered behaviour' we must consider how we bring children into the world, and how we can best support new parents and the young children in their care.

Chapter Seventeen

Community

'If we can create a society which sees the child within every adult – and the adult within every child – we will finally start to change it for the better.'
Her Royal Highness, The Princess of Wales

It's in all our interests to ensure that future generations of adults are able to lead happy and successful lives. In fact, the future of society depends on it. Parenting, therefore, brings with it great responsibility. Yet changes in our communities have made family life more challenging, often leaving parents feeling increasingly isolated and overwhelmed.

It hasn't always been this way.

BRAIN BOX

'For 99.9% of the time we have been on this planet, human beings have lived in these multi-family, extended communities, where the average number of developmentally mature individuals for every child who was developing was four to one. Which would be the ideal. Now we think it's incredible if there's a ratio of one adult to five children. We think that's enriched. But that's one-twentieth of what our brain prefers and needs.'

— Dr Bruce Perry, Child Psychiatrist

We are social beings and children need numerous enriched relational interactions for healthy brain development, as do their parents. In this final chapter, we come to our tenth pillar and perhaps the most essential 'C' of all: community.

In an excellent article on family and the changing fabric of society in recent decades, author David Brooks writes passionately in favour of a return to multi-generational living. He says it offers parents a crucial buffer against life's adversities and stress. His article begins with a description of a family scene at Thanksgiving:

'The scene is one many of us have somewhere in our family history: Dozens of people celebrating Thanksgiving or some other holiday around a makeshift stretch of family tables – siblings, cousins, aunts, uncles, great-aunts. The grandparents are telling the old family stories for the 37th time... After the meal, there are piles of plates in the sink and squads of children conspiring mischievously in the basement. Groups of young parents huddle in a hallway, making plans. The old men nap on couches, waiting for dessert. It's the extended family in all its tangled, loving, exhausting glory.'

Brooks goes on to say that extended families afford parents resilience and are a solid socialising force for children. He makes the point that extended families have more people to share unexpected burdens, such as if children fall sick in the middle of the day, or an adult in the family loses their job.

Many cultures still practise and enjoy the beautiful benefits of multi-generational living. I am in awe (and more than a little envious) of friends who are able to raise their children this way. However, as with my own family, the detached nuclear unit is now more generally the norm, with only occasional visits to family who live some distance away.

It means many children have fewer emotionally available adolescents or adults in their lives, even at school where there's typically a teacher-to-pupil ratio of one to 30. Combined with the increasing use of screens and devices, their human-to-human interactions have decreased dramatically. Child psychiatrists warn that the reduction in multi-generational human engagement and relationships is influencing our children's ability to love, to be empathic, and to function healthily in wider society.

BRAIN BOX

'We are really concerned because we see changes in the way children are in school, the way they are with each other, the way they engage in the community, the way they participate and vote, all of these things are directly or indirectly related to this capacity to be empathic, and if we're raising our children in a culture where there aren't enough opportunities to develop that brain mediated capacity, we are really in a bad trajectory.'

— Dr Bruce Perry, Child Psychiatrist

So how might we resolve the disconnect between what we require both for our *own* wellbeing and our *children*'s healthy development, and what the modern world currently provides?

To create a society with children's wellbeing at its heart, neurodevelopmental research should be applied to every policy that impacts children and their care. We might also insist that those caring for children are educated in the science of child development. We should give greater recognition to the incredibly rich experience teachers and carers can offer our children and the influence they have on their social, emotional and cognitive development. I would like to see the value of all the committed people who work in education and health settings reflected in their pay. I would want to acknowledge the tremendous role of parents caring for young children and children with additional needs and the contribution of volunteers, counsellors, kinship carers, adoptive parents, foster carers and mentors too.

In schools, an increase in the number of emotionally available adults in the classroom would give our children more one-to-one adult interaction throughout the day. Not only would this serve our children, but it would likely go a long way to reducing stress on hard-working teachers who are currently expected to achieve the impossible task of managing and meeting every need of the 20 to 30 children they care for in class each day. I would like to see more counsellors funded in schools and more time and resources invested in play-based movement and patterned repetitive exercises through music and art. As we have seen, this will help to facilitate more regulated behaviour because when the lower parts of our children's brains are restless and dysregulated, they cannot concentrate, think and learn.

I can think of plenty more to add to my wish list and you will have suggestions, too. When children develop healthily, we all stand to benefit. This is not about policymakers 'doing good' – it's about good policy.

In coming together, I believe we can effect change. We can better support our children and we can help each other too. And for this, we have a passionate and powerful advocate. Her Royal Highness, The Princess of Wales, cares deeply in this regard. She has made child development her life's work. In 2021, Her Royal Highness launched The Royal Foundation's Centre for Early Childhood to support and showcase the science to inform best practices and achieve transformative societal change.

Our children's needs are really very simple: to feel safe, stimulated, valued and loved. From the Introduction, we can recall the beautiful image painted by neuroscientist Jaak Panksepp as he reassured parents that our children's 'positive arousal neurochemicals (that make us feel so happy and loved) … lie like Sleeping Beauty waiting for someone to wake them up.'

We can attune to our children's needs more readily and easily when *our* needs are met. It is with great interest that I have observed the increasing number of like-minded people coming together in this regard, creating communities of their choosing: 'forged' families, home-share programmes, eco-villages, co-housing, intentional communities – all organically created communities where people are coming together to live mindfully in more engaged and supportive ways.

We might seek out like-minded others through exercise classes, the local library, community centre, GP surgery or our children's school. We might organise shared dinners and picnics, giving each other time to talk while our children play under our collective supervision. Organisations like mealtrain.com have harnessed the power of community goodwill, with an online portal that enables people to organise meals for friends after a birth, surgery or illness.

There is much to consider about how we wish to live and how we can improve the conditions in which our children are raised today. As well as getting better at asking for help, an excellent first step might be to consider our immediate neighbours and think about where we might offer them help too.

Parent Ponder

Joyce, mum to Ade, 5, and Shola, 8

When my husband passed away, I was very low. An older lady who lived in the flat next door knocked at the door with some cake and offered to come in each day to 'help wash the dishes and tidy breakfast things away'. I broke down in her arms, crying with gratitude. She came every day for half an hour and told me I didn't need to talk unless I wanted to. It meant so much to have this silent but loving support when I felt so alone. That one act, to me, meant the world.

Human interactions like these can create lasting bonds and offer profound opportunities for healing.

We can harness technology for the good in this regard, too. My street's WhatsApp group has been instrumental in bringing our community together, with multiple generations reaching out to offer help with dog walking, parcel collecting, babysitting and sharing goods and information. It is time for us to consider all the ways in which we can bring more adult and adolescent interactions into our children's lives. This could be through a community of faith, friends or even elderly neighbours who might enjoy, in our presence, playing a role as surrogate grandparents, alleviating the significant burden of loneliness for them in turn. However we wish to do it, we must harness the power of community and the gift it brings our children.

As David Brooks says, perhaps it is time to bring back the big tables.

Thank you for journeying with me through this book. Writing it has taken me far longer than my editor would have liked, but I was doing so while juggling my family's needs and the needs of my young clients, too. I hope that, in some small way, the effort has been worth it.

I care deeply and passionately that our children have the childhood they deserve and that you get to raise the happy family you always hoped to have. Please let me know how you get on – ways to contact me are in the resources section of the book.

As the American lawyer and writer Robert Ingersoll so elegantly said, 'We rise by lifting others'; if what you have learned has proved helpful I hope that, in the spirit of community, you feel able to take the science forward and support other families around you too.

Go well, love your children, find joy.

Endnotes

Introduction

Page 5 These feel-good neurochemicals lie, as the eminent neuroscientist Jaak Panksepp described 'like sleeping beauty, waiting for someone to wake them up'. Panksepp, Jaak (2015).

Taken from a conversation between Dr Margot Sunderland and Jaak Panksepp.

Chapter One
Construction – Why We're All in the Brain Development Business

Page 12 The analogy is inspired by the psychiatrist Dr Bruce Perry's neurosequential model of brain development.

Perry, Bruce (2023). 'The Neurosequential Model of Therapeutics'. B.D. Perry, M.D., Ph.D. https://www.bdperry.com/clinical-work. (Accessed: 04.01.2023.)

'History and Evolution'. *Child Trauma Academy*. https://www.childtrauma.org/history. (Accessed: 04.01.2023.)

Page 15 Brain Box

Porges, Stephen W. (2011). *The Polyvagal Theory: Neurophysiological Foundations of Emotions, Attachment, Communication, and Self-regulation*. New York: W.W. Norton and Company.

Page 15 The physiologist Walter Cannon was the first to describe our stress response as the 'fight or flight' response.

https://www.ncbi.nlm.nih.gov/pmc/articles/PMC1447286/

Page 18 We will also reflect on children who adopt a survival mechanism that we might refer to as 'people-pleasing' and has more recently been identified by psychotherapist Pete Walker as FAWN.
Walker, Peter (2021). *Complex PTSD From Surviving to Thriving*. Lafayette, California: Azure Coyote Publishing.

Page 18 This mechanism is typically deployed if a child's brain determines that no other options are likely to work in ensuring their survival, i.e. that they cannot fight, flee or flop. We often see it in children who have experienced trauma and abuse.
Amarillo Counseling. 'Compliance as a survival response'. *Amarillo Professional Counseling and Consultation*. https://amarillo-counseling.com/2020/04/15/compliance-as-a-survival-response/ (Accessed 05.01.2023.)

Schlote, Sarah (2023). 'History of the term "appeasement": a response to Bailey et al.' *European Journal of Psychotraumatology*. Volume XIV.1. https://www.ncbi.nlm.nih.gov/pmc/articles/PMC10078115/ (Accessed 05.01.2023.)

Walker, Pete (2003). 'Codependency, trauma, and the fawn response'. *The East Bay Therapist*. http://www.pete-walker.com/codependencyFawnResponse.htm; (Accessed 05.01.2023.)

Walker, Pete (2021). *Complex PTSD From Surviving to Thriving*. Lafayette, California: Azure Coyote Publishing.

Page 17 Brain Box
When threatened or injured, all animals draw from a 'library' of possible responses.
Levin, Dr Peter (1997). *Waking the Tiger*, Berkeley, California: North Atlantic Books.

Page 26 It's what neuropsychiatrist Dr Dan Siegel terms as having good 'vertical integration'.
Siegel, Dan (2010). *Mindsight*. New York: Bantam Books.

Chapter Two
CONSTRUCTION – The Role of the Nervous System in 'naughty'

Page 32 Brain Box
'While we may think our brains are in charge, the heart of our daily experience and the way we navigate the world begins in our bodies with the autonomic nervous system.'
Dana, Deborah (2021). *Anchored: How to Befriend your Nervous System using Polyvagal Theory*. Louisville, Colorado: Sounds True Publishing.

Page 36 We cannot stay in a heightened state of emergency for too long; the symptoms would be too overwhelming, and sitting with prolonged and heightened adrenaline and cortisol levels is very harmful to our health.
'Toxic Stress'. *Center on the Developing Child: Harvard University* (2015). https://developingchild.harvard.edu/science/key-concepts/toxic-stress/ (Accessed 04.01.2024.)

Page 37 The vagus nerve plays an incredibly important role in our physical and mental health. Evidence suggests it plays a large part in governing the immune responses and the immune responses that are involved in conditions such as heart disease, Crohn's disease, rheumatoid arthritis and Parkinson's.
Wade, Grace (2023). 'Unravelling the secrets of the vagus nerve will revolutionise medicine'. *New Scientist.* https://www.newscientist.com/article/mg25934530-500-unravelling-the-secrets-of-the-vagus-nerve-will-revolutionise-medicine/ (Accessed 04.01.2023.)

Page 37 Chiropractor and functional medicine practitioner Dr Navaz Habib, in his book *Activate Your Vagus Nerve,* describes the vagus nerve as 'the conductor of the human body symphony orchestra'.
Habib, Dr Navaz (2022). *Activate Your Vagus Nerve: Unleash Your Body's Natural Ability to Heal.* Berkeley, California: Ulysses Press.

Page 38 As toddlers our children still needed our help – in fact research suggests children under four need help with emotional regulation every 20 seconds!
Lieberman, Alicia (2017). *The Emotional Life of the Toddler.* New York: Simon & Schuster.

Page 42 'One of the most powerful sets of associations created in utero is the association between patterned, repetitive rhythmic activity from maternal heart rate and all the neural patterns of activity associated with not being hungry, not being thirsty, and feeling "safe".'
McKinnon, Laurie (2012). 'The Neurosequential Model of Therapeutics: An Interview with Bruce Perry'. *Australian and New Zealand Journal of Family Therapy, Volume 33, Issue 3: Trauma and Systemic Therapy.* pp. 210–218. https://doi.org/10.1017/aft.2012.26. (Accessed 04.01.2023.)
Bruce Perry's website: www.bdperry.com

Page 43 Brain Box
Despite the widespread belief that individual grit, extraordinary self-reliance, or some in-born heroic strength of character can triumph over calamity, science now tells us that it is the reliable presence of at least one supportive relationship...
National Scientific Council on the Developing Child (2015). 'Supportive Relationships and Active Skill-Building'. *Strengthen the Foundations of Resilience: Working Paper 13.* https://developingchild.harvard.edu/wp-content/uploads/2015/05/The-Science-of-Resilience.pdf (Accessed 04.01.2023.)

Page 44 Brain Box
Resilience results in healthy development because it protects the developing brain and other organs produced by excessive activation of stress response systems.
National Scientific Council on the Developing Child (2015). 'Supportive Relationships and Active Skill-Building'. *Strengthen the Foundations of Resilience: Working Paper 13.* https://developingchild.harvard.edu/wp-content/uploads/2015/05/The-Science-of-Resilience.pdf (Accessed 04.01.2023.)

Page 44 Overactivation of the stress response in young children can lead to a path of dysfunction
Zeedyk, Dr Suzanne (2020). *Sabre Tooth Tigers & Teddy Bears: The Connected Baby Guide to Attachment.* Great Britain: connected baby Ltd.

Dr Zeedyk's website: www.suzannezeedyk.com (Accessed 05.01.2024.)

Page 47 'When the body is in that state, that body is in the state of profound autonomic defense.'
Porges, Stephen (2021). 'Working with the Freeze Response in the Treatment of Trauma with Stephen Porges, PhD'. *National Institute for the Clinical Application of Behavioural Medicine.* https://www.nicabm.com/stephen-porges-on-the-freeze-response/#:~:text=You%20want%20the%20breaths%20to,cue%20to%20disappear%20even%20more. (Accessed 04.01.2023.) YouTube video.

Chapter Three
CALM – Addressing Our Parental Stress

Page 51 Research has identified three factors that universally lead to stress: uncertainty, a lack of information and a loss of control.
Maté, Dr Gabor (2019). *When the Body Says No: The Cost of Hidden Stress.* London: Ebury.

Page 51 Brain Box
'When we're in a state of parental frustration or stress, the deep parts of our brain that are tightly connected to our bodies are strongly activated, briefly suppressing our higher cognitive capacities for self-regulation, self-awareness and empathy.'
Hughes, Daniel and Baylin, Jonathan (2012). *Brain-Based Parenting – The Neuroscience of Caregiving for Healthy Attachment.* New York: W.W. Norton & Company.

Page 52 Parent Ponder. Taken from the BBC's The Joe Wicks Podcast Series 3, Episode 20. Kate Silverton: Getting Back to Nature.

Page 55 His research and his concept of 'somatic experiencing' is something I use for myself and in my clinical work.
Levine, Peter (1986). 'Stress'. In Coles, M.G.H., Donchin, E. and Porges, S.W. (Eds.), *Psychophysiology: Systems, Processes, and Applications*. New York: Guilford Press.

Levine, Peter (2001). *It Won't Hurt Forever: Guiding Your Child Through Trauma*. Boulder, Colorado: Sounds True.

Levine, Peter (2008). *Healing Trauma: A Pioneering Program for Restoring the Wisdom of Your Body*. Boulder, Colorado: Sounds True. Audiobook.

Levine, Peter (2014). *Sexual Healing: Transforming the Sacred Wound*. Boulder, Colorado: Sounds True.

Levine, Peter and Frederick, Ann (Contributor) (1997). *Waking the Tiger: Healing Trauma Through the Innate Capacity to Transform Overwhelming Experiences*. Berkeley, CA: North Atlantic Books.

Ramirez-Duran, Daniela (2020). 'Somatic Experiencing Therapy: 10 Best Exercises & Examples'. *Positive Psychology*. https://positivepsychology.com/somatic-experiencing/?utm_content=cmp-true. (Accessed 05.01.2024.)

Page 59 He has highlighted research suggesting asthma, anxiety, ADHD, psoriasis, and a whole host of illnesses and what he calls 'modern maladies' could be 'reduced or reversed simply by changing the way we inhale and exhale'.
Nestor, James (2020). *Breath*. London: Penguin Life.

Page 59 Yogic breathing has been shown to relieve stress, improve concentration and helps us to breathe better generally. Essentially, you isolate each nostril, breathing in through only one of them at a time and then exhaling through the other.
Young, Melissa (2022). 'How and Why to Try Alternate Nostril Breathing'. *Cleveland Clinic Health Essentials*. https://health.clevelandclinic.org/alternate-nostril-breathing/ (Accessed 05.01.2023.)

Page 58 Brain Box
Whenever you inhale
Sapolsky, Dr Robert M. (2004). *Why Zebras Don't Get Ulcers*. New York: Henry Holt and Company.

Page 59 Journalist James Nestor has dedicated an entire, and brilliant, book to raising awareness about the ...
Nestor, James (2020). *Breath*. London: Penguin Life.

Page 59 Integrative medicine specialist Dr Melissa Young explains
Young, Melissa (2022). 'How and Why to Try Alternate Nostril Breathing'.
Cleveland Clinic Health Essentials. https://health.clevelandclinic.org/alternate-nostril-breathing/ (Accessed 05.01.2023.)

Page 61 The vagus nerve is connected to your vocal cords and the muscles at the back of your throat, which explains why singing, humming, chanting and gargling can all help to improve vagal tone.
Fallis, Jordan (2023). 'How to Stimulate Your Vagus Nerve for Better Mental Health'. *Optimal Living Dynamics*. https://www.optimallivingdynamics.com/blog/how-to-stimulate-your-vagus-nerve-for-better-mental-health-brain-vns-ways-treatment-activate-natural-foods-depression-anxiety-stress-heart-rate-variability-yoga-massage-vagal-tone-dysfunction. (Accessed 05.01.2023.)

Page 61 The vibrations caused by making these sounds stimulate the vagus nerve, regulating our immune system and lowering our stress …
Ward, Rebecca. 'Regulating The Nervous System With The Voo Breathing Method'. *Insight Timer*. https://insighttimer.com/originalblueprint/guided-meditations/regulating-the-nervous-system-with-the-voo-breathing-method. (Accessed 05.01.2023.)

Chapter Four
CALM(ER) KIDS – How to De-Stress Our Children Too

Page 76 Brain Box
Neuroscience research shows that the only way we can change the way we feel is by becoming …
Van der Kolk, Bessel (2015). *The Body Keeps the Score*. London: Viking.

Page 77 Organisations and charities like Unlocking Potential (UP) and Place2Be (P2Be) can offer tremendous support to families in school settings in this regard …
Website – Unlocking Potential: https://up.org.uk
Website – Improving Children's Mental Health: https://www.place2be.org.uk

Page 77 given research shows the HPA axis is much more reactive for some children than others.
Doom, Janalee R. and Gunnar, Megan R. (2013). 'Stress physiology and developmental psychopathology: past, present, and future'. *Developmental Psychopatholology*. 25(4 Pt 2):1359-73. <doi: 10.1017/S0954579413000667>. (Accessed 04.01.2024.)

Page 80 In educating children about stress and how it's felt not just in the head but throughout the body, we encourage what psychiatrist Dr Dan Siegel calls 'vertical integration'.
Siegel, Dan (2010). *Mindsight*. New York: Bantam Books.

Page 81 Brain Box
By and large, anxiety is a defence against intense feelings which have been pushed underground.
Sunderland, Dr Margot (2018). *Draw on Your Emotions*. Abingdon, Oxon: Routledge.

Chapter Five
CONTAIN – Anger Management and Emotional Outbursts

Page 85 In the US, a 2020 survey of 2,000 parents found more than a quarter admitted their six- to eight-year-olds displayed 'the most brutal meltdowns' with parents admitting their children had hit, kicked or bitten them when they did.
https://swnsdigital.com/us/2020/04/parents-report-the-hateful-eights-are-the-hardest-age-to-raise-study-finds/

Page 85 but as the child and adult psychotherapist Violet Oaklander said, it is also one of the most misunderstood
https://vsof.org/the-many-faces-of-anger/

Page 86 Dr Allan Schore asserts that 'enhancing self-regulation should be considered the whole of child development' … Because, he says, 'just about every psychiatric disorder shows problems in emotional dysregulation'.
https://www.youtube.com/watch?v=c0sKY86Qmzo

Page 87 Brain Box
We tend to think of anger as distasteful and abhorrent, something that we would rather not experience.
https://vsof.org/the-many-faces-of-anger/

Page 88 The addiction specialist Dr Gabor Maté observes of his own patients …
Hollington-Sawyer, Stephanie, 'The Healing Force Within'. *Dr. Gabor Maté*. https://drgabormate.com/healing-force-within/.

Page 90 An emotions wheel can be a very useful tool for teaching children emotional literacy. I use a version of psychologists Dr Paul Ekman and Dr Robert Plutchik's emotion wheel.
https://www.paulekman.com/universal-emotions/

Page 92 'We are deeply feeling and deeply biological creatures ... We must come to terms with the biological sources of the human spirit.'
Panksepp, Jaak (1998). *Affective Neuroscience: The Foundations of Human and Animal Emotions*. Oxford: Oxford University Press. p. 257.

Page 102 In 2013, the London School of Economics research paper 'What Predicts A Successful Life' concluded that the 'most important predictor of adult life satisfaction is the child's emotional health, followed by the child's conduct'.
Layard, Richard, Clark, Andrew E. Cornaglia, Francesca, Powdthavee, Nattavudh and Vernoit, James (2013). 'What Predicts A Successful Life? A Life Course Model of Well-Being'. *Centre for Economic Performance*. https://www.lse.ac.uk/business/consulting/assets/documents/what-predicts-a-successful-life.pdf (Accessed 05.01.2024.)

Page 103 As child psychotherapist Violet Oaklander poignantly explained ... 'the 'good behaviour will often be driven by fear and the child's self becomes diminished due to lack of expression; his deep-felt feelings become buried inside of him.'
Oaklander, Violet (2022). *Hidden Treasure: A Map to the Child's Inner Self*. Abingdon, Oxon: Routledge.

Chapter Six
CONNECTION – Why We Must Connect Before We Command

Page 108 In my therapy room, I have a lovely book called *The Invisible String* by Karst, Patrice.
Karst, Patrice (2018). *The Invisible String*. New York: Little, Brown.

Page 115 The British psychiatrist John Bowlby defined this connection as our 'attachment'. He described it as a 'lasting psychological connectedness between human beings'.
Bowlby, John (1997). *Attachment and Loss*. Volume 1: attachment. London: Pimlico.

Page 116 The push–pull behaviour of ambivalence or disorganised attachment can often express itself as hyperactivity.
https://www.ncbi.nlm.nih.gov/books/NBK588783/

Page 120 Research shows that physical touch in the context of a secure attachment relationship is as powerful as a drug in calming the baboon.
https://pubmed.ncbi.nlm.nih.gov/18662717

Page 120 The importance of touch was highlighted in a famous experiment conducted in the 1950s by the primatologist and animal psychologist Harry Harlow.
Cited in van Rosmalen, Lenny, van der Veer, René and van der Horst, Frank C.P. (2020). 'The nature of love: Harlow, Bowlby and Bettelheim on affectionless mothers'. *History of Psychology*. 31(2). pp. 227–231. https://www.ncbi.nlm.nih. gov/pmc/articles/. (Accessed 05.01.2024.)

Chapter Seven
CREATIVITY – The Importance of Attachment Play

Page 136 One of my colleagues, psychologist Dr Lawrence Cohen, writes wonderful books about play ... His top tips include.
Cohen, Laurence J. (2001). *Playful Parenting: An Exciting New Approach to Raising Children That Will Help You Nurture Close Connections, Solve Behavior Problems, and Encourage Confidence.* New York: Ballantine Books.

Page 137 Brain Box
'I like to start every roughhousing session with a good strong connection ...'
Cohen, Laurence J. (2001). *Playful Parenting: An Exciting New Approach to Raising Children That Will Help You Nurture Close Connections, Solve Behavior Problems, and Encourage Confidence.* New York: Ballantine Books.

Chapter Eight
CURIOSITY – Curiosity is King – or Queen!

Page 143 Our children experience psychological pain when they feel excluded from friendship groups or if they feel rejected by us.
Eisenberger, Naomi I. and Lieberman, Matthew D. (2004). 'Why rejection hurts: a common neural alarm system for physical and social pain'. *Trends in Cognitive Sciences, Issue VII, Volume 8.* https://pubmed.ncbi.nlm.nih.gov/15242688/. (Accessed 04.01.2024.)

Page 145 Brain Box
'When a child feels safe, when you are emotionally available they move from explosive rage to sobbing, a release of often years of grief and fear and desperate aloneness.'
Batmanghelidjh, Camila (2007). *Shattered Lives: Children Who Live with Courage and Dignity.* London: Jessica Kingsley Publishers.

Page 149 'Because that wound is a story we tell ourselves, like "No one ever listens to me," we're always looking for confirming evidence that that's the way the world is.'
Sibboney, Claire (2023). 'This Might Be Why You're Getting so Mad at Your Kids'. *Today's Parent*. https://www.todaysparent.com/family/parenting/parenting-triggers/ (Accessed 05.01.2024.)

Page 156 The psychologist Oliver James observes that we either 'robotically reproduce, or react against, the care we received as children'.
James, Oliver with The School of Life (2014). *How to Develop Emotional Health*. Basingstoke: Macmillan. p. 47.

Page 158 'I was quite amazed at how effective it can be to say, "I wonder if you are feeling anxious about the different teacher in class today and that's why you are refusing to sit on your chair."'
Bomber, Louise (2017). *Inside I'm Hurting*. London: Worth Publishing Ltd. p. 89.

Chapter Nine
COMMUNICATION – It's a Two-way Street!

Page 161 Brain Box
'Negative looks and interactions are remembered and stored.'
Gerhardt, Sue (2004). *Why Love Matters: How Affection Shapes a Baby's Brain*. London: Routledge.

Page 163 The communications we have with our children result in 'an inner library of images that can be referred to that will become increasingly complex and loaded with associations and thoughts as the child grows up'.
Gerhardt, Sue (2004). *Why Love Matters: How Affection Shapes a Baby's Brain*. London: Routledge.

Page 164 Brain Box
'One of the main reasons children behave badly is that the way a parent is relating to a child is activating the wrong part of a child's brain.'
Sunderland, Dr Margot (2016). *The Science of Parenting: How Today's Brain Research Can Help You Raise Happy, Emotionally Balanced Children*. London: Dorling Kindersley. p. 119.

Page 165 Brain Box
'People don't realise that verbal putdowns constitute emotional abuse, which is particularly lethal in childhood when the brain is forming and the child is developing a sense of self.'
Sunderland, Dr Margot (1997). *Draw on Your Emotions*. London: Routledge.

Page 164 Research shows that not only does shame impact our children's psychology but it can impact them physiologically too. A series of studies show how acute threats to the social self – that is, how our children feel they 'fit in' – increase proinflammatory cytokine activity and cortisol, and that these changes occur in concert with shame.
Dickerson et al. (2004). 'When the social self is threatened: Shame, physiology and health', *Journal of Personality*, Dec, 72(6):1191–216.

Page 165 Even though the science is clear on the potential long-term consequences and damage to a child's mental and physical well-being, the information has yet to filter into some primary schools who still practice behaviour management policies that involve shaming children, to effect 'good behaviour'.
Dempsey, Nicola. 'Some classroom behaviour management strategies can humiliate children, with long-term consequences'. *teachwire*. https://www.teachwire.net/news/some-classroom-behaviour-management-strategies-can-humiliate-children-with-long-term-consequences/ (Accessed 05.01.2024.)

Chapter Ten
COMPASSION – How to Keep an Open Heart, Even if it Feels Like Your Child Has Closed Theirs

Page 177 Compassion is defined as the sympathy and concern we feel for the sufferings or misfortunes of others.
Simpson, A.V. (2014). 'Normal Compassion: A Framework for Compassionate'. *Springer Journal of Business Ethics*. https://link.springer.com/article/10.1007/s10551-013-1831-y#:~:text=We%20focus%20on%20the%20idea,ethical%20managerial%20and%20organizational%20implications.

Page 179 'They got a warning card, it was yellow, that said WARNING! right across it. If they did it again, they got a red card which said CONSEQUENCE and then the child would lose what we called golden time.'
ACE-Aware Scotland (2019). Susanne McCafferty – Headteacher, Bainsford Primary School. *ACE-Aware Scotland*. <https://www.youtube.com/watch?v=GyZcH6aAEog&t=306s>. YouTube video.

Page 179 McCafferty said her views changed after watching a TED Talk by the pioneering paediatrician Dr Nadine Burke Harris.
Burke Harris, Nadine (2014). 'How Childhood Trauma Affects Health Across a Lifetime'. *TEDxTalk*. https://www.ted.com/talks/nadine_burke_harris_how_childhood_trauma_affects_health_across_a_lifetime?language=en# Video.

Page 179 In England *almost half of all adults* will have experienced at least one adverse childhood experience, and nearly 10% of children will experience four ACES or more.
'ACEs – Adverse Childhood Experiences'. *Gloucestershire Healthy Living and Learning*. Website. (Accessed 08.01.2024.)
https://www.ghll.org.uk/mental-health/aces---adverse-childhood-experiences/

Burke Harris, Nadine (2014). 'How Childhood Trauma Affects Health Across a Lifetime'. *TEDxTalk*. https://www.ted.com/talks/nadine_burke_harris_how_childhood_trauma_affects_health_across_a_lifetime?language=en# Video.

Page 179 'I thought to myself, that is definitely what I am looking at. I am looking at children who are coming into school who are already in a state of anxiety and they do not need me or anyone else adding to their anxiety.'
ACE-Aware Scotland (2019). Susanne McCafferty – Headteacher, Bainsford Primary School. *ACE-Aware Scotland*. <https://www.youtube.com/watch?v=GyZcH6aAEog&t=306s>. YouTube video.

Page 180 As the interviewer Gary Robinson reflected, 'It's not about punishment, it's about kindness.'
https://www.youtube.com/watch?v=GyZcH6aAEog&t=306s

Page 185 Self-determination theory suggests that all humans have three basic psychological needs.
Ryan, R.M. and Deci, E.L. (2000). 'Self-determination theory and the facilitation of intrinsic motivation, social development, and well-being'. *American Psychologist*, 55(1), 68–78. https://doi.org/10.1037/0003-066X.55.1.68 (Accessed 08.01.2024.)

Page 186 In her study, *Empathy and the Novel*, the literary scholar and poet Professor Suzanne Keen observes that 'the desire for dominance, division, and hierarchal relationships' has weakened empathy.
https://academic.oup.com/book/5700

Page 187 'Historically, society has never been very good at valuing motherhood.'
Goddard Blythe, Sally (2017). *Raising Happy Healthy Children: Why Motherhood Matters*. Stroud, Gloucestershire: Hawthorn Press.

Chapter Eleven
CONTRACTS AND CRISIS MANAGEMENT – Dealing with Distress

Page 197 The stress response triggers neurochemical and hormonal forces that, in the words of Dr Margot Sunderland, can 'overwhelm the mind and body like wildfire'.

Sunderland, Dr Margot (2016). *The Science of Parenting: How Today's Brain Research Can Help You Raise Happy, Emotionally Balanced Children*. London: Dorling Kindersley.

Page 202 The parts of the brain activated during distress, particularly distress caused by social exclusion, are the same areas activated as when we experience physical pain.
https://pubmed.ncbi.nlm.nih.gov/14551424/

Page 211 Brain Box
'A society without structure is an extremely fertile ground for bad behaviour.'
Sunderland, Dr Margot (2016). *The Science of Parenting: How Today's Brain Research Can Help You Raise Happy, Emotionally Balanced Children*. London: Dorling Kindersley.

Page 225 When our children are comforted, the acetylcholine comes back to its base rate and the child will feel calmed.
Panksepp, Jaak (1998). *Affective Neuroscience: The Foundations of human and Animal Emotions*, Oxford University Press, Oxford, p. 257.

Page 228 'Experiences with our adult clients in therapy confirm that often the most frightening part of an incident experienced as a child was their parents' horror reaction!'
Levine, Peter and Kline, Maggie (2008). *Trauma Proofing Your Kids: A Parents' Guide for Instilling Confidence, Joy and Resilience*. Berkeley, California: North Atlantic Books.

Page 228 Always take a moment to ground yourself before you try to ground your children. Because, as Peter Levine, who developed Somatic Experiencing in his excellent book …
Levine, Peter and Kline, Maggie (2008). *Trauma Proofing Your Kids: A Parents' Guide for Instilling Confidence, Joy and Resilience*. Berkeley, California: North Atlantic Books.

Chapter Thirteen
School, Shaming and Separation Anxiety

Page 249 Epigraph
Maté, Dr Gabor (2019). *When the Body Says No: The Cost of Hidden Stress*. London: Ebury.

Page 251 When our children feel understood, it results in increased brain activity associated with reward, positive feelings and social connection.
Morelli, S.A., Torre, J.B. and Eisenberger, N.I. (2014). 'The neural bases of feeling understood and not understood'. *Social Cognitive and Affective Neuroscience.* (12):1890-6. doi: 10.1093/scan/nst191. PubMed Online Publication.

Page 253 Research has shown that children transitioning from nursery to primary school experience an increase in the stress hormone cortisol and suggests it can take as many as three to six months before cortisol concentration returns to baseline levels.
https://pubmed.ncbi.nlm.nih.gov/30253327/

Page 253 Yes, it can take an initial extra investment of our time, but better to invest it now to help our children return to calm, rather than having a child for whom separations are always associated with a sense of anxiety – and leaving them sitting with their adrenaline and cortisol coursing for the rest of the day.
Parent, S., Lupien, S., Herba, C.M., Dupére, V., Gunnar, M.R. and Séguin, J.R. (2018). 'Children's cortisol response to the transition from preschool to formal schooling: A review'. *Psychoneuroendocrinology.* 99:196-205. doi: 10.1016/j. psyneuen.2018.09.013. Epub.

Page 255 Holding in Mind Guessing Game
Website: Emma Connor, Integrative Child Psychotherapist: www.yourspacetherapies. org

Page 257 What I will say is that if your child is finding the school environment difficult, please do not feel you and they must struggle alone. Every school and local authority should have what is known as EBSA (Emotionally Based School Avoidance) guidance. EBSA is a term that covers children and young people who experience challenges in attending school due to negative feelings (such as anxiety).
Anna Freud. 'Addressing emotionally-based school avoidance'. *Anna Freud.* https:// d1uw1dikibnh8j.cloudfront.net/media/18945/addressing-emotionally-based-school-avoidance-rebrand.pdf.

Page 257 'Barriers often relate to unmet Special Educational Needs and Disabilities (diagnosed or suspected), physical or mental illness ....'
www.notfineinschool.co.uk

Page 257 'What seems to be happening in the UK educational system is that the individual pupil is seen as the whole problem rather than acknowledging that the school environment and unhelpful government policies around targets are a part of this, too.'
Perry, Philippa (2023). 'Our Son is Refusing to go to School – and We Feel So Isolated'. *Guardian.* https://www.theguardian.com/lifeandstyle/2023/jun/18/our-son-is-refusing-to-go-to-school---and-we-feel-so-isolated. (Accessed: 08.01.2024.)

Page 258 We know some children who have been bullied can suffer post-traumatic stress disorder.
'Bullying and Cyberbullying'. *NSPCC*. https://www.nspcc.org.uk/what-is-child-abuse/types-of-abuse/bullying-and-cyberbullying/. (Accessed 08.01.2024.)

Page 259 It would be best to resource playtimes with staff in sufficient numbers who have clear oversight and have been trained in both conflict resolution and understand the damaging impact bullying has on a child's still developing brain.
Muetzel, Ryan L. et al. (2019). 'Frequent Bullying Involvement and Brain Morphology in Children'. *Frontiers in Psychiatry*. 10:696. https://pubmed.ncbi.nlm.nih.gov/31607968/

Page 260 The NSPCC advises that 'if you find out your child has done something to hurt someone else, you're likely to feel angry, disappointed or any number of other strong emotions. Explain that what they're doing is unacceptable. Children and young people don't always realise what they're doing is bullying, or understand how much their actions have hurt someone.'
https://www.nspcc.org.uk/what-is-child-abuse/types-of-abuse/bullying-and-cyberbullying/

Page 261 It is worth noting that students who perceive their school to be supportive are more likely to report bullying.
Eliot, Megan et al. (2010). 'Supportive school climate and student willingness to seek help for bullying and threats of violence'. *Journal of School Psychology*. https://pubmed.ncbi.nlm.nih.gov/21094397/. (Accessed 08.01.2024.)

Page 261 While punishing a child for their behaviour might be thought to 'work' in the short-term, it is unlikely to resolve happily for the child, or those around them, in the future.
Bachman, Curt (2016). 'The Bonds That Break: Sibling Abuse Perpetration Behaviors as Correlates of Peer Bullying Perpetration Behaviors: A Structural Equation Model'. *Digital Commons at Andrews University*. 1619. https://digitalcommons.andrews.edu/dissertations/1619 (Accessed 08.01.2024.)

Page 261 Brain Box
'What punishment does, at best, is immediately suppress the behaviour. The trouble is, the research is unequivocal: what happens is the behaviour returns at the same rate.'
Quoted in: Ruggeri, Amanda (2022). 'The Truth About "Time Out"'. *BBC Family Tree*. https://www.bbc.com/future/article/20220607-what-should-you-do-when-a-child-misbehaves.

Page 261 Brain Box
If your child is being bullied by their sibling and does not yet have sufficient 'wise owl' capacity to share with you the depth of their emotional suffering, it can see them in a threatened baboon state and potentially also seeing him/her bullying other children in turn.
Bachman, Curt (2016). 'The Bonds That Break: Sibling Abuse Perpetration Behaviors as Correlates of Peer Bullying Perpetration Behaviors: A Structural Equation Model'. *Digital Commons at Andrews University*. 1619. https://digitalcommons.andrews.edu/dissertations/1619 (Accessed 08.01.2024.)

Page 262 Brain Box
'Shame is closely related to guilt, but there is a key qualitative difference.'
Ekman, Dr Paul (2009). *Telling Lies: Clues to Deceit in the Marketplace, Politics and Marriage*. New York: W.W. Norton and Company.

Chapter Fourteen
Screentime, Social Media and Self-Image

Page 265 Your cellphone has already replaced your camera ...
Source unknown.

Page 265 Steve Jobs was among tech moguls like Google CEO Sundar Pichai, former Facebook executive Chamath Palihapitiya and Snapchat CEO Evan Spiegel who all restrict the access their children have to devices.
López, Quispe (2020). '6 tech executives who raise their kids tech-free or seriously limit their screen time'. *Business Insider*. https://www.businessinsider.com/tech-execs-screen-time-children-bill-gates-steve-jobs-2019-9?r=US&IR=T#in-steve-jobs-household-dinnertime-was-reserved-for-face-to-face-conversation-with-his-children-meaning-no-ipads-or-iphones-in-sight-2

Page 265 According to Walter Isaacson, author of *Steve Jobs* ... 'The kids did not seem addicted at all to devices.'
Isaacson, Walter (2015). *Steve Jobs*. London: Abacus.

Page 266 Social media sites are designed to activate similar mechanisms in the brain as slot machines, and even cocaine.
Busby, Mattha (2018). 'Social media copies gambling methods "to create psychological cravings"'. *Guardian*. https://www.theguardian.com/technology/2018/may/08/social-media-copies-gambling-methods-to-create-psychological-cravings. (Accessed 08.01.2024.)

Stanford Graduate School of Business (2017). 'Chamath Palihapitiya, Founder and CEO Social Capital, on Money as an Instrument of Change'. YouTube Video. https://www.youtube.com/watch?v=PMotykw0SIk (Accessed 08.01.2024.)

Page 266 A Harris Poll survey in 2020 found nearly seven in ten parents of five- to 17-year-olds said their children's screen time had increased, and 60% felt they 'have no choice but to allow it'.
Broughton, Amber (2020). 'From Sinner to Saviour: Screen Time'. *The Harris Poll*. https://theharrispoll.com/briefs/from-sinner-to-savior-screen-time/ (Accessed 08.01.2024.)

Page 266 One global analysis found primary school children's screentime had increased by an extra hour and twenty minutes a day on average.
https://www.sciencedirect.com/science/article/pii/S2589537022001821

Page 266 Early data from a landmark National Institutes of Health (NIH) study that began in 2018, indicates …
Adolescent Brain Cognitive Development Website: https://abcdstudy.org

Page 267 'Unlike reading books which gives time for children to process words, images and voices, the constant absorption of on-screen images and messages affects a child's attention span and focus.'
Nelson, Carlota. 'Babies Need Humans, Not Screens'. *UNICEF*. https://www.unicef.org/parenting/child-development/babies-screen-time (Accessed 08.01.2024).

Page 267 'It shows you can produce profound changes in the brain with training. That's a big deal.'
Jabr, Ferris (2011). 'Cache Cab: Taxi Drivers' Brains Grow to Navigate London's Streets'. *Scientific American*. https://www.scientificamerican.com/article/london-taxi-memory (Accessed 08.01.2024.)

Page 268 Tristan Harris went on … to raise awareness about how manipulative devices are, going so far as to say the addiction to smartphones is causing 'human downgrading'.
Heathman, Amelia (2019). 'How smartphones and social media have been designed to "downgrade humans"' *The Standard*. https://www.standard.co.uk/tech/digital-wellbeing-screen-time-tools-smartphone-google-tristan-harris-a4153016.html. (Accessed 08.01.2024.)

Page 268 More longitudinal studies and research is needed to clarify what might constitute 'healthy' or otherwise amounts of time on a screen for older children.
'Guidelines on Physical Activity, Sedentary Behaviour, and Sleep'. *World Health Organization*. https://apps.who.int/iris/bitstream/handle/10665/311664/9789241550536-eng.pdf?sequence=1&isAllowed=y. (Accessed 08.01.2024.)

Page 270 'If there's a struggle over stopping screen use, that's usually a warning sign that they're fairly addicted to it and their brains are really craving it.'
Lopez, Kathryn, MD (2018). 'Media and Your Child: Making Choices, Healthwise'. *Upper Valley Family Medicine*.

Page 271 'I think we have created tools that are ripping apart the social fabric of how society works.'
Stanford Graduate School of Business, (2017). 'Chamath Palihapitiya, Founder and CEO Social Capital, on Money as an Instrument of Change'. YouTube Video. https://www.youtube.com/watch?v=PMotykw0SIk (Accessed 08.01.2024.)

Page 275 'It's very, very hard for children to have to share us.'
Markham, Laura. 'Helping Siblings Get Along'. *Aha! Parenting*. https://www. ahaparenting.com/guide/helping-siblings-get-along. (Accessed 08.01.2024.)

Chapter Fifteen
Siblings

Page 276 I was reminded of this while watching a Netflix documentary about Arnold Schwarzenegger.
Arnold (2023). Directed by Lesley Chilcott. [Television Documentary]. Netflix.

Page 276 'The only opponent you have to beat is yourself, the way you were yesterday.'
Murakami, Haruki (2009). *What I Talk About When I Talk About Running*. London: Vintage.

Panksepp, Jaak (1998). *Affective Neuroscience: The Foundations of Human and Animal Emotions*. Oxford: Oxford University Press.

Wolpert, Lewis (1999). *Malignant Sadness: The Anatomy of Depression*. London: Faber & Faber.

Page 277 'The language of loss is the language of pain.'
Panksepp, Jaak (1998). *Affective Neuroscience: The Foundations of Human and Animal Emotions*. New York: Oxford University Press.

Page 287 It means we are helping them achieve the crucial life skill of what Professor Peter Fonagy from the Anna Freud Centre calls 'mentalisation'.
https://www.youtube.com/watch?v=MJ1Y9zw-n7U

Anna Freud Centre (2021). 'Peter Fonagy appointed to expert panel on mental health'. *Anna Freud*. https://www.annafreud.org/news/peter-fonagy-appointed-to-expert-panel-on-mental-health/ (Accessed 08.01.2024.)

Page 296 Brain Box
'The physical comforting of a grieving child, will release natural calming opioids in the brain, coupled with the lovely emotion chemical, oxytocin.'
Sunderland, Dr Margot (2022). *Helping Children with Loss*. Abingdon, Oxon: Routledge. www.speechmark.net

Chapter Sixteen
Difference, Difficulties and 'Disorder'

Page 293 Epigraph 'This might sound simple, but ...'
Burke Harris, Dr Nadine (2018). *The Deepest Well: Healing the Long-Term Effects of Childhood Trauma and Adversity*. London: Bluebird Publishing.

Page 295 Child psychiatrist Dr Bruce Perry suggests school staff record the number of positive interactions they have with children who are struggling.
Cited in Brous, Kathy (2014). 'Perry: Rhythm Regulates the Brain'. *Kathy Brous*. https://attachmentdisorderhealing.com/developmental-trauma-3/. (Accessed 08.01.2024.) [Perry 2008]

Page 296 Brain Box.
'The physical comforting of a grieving child, will release natural calming opioids in the brain ...'
Sunderland, Margot (2022). *Helping Children with Loss*. Abingdon, Oxon: Routledge.

Page 298 As the clinician and trauma specialist Dr Gabor Maté summarises it, trauma 'leaves an imprint in your nervous system ...'
Maté, Dr Gabor and Maté, Daniel (2022). *The Myth of Normal: Trauma, Illness & Healing in a Toxic Culture*. London: Vermilion.

Page 299 Dr Maté says trauma impacts our health and behaviour because 'children, especially highly sensitive children, can be wounded in various ways ...'
Maté, Dr Gabor and Maté, Daniel (2022). *The Myth of Normal: Trauma, Illness & Healing in a Toxic Culture*. London: Vermilion.

Page 299 Unresolved childhood trauma can significantly impact our future health.
Violence Prevention (2021). 'About the CDC-Kaiser ACE Study'. *Centers for Disease Control and Prevention*. https://www.cdc.gov/violenceprevention/aces/about.html (Accessed 08.01.2024.)

Page 299 High doses of adversity in childhood can not only affect brain structure and function, they can affect a child's still-developing immune system …
Burke Harris, Dr Nadine *The Deepest Well: Healing the Long-Term Effects of Childhood Trauma and Adversity*. London: Bluebird Publishing.

Page 300 The trauma specialist Dr Peter Levine says, 'Trauma is perhaps the most avoided, ignored, belittled, denied, misunderstood, and untreated cause of human suffering.'
Levine, Peter (1999). *Healing Trauma Study Guide*. Boulder, Colorado: Sounds True Publishing. p. 5.

Page 301 We can start by dosing up on our happiness hormones: dopamine, oxytocin, serotonin and endorphin, or DOSE for short!
Website – UC Berkeley's Greater Good Science Center (GGSC): https://greatergood. berkeley.edu/ (Accessed 08.01.2024.)

Page 301 Doing things that help us DOSE up are not just 'nice to haves', they are proven to counter the impact of toxic stress.
Burke Harris, Nadine (2018). 'Dr Nadine Burke Harris: Healing the Long-Term Effects of Childhood Adversity'. *Commonwealth Club of California*. https://www. youtube.com/watch?v=MDTW89Ycxw0 YouTube Video.

Page 301 In fact, Dr Nadine Burke Harris's studies have shown that high-quality nurturing relationships can actually alter a child's brain structure, which can be measured using MRI technology.
Burke Harris, Nadine (2018). 'Dr Nadine Burke Harris: Healing the Long-Term Effects of Childhood Adversity'. *Commonwealth Club of California*. https://www. youtube.com/watch?v=MDTW89Ycxw0 YouTube Video.

Page 303 Dr Perry's research in the United States suggests that 30-40% of children there will be exposed to domestic violence …
Perry, Dr Bruce and Gras, Patricia (2010). 'Dr. Bruce Perry, Childhood Development on LIVING SMART with Patricia Gras'. *Houston PBS*. https://www. youtube.com/watch?v=vak-iDwZJY8. YouTube Video.

Page 304 There has been a surge in the diagnosis of children who are said to have neurodevelopmental and behavioural disorders in recent years …
Werkhoven, Sander, Anderson, Joel H. and Robeyns, Ingrid A.M. (2022). 'Who benefits from diagnostic labels for developmental disorders?'. *Developmental Medicine Childhood Neurology*. 64: 944–949. https://onlinelibrary.wiley.com/doi/ full/10.1111/dmcn.15177 (Accessed 08.01.2024.)

Abdelnour, Ellie, Jansen, Madeline O. and Gold, Jessica A. (2022). 'ADHD Diagnostic Trends: Increased Recognition or Overdiagnosis?' *The Journal of the Missouri State Medical Association*. 119(5): 467–473.https://www.ncbi.nlm.nih.gov/pmc/articles/PMC9616454/) (Accessed 08.01.2024.)

Page 304 Clinical psychologist Dr Lucy Johnstone is passionate that parents feel sufficiently informed when it comes to the diagnosis of their children.
Johnstone, Lucy. *A Straight Talking Introduction to Psychiatric Diagnosis*, PCCS Books (Second Edition, 2022).
www.adisorder4everyone.com

Page 306 According to Dr Nadine Burke Harris, the rate of misdiagnosis for ADHD is alarmingly high.
Aces Too High – Website: https://acestoohigh.com/

Page 308 The adverse childhood experience (ACE) study found that the more adversity and trauma a person experiences, the higher the chance of being diagnosed with ADHD, conduct disorder or being on the autism spectrum.
https://pubmed.ncbi.nlm.nih.gov/9635069/

307 Brain Box: Dr Margot Sunderland
Sunderland, Dr Margot. 'The Muddle Between Trauma and Psychiatric Diagnosis of ADHD and Autism Spectrum'. *The Centre of Child Mental Health*. Webinar. https://www.childmentalhealthcentre.org/webinars/webinars-for-schools/product/143-the-muddle-between-trauma-and-psychiatric-diagnosis

Page 308 'Child psychiatrist Dr Sami Timimi is a critic of the concept of ASD and ADHD, pointing out that the "so-called tests" do not require the behaviours to be present in all contexts.' Sami Timimi Consultant Child and Adolescent Psychiatrist
Sami Timimi – Website: samitimimi.co.uk

Page 309 It can be argued that this is more beneficial in the long run as medication does not 'solve' ADHD, and once medication is stopped, the behaviour often returns.
Brown, Richard P., MD and Gerbarg, Patricia L., MD (2012). *Non-drug Treatments for ADHD – New Options for Kids, Adults and Clinicians*. New York: W.W. Norton and Company.

Page 309 Brain Box
'The use of psychostimulants in children with attention problems …'
https://www.cambridge.org/core/journals/australian-and-new-zealand-journal-of-family-therapy/article/abs/neurosequential-model-of-therapeutics-an-interview-with-bruce-perry/46492F8C5926E78EDB30A67177CE984C

Page 310 We know that, when children are helped to grieve, process, and make sense of what has happened in their lives their previous symptoms and distressing behaviour are often alleviated.
Lupien, Sonia J. et al. (2009). 'Effects of stress throughout the lifespan on the brain, behaviour and cognition'. *Nature Reviews Neuroscience*. 10: 434-445. https://www.researchgate.net/profile/Christine-Heim/publication/24376619_Lupien_SJ_McEwen_BS_Gunnar_MR_Heim_C_Effects_of_stress_throughout_the_lifespan_on_the_brain_behaviour_and_cognition_Nat_Rev_Neurosci_10_434-445/links/53ef7d3f0cf2711e0c42f3f6/Lupien-SJ-McEwen-BS-Gunnar-MR-Heim-C-Effects-of-stress-throughout-the-lifespan-on-the-brain-behaviour-and-cognition-Nat-Rev-Neurosci-10-434-445.pdf. (Accessed 08.01.2024.)

Page 311 Nearly 20 years ago neuroscientist Jaak Panksepp warned that children moving less, and sitting still more in classrooms, could be contributing to the increase in the rate of diagnosis of ADHD.
Robinson, Sir Ken (2011). 'ADHD: The Tonsillectomy of the 21st Century?' *Fora. tv*. https://www.youtube.com/watch?v=HInN7t4Zl04 YouTube video.

Pansepp, Jaak (2007). 'Can PLAY Diminish ADHD and Facilitate the Construction of the Social Brain?'. *Journal of the Canadian Academy of Child and Adolescent Psychiatry*. 16(2): 57–66. https://www.ncbi.nlm.nih.gov/pmc/articles/PMC2242642/. (Accessed 08.01.2024.)

Page 311 We now know, for instance, that a foetus in the womb feels a mother's stress directly.
MediBulletin Bureau (2018). 'Fetal scans Confirm Maternal Stress Affects babies' brains', *MediBulletin*. http://medibulletin.com/fetal-scans-confirm-maternal-stress-affects-babies-brains/. (Accessed 08.01.2024.)

Page 311 As far back as 2004, researchers reported that infants born to women who were stressed or depressed …
Tarkian, Laurie (2004). 'Tackling stress and depression back to the womb'. *New York Times*.

Page 311 'We know prenatal depression and stress and anxiety can predict behaviour problems in the child …'
Maté, Dr Gabor and Maté, Daniel (2022). *The Myth of Normal: Trauma, Illness & Healing in a Toxic Culture*. London: Vermilion. p. 145.

Chapter Seventeen
Community

Page 315 Brain Box
'For 99% of the time we have been on this planet, human beings have lived ...'
Perry, Dr Bruce and Gras, Patricia (2010). 'Dr. Bruce Perry, Childhood Development on LIVING SMART with Patricia Gras'. *Houston PBS*. https://www.youtube.com/watch?v=vak-iDwZJY8. YouTube Video.

Page 316 'David Brooks writes passionately in favour of a return to multi-generational living.'
Brooks, David (2020). 'The Nuclear Family Was a Mistake'. *The Atlantic*. https://www.theatlantic.com/magazine/archive/2020/03/the-nuclear-family-was-a-mistake/605536/ (Accessed 08.01.2024.)

Page 317 Brain Box
'We are really concerned because we see changes in the way children are in school, the way they are with each other, the way they engage in the community ...'
Perry, Dr Bruce and Gras, Patricia (2010). 'Dr. Bruce Perry, Childhood Development on LIVING SMART with Patricia Gras'. *Houston PBS*. https://www.youtube.com/watch?v=vak-iDwZJY8. YouTube Video.

Page 318 'this will help to facilitate more regulated behaviour because when the lower parts of our children's brains are restless and dysregulated, they cannot concentrate, think, and learn.'
Goddard Blythe, Sally (2023). *Reflexes, Movement, Learning and Behaviour*. Gloucestershire: Hawthorn Press.

Goddard Blythe, Sally (2005). 'Releasing Educational Potential Through Movement: A Summary of Individual Studies Carried Out Using the INPP Test Battery and Developmental Exercise Programme for Use in Schools with Children with Special Needs'. *Child Care in Practice*. 11:4, 415-432, DOI: 10.1080/13575270500340234 (Accessed 08.01.2024.)

Page 319 'the beautiful image painted by neuroscientist Jaak Panksepp as he reassured parents that our children's 'positive arousal neurochemicals ...'
This quote is taken from a conversation between Dr Margot Sunderland and the neuroscientist, Jaak Panksepp, in 2015.

Weston, Kath (1991). *Families We Choose: Lesbians, Gays, Kinship*. Oxford: Columbia Press.

RESOURCES

The books that are listed in the endnotes are a valuable resource and come as recommended reading.

The following organisations also offer a wealth of knowledge and expert advice. I will update the list of websites on my social media channels @katesilverton (Instagram) and at www.katesilverton.com I hope to see you there.

Children's Charities and Mental Health Support

Action for Children
www.actionforchildren.org.uk

Anna Freud National Centre for Children and Families
www.annafreud.org

A Disorder 4 Everyone
AD4E suggests that there are more helpful ways to understand emotional distress than seeing it as medical illness or disorder.
www.adisorder4everyone.com

The Centre for Child Mental Health
www.childmentalhealthcentre.org

Winston's Wish
A charity that helps children, teenagers and young adults affected by bereavement.
www.winstonswish.org

Child Bereavement UK
www.childbereavementuk.org

Young Minds
Supporting children, young people and parents. They have a parent support helpline
www.youngminds.co.uk

Schools Support
Mentally Healthy Schools
www.mentallyhealthyschools.org.uk

Place2Be
www.place2be.org.uk

Trauma Informed Schools UK
www.traumainformedschools.co.uk

Other Useful Links

IFS Institute [Internal Family Systems]
ifs-institute.com

NSPCC
www.nspcc.org.uk
For support and information on what to do if you are worried about a child.

Childline
www.childline.org.uk

Mind
www.mind.org.uk

Samaritans
www.samaritans.org

Finding a Therapist or Counsellor

The following organisations have registers of therapists and they require all therapists
and counsellors to attend accredited courses which require them to have their own
counselling. This is not a condition in all counselling training but in my view it is
essential for safe practice. Feel free to ask about the training and development of any
therapist you contact, it's very important.

BACP British Association for Counselling and Psychotherapy
UKCP UK Council for Psychotherapy
BAPT British Association of Play Therapists
PTUK Play Therapy UK
BAAT British Association of Art Therapists
IATE Institute for Arts in Therapy and Education
AFT Association of Family Therapists

ACKNOWLEDGEMENTS

This book has been the single biggest challenge of my working life. There were (almost daily) wobbles about whether I could do it and worries about whether I would ever find the time. There are many people I must thank, therefore, who ensured I stayed the course. I hope I can do justice to them here. The book is the culmination of over two years of writing and more than two decades of research. I wrote it in a small room at the end of our garden (which, in London, means just three strides from the back door) and was sustained by numerous cups of tea and chocolate from my husband and cheerleading visits from the children when they returned from school. It wasn't written fast enough for any of us, but there was so much to say, and I wanted to get it right. I also wanted to do justice to caring for my own family in the process, as well as supporting you and your families too, of course.

I wanted to deliver a book that justified the faith my editor, Michelle Signore, and her team at Bonnier had in me from the start. Michelle's commitment even extended to her making trips to my 'office' armed with salads and sandwiches and 'mum stuff' questions, spurring me on with her enthusiasm and personal feedback when my advice had 'worked'. Her patience has been tested numerous times, given the countless deadlines I missed due to my clinical schedule and my own 'mum stuff' at home. Thank you, Michelle; you have been a joy to work with. Your patience and faith have ensured this book is the one we always hoped it would be. And to the entire team at Bonnier, especially Nikki Mander, Madiya Altaf, Natalia Cacciatore and Jake Cook, thank you for your effervescence, energy and ongoing support. I appreciate how much it has taken behind the scenes to get us across the line!

My agents Bev, Tom, Aoife, Liz, and the brilliant team at Bev James Management have been an incredible source of support and have sustained my faith while on this long, lumpy, solitary road of writing. Thank you especially to Tom for holding the line when all of mine were wobbling!

Thanks and thoughts go to Amy Warren and Adam Parfitt for their invaluable early input into my flabby first drafts, ensuring I could finally write, seeing much more clearly through the 'trees'!

In my current capacity as a mental health professional, I am surrounded by people who work in service to others, supporting children and families in need. It is a privilege to count them as more than colleagues, and I wish to thank them for being so generous with their time and expertise. They have supported me in my research, my clinical practice, and in reading initial drafts: Noa Baum, Dr Lawrence Cohen, Emma Connor, Diana Dean, Professor Peter Fonagy, Julie Harmieson, Laura Henry-Allain, Professor Lucy Johnstone, Dr Gabor Mate, Professor Eamon McCrory, Jo Moon, Dr Bruce Perry, Dame Benita Refson, Christina Rousseau, Dr Margot Sunderland, Dr Sami Timimi, Sir John Timpson, Sarah Turner, Jo Watson, Dr Suzanne Zeedyk and the many clinicians, colleagues and practitioners from whom I have learned so much.

Noa, I could not have wished for a wiser, more containing presence in supervision this year. Thank you for being so generous with your time, for your invaluable insight and feedback, and for the compassion you demonstrate for the children in our care. To Sarah, likewise. Your smile, warmth and grace were my weekly welcome in school. Thank you for making my first long-term placement such a memorable one. And to Jo Moon, again, thank you for your exceptional holding, warmth, and always wise words. I want to thank all the schools I have worked with and the children you entrusted to my care. To the parents I have worked with, it has been a privilege to be with you and to see your love and commitment to your children first-hand.

To all at The Institute for Arts In Therapy and Education and at Place2Be: your exceptional training and support have enabled me to walk this path as a qualified child counsellor today.

Susan Law, whose gifts of healing have proved so profound and whose wisdom has afforded me such a vital guide. Thank you for being with me for this part of the journey; I look forward to the journey to come.

To all those no longer with us but who continue to walk alongside, especially my father, Terence George. Your presence is with me always.

Korda Ace, for your creative grace and gorgeous illustrations; and Martin, to whom I am indebted for showing me the way. As Yoda might say, 'Grateful, I am'.

To my brilliant, talented friends who loaned an ear, as well as their expertise and experience: Lisa Shortland, houseparent and pastoral educationalist extraordinaire; Rosie Nixon, a passionate, kind and creative force for good; and Natalie Lesser, for feeding my soul and for your proofreading perfection: thank you for being the most beautiful human beings and friends. And to dear friends near and far, who have been such an incredible source of support, even when spinning their own personal and professional plates too: Dipika – forever thanks for the pickups and playdates; Saira, Caroline, Kim, Cinta, Claire, Lucinda, Dani, Jonty and Tye, Paddy and Mel, Ali M, Amanda, Susanna and Sara. To Cilla, thank you for keeping us all sane – we miss you. And to Karen and Ariele, whom I have missed so much, too.

I want to acknowledge the children's charities who do incredible work advocating for children, enabling them to use their voices and, indeed, for their voices to be heard. Among them: The Anna Freud National Centre for Children and Families, Place2Be, Unlocking Potential (UP), UsForThem, Barnardo's, Save The Children, the NSPCC, Action for Children, National Children's Bureau, the Children's Society, The Royal Foundation and Foundation for Early Childhood.

To the many parents and families I am honoured to have helped support. Thank you for graciously allowing me to draw upon elements of your stories for this book. And to the children whose identities remain anonymous but whose presence is imprinted on every page and in my heart.

Mum, Claire and Amy, your company and love I cherish – always.

And Clemency and Wilbur. There are too few words to express how much I love you – it might take another book, but let's not go there! Thank you for allowing Mummy to share some of your stories, for your courage and compassion, for what you have taught me, and for what you teach me still. I am so proud of who you are and so excited to see the adolescents and adults you become. I love you – let's get back to baking!

And finally, to Mike: my husband, soulmate, and best friend. What a road we have travelled! And what adventures are still to come. We are so lucky to have you and we love you so much. Thank you for sustaining me these past few years with so much more than mugs of tea... (although they helped.) I love you. So glad we made it to the countryside. I promise, no more books ... at least not until the kids turn thirteen...

INDEX